The Psychology
of Well Being

The Psychology of Well Being

WILLIAM M. MILEY

PRAEGER

Westport, Connecticut
London

Library of Congress Cataloging-in-Publication Data

Miley, William M., 1941–
    The psychology of well being / William M. Miley.
    p.   cm.
    Includes bibliographical references and index.
    ISBN 0–275–96275–X (alk. paper)
    1. Clinical health psychology.   2. Mental health.   3. Health
behavior.   I. Title.
    R726.7.M55   1999
    610—dc21   98–44533

British Library Cataloguing in Publication Data is available.

Library of Congress Catalog Card Number: 98–44533
ISBN: 0–275–96275–X

First published in 1999

Praeger Publishers, 88 Post Road West, Westport, CT 06881
An imprint of Greenwood Publishing Group, Inc.

Printed in the United States of America

The paper used in this book complies with the
Permanent Paper Standard issued by the National
Information Standards Organization (Z39.48–1984).

10 9 8 7 6 5 4 3 2 1

Copyright Acknowledgments

The author and publisher are grateful for permission to reproduce portions of the following copyrighted material.

Box 2.1: from Davis, C., Brewer, H., & Ratusny, D. (1993). Behavioral frequency and psychological commitment: Necessary concepts in the study of excessive exercising. *Journal of Behavioral Medicine, 16,* 625–626. Reproduced by permission of Plenum Publishing Corporation and the author.

Box 3.2: Copyright 1993 by Consumers Union of U.S., Inc., Yonkers, NY 10703-1057. Reprinted by permission from CONSUMER REPORTS, June 1993.

Table 3.1: from Brownell, K. D., & Wadden, T. A. (1992). Etiology and treatment of obesity: Understanding a serious, prevalent, and refractory disorder. *Journal of Consulting and Clinical Psychology, 60,* 512. Copyright © 1992 by the American Psychological Association. Reprinted with permission.

Box 3.3: from *The Press* of Atlantic City, August 9, 1994. Copyright by the Associated Press. Reproduced by permission.

Box 4.1: from Sobell, M. B., & Sobell, L. C. (1993). *Problem drinkers: Guided self-change treatment.* New York: Guilford Press, pp. 21–22. Reproduced by permission.

Box 4.3: from Todd, T. (1994). Growing young. *Texas Monthly, 22,* pp. 46–50. Reproduced by permission of the author.

Figures 5.1 and 5.2: from Smith, J. C. (1993). *Understanding stress and coping.* New York: Macmillan, pp. 40, 44. Copyright © 1993. Reprinted by permission of Prentice-Hall, Inc., Upper Saddle River, NJ.

Boxes 5.1 and 5.2: from Girdano, D. A., Everly, G. S., & Dusek, D. E. (1990). *Controlling stress and tension* (3rd ed.). Englewood Cliffs, NJ: Prentice-Hall, pp. 66–67, 124–125. Copyright © 1990 by Allyn & Bacon. Reprinted by permission.

Boxes 5.3 and 6.1: from *Stress management for wellness,* second edition by Walt Schafer. New York: Holt, Rinehart and Winston. Copyright © 1992 by Holt, Rinehart and Winston, reprinted by permission of the publisher.

Box 6.3: from Resnick, S. (November 1988). Stress management: A necessary and useful tool. *Carrier Foundation Letter,* No. 138, p. 3. Copyright by The Carrier Foundation. Reprinted by permission.

Figure 8.1: from Margolis, S., & Goldschmidt-Clermont, P. J. (1995). *Coronary heart disease.* The Johns Hopkins White Papers. Baltimore, MD: The Johns Hopkins Medical Institutions, p. 5. Text: Reprinted with permission from The Johns Hopkins White Papers, Coronary Heart Disease 1995 © Medletter Associates, 1995. The White Papers are updated and published annually. For further information, please call (800) 829-9170. Illustration: Robert Duckwall, Courtesy of The Johns Hopkins University Department of Art as Applied to Medicine © The Johns Hopkins University, 1995.

To Grace, Mike, Eileena, Melinda, Laura, Steve, Imani, and future generations of healthy people.

Contents

Illustrations   xiii

Preface   xv

Acknowledgments   xvii

I. History

1. The Mind and the Body   3

   Historical Dualism   4

   The Biomedical Model   5

   Health Psychology and Behavioral Medicine   7

   Roles for a Psychology of Well Being   8

   Summary   10

II. Lifestyle

2. Exercise   15

   Exercise and Health   16

   Reasons for Not Exercising   18

   Aerobic Exercise   19

   Exercise and Emotional Fitness   20

   Running Addiction   22

   Exercise and Coronary Heart Disease (CHD)   23

   Exercise Adherence   28

	Exercise and Aging	31
	Summary	33
3.	Obesity and Weight Control	35
	Obesity	36
	Theoretical Models of Obesity	38
	Health Risks of Obesity	44
	Weight Control	48
	Eating Disorders	56
	Bulimia	62
	Eating Disorders in Athletes	63
	Eating Disorders in Males	64
	What's a Body to Do?	65
	Summary	65
4.	Unhealthy Behavior	69
	Alcohol	71
	Smoking	81
	Other Drugs	89
	Summary	95

III. Stress

5.	Stress Theory	101
	A Short History of Stress	102
	Controversy about the Stress Concept	104
	General Adaptation Syndrome	105
	Contemporary Studies on Stress	110
	Glucocorticoids	111
	Gonadosteroids	112
	Peptides	113
	Problems of Measurement	113
	Coronary Heart Disease and Stress	114
	Post-Traumatic Stress Disorder (PTSD)	117
	Summary	118
6.	Coping with Stress	123
	Psychoanalytic Theory	124

Process Theory 125
Staying Healthy under Stress: Hardiness 127
Learned Helplessness and Explanatory Style 128
Self-Efficacy and Hope 129
Social Support 130
Stress Management 131
Summary 135

IV. Chronic Diseases and Behavior

7. Diabetes 141
   Anatomy and Physiology 142
   Hypertension, Atherosclerosis, and Coronary Artery Disease 147
   Stress and Diabetes 148
   Diabetes Management 153
   Summary 156

8. Coronary Heart Disease 159
   Anatomy and Physiology 160
   Development of Disease 164
   Biological Treatments 166
   Traditional Risk Factors 168
   Psychosocial Risk Factors 172
   Rehabilitation 173
   Depression after a Heart Attack 176
   Summary 177

9. AIDS 179
   Statistics on AIDS 180
   Immunity 181
   Psychoneuroimmunology 186
   Psychosocial Interventions and Immune Function 188
   Women and AIDS 190
   Summary 193

10. Cancer 195
    Description of Cancer 196
    Factors Suspected of Increasing Risks of Cancer 198

Factors Suspected of Decreasing Risks of Cancer 203
Psychological Interventions with Cancer Patients 205
Summary 210

V. The Future

11. The Future of Health and Well Being 215
Cardiovascular Disorders 216
Adherence Models 217
Healthy Living and Health Delivery 217
Ethnic, Cultural, and Gender Issues 219
Caregiver Stress 219
Self-Help 220

References 221
Index 253

Illustrations

BOXES

2.1	Self-Test on Exercise Addiction	24
2.2	A Research Tidbit: The Influence of the Physician on Exercise	30
3.1	A Research Tidbit: Weight and Ethnicity	37
3.2	Is Your Weight Bad for Your Health?	46
3.3	In the News	58
4.1	Problem Drinkers: A Unique Category of Drinkers	80
4.2	Personality and Smoking	86
4.3	Fountain of Youth?	94
5.1	Assess Yourself: Student Stress Questionnaire	107
5.2	Assess Yourself: What Is Your Sense of Control?	109
5.3	Assess Yourself: What Is Your Pace of Life?	116
6.1	Simple Breathing Techniques That Can Be Used Quickly to Reduce Stress in the Immediate Situation	132
6.2	The Benson Relaxation Response	133
6.3	Assertiveness Training	135
7.1	Diabetes Risk Test	143
7.2	Diabetes Facts and Figures	146
7.3	Type 1 and Type 2 Diabetes	149

8.1   Cardiovascular Disease: What Are Your Risk Factors?   165
8.2   What Are Your Usual Reactions?   174

FIGURES

5.1   The Major Endocrine Glands, with the Heart and Kidneys
      as Reference Points   103
5.2   The Stages of the General Adaptation Syndrome   105
8.1   Anatomy of the Heart and the Coronary Arteries   161
8.2   Electrical Activity in the Heart   162
10.1 Age-Adjusted Cancer Death Rates, Males by Site,
      United States, 1930–1993   200
10.2 Age-Adjusted Cancer Death Rates, Females by Site,
      United States, 1930–1993   201

TABLE

3.1   Methods for Enhancing Maintenance of Weight Loss
      Based on Research and Clinical Experience   51

Preface

I must confess that one of my goals in writing this book was to indulge my passion for continuing to learn as much as possible about theories and practices that enhance the quality of life. In reading, thinking, and writing about the many exciting developments in this area, I find applications everywhere. As a clinical and health psychologist, I see people for mental health reasons, and I have come to believe that health and lifestyle issues are fundamental not only to physical health but mental health as well. For example, exercise may be of significant benefit for mild to moderate depression, it improves self-image, and good ideas seem to pop into one's head while doing it. Personally, I try as much as possible to use health-enhancing principles in my own life in areas such as diet, exercise, and other positive lifestyle behaviors. I hope students learn as much by reading this text as I did in writing it and that my enthusiasm for this field comes through in my writing.

I have included in this book, where appropriate, boxes to enhance a topic and make it more meaningful, and I have presented exercises in several chapters which apply theoretical knowledge to everyday use. I have included chapter outlines at the beginning of each chapter and glossaries at the end which define and explain new terms highlighted in the text, and I have ended each chapter with a summary.

This book does not assume any previous knowledge of psychology or the health professions, but it should be of value to psychology majors, students in the social sciences, and others who are interested in theories and behaviors that enhance the quality of life.

Acknowledgments

I wish to thank the following colleagues and friends for reading earlier drafts of selected chapters from this book: Michael Frank, John F. McInerney, and Lewis Leitner. I also wish to thank The Richard Stockton College of New Jersey and its Research and Development Committee for generous support in time and money in preparing this manuscript. I owe a debt of gratitude to the many students who have read and commented on earlier versions of this work. Finally, I would like to thank my family for their perseverance and patience while I was preoccupied with this task.

PART I

History

CHAPTER 1

The Mind and the Body

In this chapter we will consider the following subjects:

- A short history of the mind–body problem
- How the biomedical model came to be
- The advent of general systems theory
- The increasing importance of health psychology
- The advent of behavioral medicine
- A psychology of well being

Mary, at middle age, has had many symptoms of various kinds of diseases. She has been to many different physicians who have taken care of the symptoms as best they could, and have then waited until the next round of symptoms occurred. Shuffling from doctor to doctor began to be a way of life for her. Many of the physicians that she had dealings with did not consider the possibility that psychosocial factors may have been involved in her many symptoms. Eventually, Mary found a physician who referred her to a psychologist who dealt with her many anxieties and depressed mood about getting old. Through proper consideration of Mary's mind as well as her body, her symptoms improved, and she was able to face life in a more positive manner. In this chapter, we will advocate and discuss some of the powerful psychological strategies that can be brought to bear on physical problems to alleviate human suffering. We will start with some earlier views on how the psyche (mind) was thought to interact with the body.

HISTORICAL DUALISM

Some of the earliest views about the mind–body problem came from the Egyptians who localized thought in the heart but judgment in the head or kidneys (Boring, 1950). In ancient Greece, Aristotle also favored the life force in the heart. Pythagoras and Plato thought of the brain as the seat of the mind and intellect. However, for Plato, the mind could never be explained because it did not have a material existence. Herophilus thought of the brain ventricles as places for vital forces or spirits called *pneuma*, and Galen, a later Greek physician living in Rome, taught that these pneuma flow from the ventricles to the heart and were distributed to the body by the arteries (Boring, 1950). During the Renaissance, Descartes (1596–1650) proposed that the soul was separate from body but that the body and soul interacted through the pineal gland located in the brain. He came to this conclusion when he recognized that the pineal gland did not appear to be bilateral as other brain structures were, and therefore it related very well to his conception of a whole, undivided consciousness. Descartes believed that the pineal gland was the site where the mind affects the flow of the spirits so that they can influence bodily structures.

This interactionism, however, posed problems that have vexed philosophers over the centuries. For example, how can a nonmaterial force, which has no corporal extension and does not occupy space, affect structures that do have extension and do occupy space? This philosophical puzzle is known as the Cartesian impasse. Descartes, who was a devout Catholic, became extremely worried when he heard that the Vatican had forced Galileo to renounce his teaching that the earth revolves around the sun. Galileo's ideas ran counter to the Church's teaching that the earth and humans were the center of the universe. Frightened that his ideas would also incur the wrath of the Church (his astronomical views coincided with those of Galileo), Descartes withheld writing about his views on the physical and nonphysical worlds while he was alive, and they were published posthumously. Descartes believed that the body operated according to physical laws much like intricate machines and that the mind was nonmaterial. The machine analogy was appropriate for Descartes' time because machines were becoming popular as time-savers and entertainment devices.

In the late 1700s and early 1800s, some people were beginning to recognize the mind as subject to disease. For example, Phillipe Pinel (1745–1826) in France agitated for improved treatment of the insane. At that time, it was thought that possession by demons caused insanity. Pinel and others believed that treating the insane more humanely by unchaining them and spending time with them would positively affect the brain and improve the disease process. Noting that the insane did improve with more humane treatment, those concerned with health in Europe began to develop a more physical approach to the mind–body problem.

Around this time, Franz Joseph Gall (1758–1828) observed that bumps and grooves on individuals' heads were related to mental processes that he believed lay underneath. That is, certain parts of the brain that were related to individuals' psychological strengths and weaknesses were exhibited in certain bumps and indentations on the external skull. This led to the field of *phrenology* which became very popular in Europe. Even though this field has now been thoroughly discredited, it did further the idea that physical and mental structures were basically the same thing. Gall's work also promoted the view that certain areas of the brain control different behaviors (Schneider & Tarshis, 1995). This work promulgated the concept of *localization of function*, which is still important in understanding brain and behavior relationships.

THE BIOMEDICAL MODEL

The *biomedical model* has been popular in this country for the last 300 years. The model assumes that there are biochemical and neurophysiological reasons for a particular disorder. This biomedical model has been extremely successful in medicine. It developed when the Church in previous centuries relegated the mind to a spiritual nonmaterialistic area that cannot be explained by physical means. Those who worked with the biomedical model believed mind was better left to philosophy and religion. Thus, medicine tended to disregard the psychosocial aspects of a particular illness and concentrated on the physical symptoms. The biomedical model continued to develop with the advent of the theory that disease takes place in the cell rather than in the humors of the body or by evil spirits. Bodily symptoms became the only reasons for the diagnosis of an illness (Kaplan, 1975).

The biomedical model assumes an important and productive scientific principle known as *reductionism*. That is, it assumes that an explanation can be found by reducing a problem to its simplest parts. Then, one determines whether these parts (variables) cause a particular outcome, such as a disease. Scientists then manipulate these critical variables, or independent variables, to see whether they can affect the phenomenon in which they are interested. In medicine this method is used to determine causes of disease. Medical attempts are made to isolate and eliminate the critical causes of a disease and thereby eliminate the disease. For example, in infectious diseases, bacteria and viruses are causes and can be controlled in many cases by appropriate medication.

Reductionism is the essence of Occam's Razor—a philosophical principle which states that the simplest solution to a problem is the best one. In psychology, the principle is known as Morgan's Canon, which states:

"in no case may we interpret an action as the outcome of the exercise of a higher psychical faculty, if it can be interpreted as the outcome of the exercise of one which stands lower in the psychological scale" (Morgan, 1894, p. 53). Basically, this seminal idea states that the best theories are those that have the fewest and simplest assumptions and are still able to provide a complete explanation of the problem. However, when an assumed simple theory does not provide a complete explanation, then it becomes less useful. Such is the case with the biomedical model. As Engel (1977) stated, the biomedical model ignores the personality of the individual, the social milieu such as family and friend interactions, and the cultural environment in which individuals find themselves. For example, whether one copes with a particular disease in a hopeless or helpless fashion, or whether one begins to practice active coping skills in dealing with the disease determines whether the individual deteriorates or improves.

Bertalanffy (1968) has suggested that one way to look at the person with disease is through *general systems theory*. This perspective suggests that a hierarchy of systems interact with smaller subsystems in continually interchanging ways. For example, starting at the most elemental level the individual is made up of cells, organs, and systems that determine the person as a biological entity; this person is in turn affected by larger systems such as family and friends, local community, ethnic and cultural groups, and at the most general level, the world. All of these factors play a role in the individual's particular response to disease. As a practical matter, health professionals cannot take into adequate consideration all of these different variables when dealing with a sick person. However, the biomedical model seems to overlook critical psychosocial variables that are known to play a role in health and disease.

Nowhere does the biomedical model seem more inadequate then in the area of chronic pain. By definition, chronic pain continues beyond a time when an individual's physical trauma would normally be healed, and it persists in spite of the best efforts of health care providers (Turk & Nash, 1996). According to Turk and Nash (1996), the average duration of pain in specialized pain clinics exceeds seven years, and there are reports of chronic pain for 20 or 30 years. Chronic pain causes suffering not only for the patient involved but also for care takers, health providers, family members, friends, co-workers, and employers. In addition, it often produces financial difficulties. According to Turk and Rudy (1990), the characteristics of patients referred to pain clinics include high levels of psychopathology and psychological distress, frequent use of the health care system, complaints of constant pain with few pain-free periods, prior surgeries, and use of narcotic medication. Using a biomedical model to approach these problems is generally ineffective.

Turk and Nash (1996) have basically attacked chronic pain from a general systems approach. They conceptualize pain as derived from organic processes, psychological processes that entail emotional, motivational, and behavioral contributions, family relations, historical antecedents, and present context. Their *biopsychosocial model* of chronic pain emphasizes cognitive behavior transactions involving cognitive reassessment, reinterpretation, developmental problem solving, and coping skills. The model also emphasizes the interactions between the biomedical approach and psychosocial factors that are related to the treatment of chronic pain. Interdisciplinary pain clinics have developed to deal with the physical aspects of chronic pain, such as loss of muscle strength, tone, and flexibility, to improve body mechanics, and to assist in homemaking activities, occupational tasks, and self-pacing. Psychologists teach self-management techniques to help improve communication among family, friends, and health care providers.

In practice, it is sometimes difficult to utilize a general systems approach. Multidisciplinary pain clinics are best equipped and seem generally able to deal with the biopsychosocial aspects of the chronic pain experience. However, in the day-to-day busy practices of many health care providers, this approach is frequently difficult. For example, in a recent study done in England (Howe, 1996), many physicians felt that they did not have enough time. In this study, nineteen practitioners were recruited in Sheffield, England, by random selection. They were asked questions that were related to their relative inability to identify psychological distressed individuals and their reasons for it. At least in this study, better psychosocial training for general practitioners may improve their skills in picking up psychosocial stress. However, putting this training into practice at the practitioner–patient level may be difficult because adequate time did not seem to exist for these general practitioners to use their psychosocial skills in an appropriate manner. They were forced to focus on presenting physical symptoms rather than on psychological distress.

With the advent of managed care, time constraints for health professionals will likely get more stringent rather than less so. It remains an extremely powerful challenge at the most basic level to provide more time and training to use the biopsychosocial model in dealing not only with patients' medical symptoms, but also with the psychological and social milieu that affects them.

HEALTH PSYCHOLOGY AND BEHAVIORAL MEDICINE

A new field that was started in the early 1970s integrated psychology into physical illness. This new field grew out of behaviorism and was called *behavioral medicine*. It monopolized classical conditioning and operant conditioning as ways to enhance, suppress, or modify problem behaviors such as phobias and anxieties. The founder of the field, Neal Miller, developed biofeedback to control various internal biological systems in order to improve individual health. Mind–body links became more and more prevalent, and sensitivity developed across the health community in general regarding mind–body links. Health psychology developed in the late 1970s within the field of psychology. It rapidly became a large enough contingent in psychology to have its own division, the Division of Health Psychology, in one of the two national psychology organizations, the American Psychological Association. Health psychology also became a significant part of the broad-based discipline of behavioral medicine. At present, behavioral medicine has a large, diverse membership consisting of the disciplines of psychology, psychiatry, public health, sociology, anthropology, occupational and physical therapy, nursing, and nutrition. Health psychology is one of the disciplines found in this broad and diverse field. The integration of health psychology into behavioral medicine has helped to form a new psychology of well being.

ROLES FOR A PSYCHOLOGY OF WELL BEING

According to Richard Suinn (1996), two national movements in the United States have created a crisis for psychologists: national health care reform and managed care. What roles do psychologists play in this changing health care market, and what unique abilities do they bring to the table? Psychologists have a unique opportunity to redefine their roles in the health care system. Psychologists, more than ever before, should be able to demonstrate their abilities to diversify into primary health care. According to Suinn (1996), it is crucial to identify psychology as contributing to all individuals using health care systems, not only those in need of psychotherapy. To show this, psychologists must inform the public that psychological services include primary health care and not simply mental health care. Suinn covers two areas of service: services to protect health and prevent disease, and services to help the patient once the physical disease has occurred. As Suinn points out, poor health is costly. Total health care costs in the United States totaled $800 billion in 1992 (U.S. Congressional Budget Office, 1992). Factoring in lost productivity, total costs of health care are estimated to be 30 percent of the gross national product (Bernard & Krupat, 1993, in Suinn, 1996).

Psychological services can reduce these costs. For example, stress management programs can reduce surgical recovery time (Wells, Howard, Nowlin, & Vargas, 1986). Pain clinics can produce lifetime savings from medical costs, disability payments, and loss of potential earnings (Steig & Williams, 1983). Jacobs (1987) estimated cost reductions of over $7 million using psychological programs on reducing hospital stays and outpatient visits. These programs used certain procedures to control stress and pain. Suinn (1996) indicates that biofeedback training has led to a 72 percent reduction of time in hospital and a 63 percent reduction in clinic visits. At the same time, pain control programs have led to 72 percent reductions in hospital stays and 50 percent reductions in clinical visits (Jacobs, 1987). Linden, Stossel, and Maurice (1996) indicated that psychological interventions with cardiac patients reduced mortality by 42 percent and morbidity by 61 percent, compared to treatments using traditional medical and physical components.

In health protection, the leading causes of death are smoking, alcoholism, obesity, hypertension, and poor physical fitness. A large number of programs have demonstrated success in all of these areas (see Suinn, 1996). Anger management (Nakano, 1990; Suinn, 1990) is available for controlling the critical anger/cynicism component of Type A behaviors. It may be possible in the near future to deal with buttressing the immune system against the ravages of stress. For example, caregivers of patients with Alzheimer's disease show high stress, poor immune function, and higher infection rates (Kiecolt-Glaser, Dura, Speicher, Trask, & Glaser, 1991). Stress management programs may prove of immense value in helping these individuals.

There are psychological programs that deal with recovery from disease, especially heart disease, which is a major killer in the United States. Psychological services include neuropsychological assessments, psychosocial and cognitive rehabilitation, and supportive counseling (Suinn, 1996).

For cancer patients, psychologists provide supportive therapy during initial diagnosis and training in coping with the side effects of chemotherapy, pain management, grief counseling, and psychotherapy for cancer survivors (e.g., B. L. Anderson, 1992; Spiegel, Bloom, Kraemer, & Gottheil, 1989).

In HIV infection and AIDS, psychologists are helping to identify the psychosocial variables that increase risk-reducing behaviors and to develop control of alcohol and drug abuse which decrease risk-reducing behaviors (Stall, Coates, & Hoff, 1988). Psychologists are involved in changing peer norms and individual behaviors that increase high-risk behaviors (e.g., Kelly et al., 1991).

In diabetes control, psychologists are offering stress management programs and psychological support, weight control programs, and education in self-care programs (e.g., Feinglos & Surwit, 1988; Wing, Epstein, Nowalk, & Lambarski, 1996).

Psychologists have been making significant progress in reducing medical costs, clinical stays and clinical visits, and the general costs associated with health care. The time is ripe for a psychology of well being.

SUMMARY

The psychology of well being has roots going back to ancient Greece and Rome. The prevailing view of the ancients was that the mind and the body were separate. The mind could never be explained on a materialistic basis. It was thought to operate through pneuma, or spirits, that governed thoughts and behaviors. Descartes suggested that the mind and body, though separate, interact at the pineal gland. Gradually through the 1700s and 1800s, behaviors were thought to have a more physical basis. Gall suggested that behaviors could be determined by the lumps and indentations on a person's skull. He thought these irregular features of the skull indicated underlying psychological attributes. Even though disproved, the idea suggested that the physical brain and behavior were intimately related.

As the belief in the physical basis of behavior became dominant, the biomedical model developed as a powerful way to explain mental and physical illness. The biomedical model was hugely successful, but psychosocial variables remained largely ignored. To meet this need, general systems theory and the biopsychosocial model of health and disease developed. These concepts indicate that psychosocial and environmental variables, as well as biological ones, determine health and disease.

Modern-day applications of principles derived from general systems theory and the biopsychosocial model have shown important improvements in preventative health and recovery from chronic diseases. With the application of procedures such as stress management, cognitive restructuring, and biofeedback, individuals stay well and recover faster from illnesses, with considerable cost reductions in the health care system. It is now time to embrace a psychology of well being.

Food for Thought

1. Describe how Descartes came to terms with the pneuma theory. Why was the pineal gland chosen as the point of intersection of mind and body? What is the Cartesian impasse?
2. What was Franz Joseph Gall's theory? Why did it make sense to him? What was the positive contribution of his work to medicine and psychology?
3. What is reductionism? Why is it so important in science? How does the biomedical model make use of reductionism?
4. Describe the biopsychosocial model. Why is it such an advancement over the biomedical model? Are there any difficulties with it? Explain.

GLOSSARY

behavioral medicine: an interdisciplinary field of study integrating the behavioral, social, and medical sciences.

biomedical model: a model that emphasizes the biological aspects of health and disease.

biopsychosocial model: a model that emphasizes psychological, social, and cultural aspects of health and disease as well as biology.

general systems theory: a theory concerned with the interaction of biological, psychological, social, cultural, and environmental determinants of behavior.

localization of function: a theory that particular parts of the brain carry on specialized psychological functions.

phrenology: a theory that bumps and indentations on the skull can determine an individual's psychological attributes.

pneuma: spirits or metaphysical forces that were thought to govern the mind's actions during ancient and medieval times. It was supplanted by the biomedical model.

reductionism: a theory that explains a complex phenomenon like behavior by reducing it to its simplest and most important elements.

PART II

Lifestyle

CHAPTER 2

Exercise

In this chapter we will consider the following subjects:

- Meaning of exercise
- Difficulties in starting an exercise program
- Mental and physical benefits of exercise
- Exercise addiction
- Exercise and chronic diseases
- Older adults and exercise

In the early days of the running boom, right after the publication of Kenneth Cooper's first book on *aerobics* (1968), interest in aerobic fitness and health peaked. Cooper's book was based on research he did with Air Force recruits at Lackland Air Force Base in San Antonio, Texas, and was very persuasive to a health-conscious public. Races and running clubs sprang up everywhere. After a few years, however, the upswing in running began to plateau. Some of the runners just got tired of it, some became injured too often, and others began to *cross-train* in other sports such as swimming and cycling. Some of these cross-trainers participated in the developing sport of the triathalon which required proficiency in the three sports of running, swimming, and cycling. Others cross-trained to reduce or stop overuse injuries that occurred with running.

The message carried from the early era of the running boom was that most people cannot tolerate long-term, exclusively high-level activity such as running, which produces physical shock to the lower extremities.

Physical injuries and mental burnout from the everyday workouts were the results. However, the physical and mental problems of runners, cross-trainers, and other intensive exercisers were, and are, the concerns of only a small subset of the American population. These athletes consist of no more than 8 percent of all men and 7 percent of all women (Caspersen, Christenson, & Pollard, 1986). Exercise needs to be studied for its benefits among people who will not exercise this intensely.

EXERCISE AND HEALTH

Exercise does seem to be important to people in the general population who are not part of the above small group, and if you ask around it seems that everyone is engaging in some physical activity. Sometimes you hear comments like "I've been on my feet all day; I get plenty of exercise." "Chasing the kids around gives me plenty of exercise." Although some people may think this is exercise, it may not be enough. According to a select panel of experts (Pate et al., 1995), sanctioned by the Centers for Disease Control and Prevention and the American College of Sports Medicine, "Every U.S. adult should accumulate 30 minutes or more a day of moderate-intensity physical activity on most, preferably all, days of the week." Neither standing on one's feet and occasionally moving from here to there, nor sporadic chases after children may capture the large muscles of the body consistently or forcefully enough to fulfill these requirements. However, the daily requirement is a cumulative requirement, and it can be done in more than one session (Surgeon General's Report on Physical Activity and Health, 1996). Brisk walking, or expending 200 kilocalories a day, will fulfill these requirements (Pate et al., 1995). This would necessitate a walk of about two miles.

An analysis of eight national surveys (Stephens, Jacobs, & White, 1985), conducted in the United States and Canada between 1972 and 1983, suggested that only 20 percent of people in North America were exercising enough to achieve cardiorespiratory fitness. Some 40 percent were active to some lesser degree and were still receiving some health benefit; approximately 40 percent of the population were entirely sedentary, which self-reports may underestimate. Of course, these were major surveys and there were methodological problems such as the validity of self-reports. Interpretations of these results are also dependent on how each of the surveys defines exercise and how intense the exercise is. Lack of agreement on parameters could easily produce differences in outcome. These studies were not prospective and did not survey individuals over time, nor were they blind or double-blind experiments, an almost impossible task in the exercise field since it is very hard to conceal whether or not subjects are exercising. However preliminary these studies are, they are cause for concern with their indication that such a large percentage of the population is sedentary.

As mentioned at the beginning of this chapter, it appears that the running boom and exercise boom of the 1970s and 1980s may be leveling off and may even be declining. Since we control the amount of exercise we get, it would be helpful to determine ways in which we could increase the level of exercise in this country. Knowing that exercise has so many health benefits it is important to educate the public about them. On the positive side, older Americans (50 and over) have increased their activity level more than younger adults (Stephens, 1987), but older Americans still show low levels of exercise, as we will see later in this chapter.

Motives for exercise include exercise as a social experience, as a way to health and fitness, as a release for tension and pent-up emotions, and as a significant challenge in one's life (Kenyon, 1968).

Running seems to satisfy all of these motives; so for these reasons, as well as the aerobics revolution for health, it has developed into one of the most popular participant sports in the United States. Consequently, a larger body of research has been built up around running than many other sports because researchers have access to so many willing subjects who themselves often want to know more about their activity. (By the way, it is considered poor form to call a runner a jogger. Runners say they move faster and are more serious about their activity.) Many running clubs have been established throughout the country, and lots of newsletters and sports equipment (especially shoes) dedicated to runners are in evidence.

According to Johnsgard (1985), once runners start, several motives encourage them to continue running. These motives include maintaining fitness, having a chance to be alone with one's own thoughts, challenging one's physical and mental limits, competing, developing good feelings, gaining a sense of identity as a runner, controlling weight, and developing friendships. In a study on runners, Carmack and Mertens (1979) asked 250 men and 65 women why they began to run and why they continued running. Getting in shape and staying there topped the list of reasons for both men and women; enjoyment was second as a motive for beginning and continuing; weight control was third for beginning and fourth as a reason for continuing.

Exercise clearly helps one maintain optimal body weight and optimal *muscle-to-fat ratios*, prevent coronary heart disease, keep cholesterol within normal limits, and prevent adult onset diabetes or type 2 diabetes (Surgeon General's Report on Physical Fitness and Health, 1996). There is also some evidence that exercise helps to keep blood pressure under control, promotes bone density, and helps prevent lower back pain. It may also help prevent lung disease, kidney failure, and various forms of arthritis (Bouchard, Shepherd, Stephens, Sutton, & McPherson, 1990, pp. 4–28). In sum, physical fitness seems to have the ability to prevent and delay disease and disability, and to improve quality of life and possibly even extend it (Blair, Kohl, Gordon, & Paffenbarger, 1992). However, it is generally agreed that more long-range longitudinal (prospective) studies are needed to reinforce these perceptions.

REASONS FOR NOT EXERCISING

Lack of time is one of the frequently cited reasons for not exercising (Willis & Campbell, 1992, pp. 15–16). However, if one analyzes what goes on during an individual's day, lack of time is not the problem. It is usually a matter of what a person wants to do at particular times during the day. For example, people will spend large amounts of time watching television, socializing, or engaging in a variety of other activities rather than exercising. Exercise is something many people do not consider a joyful activity, and therefore they find other things to do in its place.

Another reason frequently heard for not exercising is feeling fatigued (Willis & Campbell, 1992, p. 16). However, we know that individuals seem to rejuvenate after exercising; the fatigue accumulated during the day seems to dissipate.

Lack of exercise facilities nearby is another excuse for not exercising (see Dishman, 1990, p. 85). This problem is disappearing rapidly with the almost daily establishment of health clubs and other exercise facilities. There is also a myriad of home exercise products (although, they often collect dust or are used as clothes hangers). One does not necessarily need exercise facilities or equipment in order to exercise. For example, walking, biking, and jogging can all be done with minimum facilities and equipment. In fact, walking is almost universally recognized as one of the most important exercise habits one can develop. It is relatively nontraumatic to the musculoskeletal system, improves cardiorespiratory fitness, and aids in weight control. However, living in dangerous neighborhoods is a mitigating circumstance against walking, particularly in the evenings. In this case, it may be possible to travel to shopping malls or other enclosed and more protected areas and walk there.

Lack of knowledge about how to get in shape is another problem. Quackery and misinformation abound in the exercise world. Misinformation and quick fixes are frequently seen on television and in advertisements for exercise equipment. For example, motorized exercise equipment popular in some exercise facilities that does not require active muscle effort, but moves the body through a range of motion passively, has limited effectiveness in developing physical fitness. Not receiving the correct information, or being swayed by simplistic and exaggerated claims to fitness, can discourage individuals from ever achieving optimal fitness for themselves when they do not see physical change in a reasonable amount of time.

AEROBIC EXERCISE

In the last 100 years we have become subject to a tremendous increase in stress caused by technological advances coupled with a reduction in physical activity in our lives. As tension mounts in our daily lives, there are fewer ways to release this tension and the anxiety that develops. This causes an overflow of many of the hormones related to stress, with eventual mental and physical collapse. As we go along, we tend to believe that this level of sedentary activity coupled with increased stress in modern-day society is a normal state of affairs. As mentioned earlier, only 8 percent of all men and 7 percent of all women regularly perform the type of vigorous activity recommended (Caspersen, Christenson, & Pollard, 1986). We seem to lack physical activity in our lives. Because of the technological revolution, many activities that required physical effort such as going to school and work, the job itself, and managing a household, are much less physically demanding than they were at, say, the turn of this century. According to an earlier report by the American College of Sports Medicine (1991), we should be engaging in large-muscle activity that is rhythmic and repetitive (for example, walking, running, rowing, jumping rope, cycling, and swimming) for at least 20 minutes three to four times a week. This should be at a level of intensity that is at 50 to 85 percent of our maximal aerobic capacity. (A rough estimate of maximal capacity is easily determined by 220 minus your age, times 50 to 85 percent.) However, the new recommendations (Pate et al., 1995; Surgeon General's Report on Physical Activity and Health, 1996) note that the majority of health benefits can be attained with a cumulative 30-minute daily physical activity program outside of formal exercise programs and are equivalent to the older recommendations. The new recommendations may also have been made because Caspersen et al. (1986) indicated that so few adults were achieving the earlier requirements.

Through years of evolution, our bodies have developed a need for vigorous physical activity regularly in our lives. Even mild to moderate amounts of physical activity are better than nothing and may add to our physical well-being and life expectancy (Paffenbarger, Hyde, Wing, & Hsieh, 1986). It is important to engage in some level of physical activity, and it does not need to be exhausting and difficult. For example, walking, hiking, slow cycling, and comfortably paced swimming could all confer some health benefits (Blair, Kohl, Gordon, & Paffenbarger, 1992).

The biggest problem with exercise is going from doing nothing to doing something. With their easy availability and immediate reinforcement abilities, it is much easier to turn to mood-altering chemicals such as alcohol, cigarettes, and other drugs in order to achieve some relief from the stress and strains of everyday life, and to relieve anxiety and depression. However, they work so well mainly because of their reinforcing and positive-incentive value (e.g., Pinel, 1993, p. 445). They make the drug user feel good right away and produce a strong drive to use the drug again. There is evidence that exercise might be as effective as drugs in improving mood but without the side effects of these other methods (e.g., King, Haskell, Taylor, & DeBusk, 1989; Taylor, Sallis, & Needle, 1985). The lack of immediate mood improvement following the beginning of an exercise program (delay of reinforcement) is a problem for behavioral control. The feeling good state that reinforces exercise and motivates one to stay with it (positive-incentive value) usually comes much later after physical fitness has improved. Motivational techniques must be developed to get the exercising individual through the first few difficult weeks of an exercise program. As it is, dropout rates in the first few weeks from supervised exercise programs in North America and Scandinavia have remained at about 40 to 50 percent for about the last 20 years (Dishman, 1990, p. 94).

EXERCISE AND EMOTIONAL FITNESS

Many studies in recent years have shown that exercise has a positive effect on emotions, and in particular, anxiety and depression (Surgeon General's Report on Physical Activity and Health, 1996). For example, Griest et al. (1981) showed there was a significant reduction in depression among individuals who participated in running therapy as compared to psychotherapy techniques, and they responded better than many individuals did on antidepressant medication. Roth and Holmes (1987) found that college students who reported a high number of negative life events showed improved health after engaging in physical exercise over an eleven-week period. They experienced a greater drop in depression when compared to a relaxation training group or a group that received no treatment at all. Another study reported similar findings with female undergraduates exercising (McCann & Holmes, 1984).

On the negative side, Weinstein and Meyers (1983) concluded that the available literature failed to support the position that running plays a significant role in modulating depression and other mood problems. These researchers believe that the research in this area is not well done. Also, most of the research in the area is cross-sectional and correlational in nature, and begs the question of the cause-effect relationship between running and the reduction of depression. However, studies that have been done seem to agree that chronic exercise is related to decreased depression. Simons, Epstein, McGowan, Kupfer, and Robertson (1985) were guardedly optimistic about the effects of exercise on positive mood changes. A meta-analysis consisting of an analysis of 261 studies relating to exercise and depression revealed that exercise significantly decreased depression (McCullagh, North, & Mood, 1988). North and McCullagh (1988) showed that the large decreases in depression were associated with longer exercise programs and increases in the frequency of exercise sessions. One study (Doyne et al., 1987) indicated that both running and weight training can have a significant effect in reducing depression.

Sime (1984) suggested several different explanations for the effects of exercise on depression: increases in the availability of the neural transmitter, norepinephrine which may be less available in depression, increased feelings of mastery and self-control, and improvements in body image and self-concept. Other factors may be distraction from the symptoms of depression, substitution of good habits for bad habits, and exercise-induced mood alterations (Dishman, 1986).

Dienstbier, LaGuardia, Barnes, Tharp, and Schmidt (1987) have proposed that emotionally healthy individuals are more difficult to arouse than anxious individuals. However, when they are in difficult and stressful situations, they experience a rapid upswing of adrenal gland hormonal output and arousal, but then they return to the normal base rate much more quickly than emotionally less fit individuals. Dienstbier and colleagues called this type of response *toughness*. They suggested the best way to increase toughness is through aerobic exercise. "Even a modest physical training program should, therefore, have an impact on toughening" (Dienstbier et al., 1987). Some of the physiological benefits include lower arousal base rates, decreases in heart rate and blood pressure, improved glucose utilization, and relative increases in high-density lipid protein (the good cholesterol). Direct psychological benefits include feelings of mastery and improved body image from lowered weight and body fat distribution changes.

Some aerobic activities such as running do pose a risk of injury, especially to the joints and muscles. For example, many runners experience injuries, especially to the knees, which incapacitate them for days or quite a bit longer. One way to offset this injury is to cross-train. This approach uses a variety of different aerobic and nonaerobic exercises during the week to rest and counterbalance muscles that are used exclusively for running. We have no good long-term studies on the effects of cross-training versus running as an exclusive activity, but each has benefits and costs. Cross-trainers tend not to be at the top of the running elite but are more injury free. For most exercisers, cross-training is a price worth paying.

RUNNING ADDICTION

Although there has been a lot of comment in the last few years about *running addictions* in which individuals have withdrawal symptoms if they have to stop running, other forms of aerobic exercise and weight lifting may also be considered possible candidates for this addiction. Morgan (1979) indicated that negatively addicted runners seem to need exercise to cope with life, and they also experience withdrawal within the first 24 to 36 hours after ceasing. They seem to experience many of the same withdrawal symptoms that stopping opiates, alcohol, and nicotine may produce. These symptoms include apathy, sluggishness, tension, lack of appetite, headaches, and sleeplessness. In the case of aerobic exercisers, however, if the exercise break is planned, apparently the withdrawal symptoms do not take place (Crossman, Jamieson, & Henderson, 1987). Even slight variations in training may have negative effects on regular runners (Thaxton, 1982). Thaxton's study showed elevated depression scores and higher Galvanic Skin Response scores (which suggest elevated anxiety) in a group of runners who missed a regular workout. These results suggest that stress was higher in these runners when compared to others who did not miss their workout.

One author (Glasser, 1976) suggested that running addictions were positive rather than negative. That is, if exercise improves psychological well being and physical strength, then individuals have a positive addiction. For an addiction to be positive, it must be something that one chooses to do and that one can become proficient in on one's own, something that one must be willing to spend time consistently on, and something that one must persevere long enough to become positively addicted to. This positive addiction will then produce withdrawal symptoms such as fatigue, tension, and anxiety when an exercise session is missed. A study of more than 340 runners found that most runners experience withdrawal symptoms when they are unable to run (Robbins & Joseph, 1985). Over 50 percent reported restlessness, irritability, frustration, guilt, and fatigue. Interestingly, this effect does not seem to occur in swimmers (Crossman et al., 1987). The swimmers showed no significant changes in mood during a layoff period from swimming training.

A running addiction can become negative when the runner's social life is severely affected. For example, family relations, relations with friends, common interests, feelings of not wanting to work, and feeling tired most of the time may be related to a negative addiction (Robbins & Joseph, 1980). Some even run on severe injuries and stress fractures. If runners seem to need ever-increasing dosages of running and seem to neglect other aspects of their lives, then they are likely to be negatively addicted (Morgan, 1979).

One physiological explanation for exercise addiction is the sympathetic arousal hypothesis of Thompson and Blanton (1987). In their view, exercise dependence is mediated by reductions in sympathetic output during exercise because of efficiency in energy use. This lowered sympathetic output produces an ever increasing level of exercise to produce increases in physiological arousal that the individual finds pleasurable. This increase in arousal produced by exercise is related to the properties of catecholamines such as norepinephrine and serotonin. The feelings of fatigue and cognitive slowdowns that occur when addicted individuals are not exercising support this hypothesis. Researchers are not sure what this exercise addiction is but do know that it sometimes interferes with social, recreational, and professional activities as much as any other drug addiction.

Box 2.1 provides a sample test on exercise addiction.

Runner's High

Apparently, some runners experience a positive mood-state sometimes called the *runner's high* during runs. Some runners report that it is very positive and sometimes produces a mystical experience and altered state of consciousness. According to Willis and Campbell (1992), the experience is completely absorbing. It's a peak experience sometimes of wonder, awe, reverence, humility, and surrender, positive experiences of elation and joy are accompanied by loss of fear, anxiety, inhibition, and restraint. Not all runners experience this runner's high. Depending on the study, as few as 9 percent to as many as 78 percent of all runners have this experience (Sachs, 1984). According to Sachs, even the ones who do experience these euphoric feelings do not experience them more than about 30 percent of the time. For many, the "high" comes from finishing the run or exercise program. Morgan (1985) suggested that this runner's high may occur from distraction from stress; from elevation of the neural transmitters, norepinephrine and serotonin; and possibly from elevation of endorphins. However, the research on this topic remains preliminary and speculative. (Personally, I have heard few, if any, regular exercisers report this effect.)

EXERCISE AND CORONARY HEART DISEASE (CHD)

In the early 1970s, Dr. Ralph Paffenbarger and his colleagues (Paffenbarger, Laughlin, Gima, & Black, 1970) published data on more than 3,600 San Francisco longshoremen whom they had tracked for about 20 years. They found that longshoremen who had physically demanding jobs had a lower death rate from CHD than their colleagues who had jobs that were less physically demanding. Sedentary workers had a death rate from CHD that was 80 percent higher than that of the more active

Box 2.1
Self-Test on Exercise Addiction

Test yourself to see if you are an addicted exerciser. In general, the closer your score is to 80, the more likely you are addicted to exercise.

Commitment to Exercise Scale

Instructions: the following are statements describing attitudes to exercise. Respond by marking on the line beside each statement the point which best describes your position on the continuum. The right end of the scale is worth 10 points, and the left end of the scale is worth zero points.

1. How important do you think it is to your general well-being not to miss your exercise sessions?

---

not at all   very
important   important

2. Does it upset you if, for one reason or another, you are unable to exercise?

---

never   always
upset   upset

3. If you miss an exercise session, or several sessions, do you try to make them up by putting in more time when you get back?

---

never   always

4. Do you have a strict routine for your exercise sessions, e.g., the same time of the day, the same location, the same number of laps, particular exercises, and so forth?

---

no routine   strict routine

5. Do you continue to exercise at times when you feel tired and unwell?

---

never   always

6. Do you continue to exercise even when you have sustained an exercise-related injury?

---

never   always

(continued)

Box 2.1 *(continued)*

7. Do you feel guilty that you have somehow "let yourself down" when you miss your exercise session?

_____

not at all   a great deal

8. Are there times when you turn down an invitation to an interesting social event because it interferes with your exercise schedule?

_____

never   always

Source: Davis, C., Brewer, H., & Ratusny, D. (1993). Behavioral frequency and psychological commitment: Necessary concepts in the study of excessive exercising. *Journal of Behavioral Medicine, 16,* 625–626. Reproduced by permission of Plenum Publishing Corporation.

longshoremen. Paffenbarger and his colleagues matched on other risk factors for CHD such as smoking habits, blood pressure levels, and height to weight ratios by comparing men who had jobs that involved different amounts of physical activity but had similar coronary risk factors. Matching prevented the activity data from being confounded by other coronary risk factors and allowed the researchers to determine if it was truly physical activity that was having an impact on CHD death rates. Other risk factors also had independent effects on CHD rates. They found heavy smokers had a death rate from CHD double those who did not smoke or who were light smokers. Those who had high systolic blood pressure (above 140 mm/hg) had a risk factor that was 89 percent higher than those with normal blood pressure. Those with a height to weight ratio that indicated obesity had a death rate that was 35 percent higher than those with normal height to weight ratio.

In 1976, Cooper and his colleagues (Cooper et al., 1976) investigated whether the level of cardiovascular fitness correlated with CHD risk factors such as smoking, obesity, and high blood pressure. Cooper et al. used cardiorespiratory fitness levels (very poor, poor, fair, good, excellent) to categorize men whose average age was about 44½ years old. These researchers concluded that their data showed an inverse relationship between levels of cardiorespiratory fitness and variables related to a higher CHD risk. That is, the higher the cardiorespiratory fitness, the less the risk of CHD. The more inversely related the categories were, the more marked the differences between the groups in CHD risk. The researchers suggested that their data supported the notion that higher levels of physical fitness appeared to protect individuals from CHD. Later studies by Paffenbarger, Wing, and Hyde (1978) and by Morris, et al. (1980) confirmed and extended these results, which indicated that individuals who were more active tended to have much less CHD.

All of these studies were correlational, and it was difficult to ascertain cause-effect relationships. For example, do people who are prone to healthier constitutions exercise more, or does exercise produce healthier constitutions? Also, it is sometimes difficult to determine whether earlier preexisting conditions may contribute to an individual's poor health.

In 1983, Peters, Cady, Bischoff, Bernstein, and Pike examined the physical work capacity of 2,779 men. Coronary risk factors were also noted, such as blood pressure and smoking. The researchers followed the men for about five years, and there were 36 heart attacks at the end of this period. Physically unfit men were twice as likely to have heart attacks as were the physically fit men.

In 1984, Paffenbarger, Hyde, Wing, and Steinmetz followed Harvard alumni on the amount of calories expended in physical activity for a week based on self-reports. College athletes who became inactive after graduation were 49 percent more likely to develop cardiovascular disease than their more active cohorts. Sedentary students who became active after graduation had less than one-half the CHD risk factor of their sedentary cohorts. Researchers found a strong inverse relationship between the amount of physical activity and cardiovascular and respiratory diseases. However, in large-scale epidemiological studies such as this one, it is difficult to determine whether physical activity was the single most important factor in reducing coronary risk factors. Reviewing risk factors such as high blood pressure, elevated cholesterol levels, cigarette smoking, obesity, and physical inactivity, Crandall (1986) concluded that research, though based on self-reports and correlational in nature, overwhelmingly indicates that physical activity such as running can lower coronary risk factors, and the more one exercises the more beneficial it is.

Controversy: Running and Heart Disease

In 1972, Dr. Thomas Bassler, pathologist at Centinella Hospital in Los Angeles, reported in *The New England Journal of Medicine* that he was unable to find a single death due to coronary atherosclerosis among marathoners of any age. Parenthetically, a marathon is 26.2 miles or 42 kilometers. He reported that in order for marathoners to be included in his data, they would have had to have completed a marathon in under four hours. Bassler would only consider bona fide autopsied cases. He and his colleagues (Bassler & Cordello, 1976; Bassler & Schaff, 1976) could not find any deaths from heart disease in anyone who finished a marathon. Other qualifications in this marathon hypothesis were that the individual must have the ability to cover the 42K on foot, but this person could do it by walking, running, or cross-country skiing. There were some inconsistencies in this hypothesis; for example, walking the distance would take more than four hours. Bassler also seemed to be ambiguous about beer drinking as a plus in preventing CHD (Olsen, 1982). By 1980, Bassler had modified his hypothesis, stating that the marathon runner's lifestyle was most critical in preventing degenerative diseases such as CHD.

The controversy raged for several years in the 1970s, with detractors arguing that Bassler had produced no scientific evidence based on methodologically sound scientific criteria to back up his claims. Bassler noted for every incidence of evidence refuting his hypothesis that the runners either were not marathon runners or had died of other conceivable causes.

In 1979, Noakes, Lionel, Opie, Rose, and Kleynhans reported on five deceased, autopsied marathon runners, four of whom, it had been determined, had advanced atherosclerosis. Noakes and Opie (1979) also pointed to five living marathon runners who had suffered heart attacks and who had angiography confirming myocardial infarction. They pointed out that marathon running and the lifestyle that it encourages probably prevent the development of and spread of CHD, but the protection is not as absolute as Bassler had claimed.

The big fear was that based on Bassler's hypothesis many runners, especially marathon runners, would ignore symptoms of heart disease and continue training in order to reverse the symptoms. Opie (1975) looked at sudden death among athletes. In the 19 deaths from CHD that he studied, 13 of these men had physical symptoms prior to their deaths such as chest pain. However, Opie noted that almost all of them ignored their symptoms and continued at the same level of physical training. In discussing this controversy, Crandall (1986) noted that many researchers had misgivings about the marathon protection hypothesis propagated by Bassler. However, Crandall pointed out that Bassler was generally very conservative in his statements. He often modified his statements with the verbs "appears" or "suggests," rather than making blanket endorsements. Based on a review of evidence in the 1970s and 1980s, Crandall (1986) concluded that running does not prevent CHD. He indicated that even the ability to run a marathon does not indicate that no CHD is present.

On observing the running phenomenon in the 1970s and 1980s, it did appear (although I know of no scientific evidence in this regard) that many runners ignored diet, believing that their exercise program would protect them. Diet seemed important only as a means to reduce body weight and decrease running times in races. I remember one T-shirt proclaiming, "I run so I can pig out."

One death that stands out among all the others is that of Jim Fixx, a well-known runner and author of two best-selling books on running. He died while on a ten-mile run that he took almost every day. His premature death can at least be partially understood by his personal and genetic history. He started running late in life after being sedentary for many years, he was a heavy smoker until he started running seriously, and he had a strong family history of heart disease. He is purported to have also ignored early warning signs that he had CHD. According to runners who knew Jim Fixx, he also believed that his ten-mile runs would protect him against the heart disease that ran in his family. He was on the lecture circuit because of the popularity of his books, and likely he had to eat whatever was at hand in airports and other away-from-home eating places. No doubt much of this fare was high fat and contributed to his atherosclerosis.

Jim Fixx's story cannot be dismissed lightly because of his negative genetic and personal history. Crandall (1986) has summarized a great deal of evidence that intense physical activity such as running a marathon does *not* absolutely protect against CHD in individuals—even in those who do not have Fixx's negative genetic and personal characteristics. There is even evidence that cardiac arrest occurs more frequently during exercise than during nonexercise periods. However, a few caveats are in order here. It is true that cardiac arrest is more likely during exercise, but the well-conditioned person has much less likelihood of having a cardiac arrest anytime than the deconditioned person. Also, the probability of a heart attack is much higher during exercise for a person who is not in shape than for one who is. Thompson and Mitchell (1984), for example, state that exercise risk does not equal the long-term beneficial effects of physical activity. It is clear now that exercise of any intensity does not protect against degenerative diseases such as CHD, and that all lifestyle factors and genetics must be considered in the total package in preventative health care. However, as Crandall (1986, pp. 222–223) states in a small study that he did with 113 joggers who were 55 and over and "were certainly not elite in health," even though running does not provide absolute immunity from heart disease, it does seem to produce "a higher quality of life."

EXERCISE ADHERENCE

At the other end of the continuum of committed marathon runners are individuals who start exercise programs. Continuing to exercise after starting an exercise program is called *adherence*. This basically means sticking to or faithfully conforming to a standard of behavior in order to meet some goal (Willis & Campbell, 1992, p. 20). As mentioned earlier, the primary reason given for dropping out of an exercise program is lack of time (Oldridge, 1982; Willis & Campbell, 1992, p. 22). Other factors are:

- too much time away from work and family
- illness in the family
- lack of interest in the exercise program
- too far or inconvenient to travel to an exercise center
- too expensive
- exercise programs offered at inconvenient days and times
- difficulty in transportation

In their review of the literature, Willis and Campbell (1992) suggested that there appeared to be a direct relationship between the individual's activity level as a child and as an adult. Growing up with an involvement in exercise and sports activity seemed to play a significant role in physical activity in adulthood. Even activity just prior to present exercise behavior is positively related to adherence. Those who were most active before the evaluation of exercise activity continued to be the most active, and those the least active continued to be the least active (Kruse & Calden, 1986).

Another relevant factor is use of leisure time. For example, those who are inactive during their leisure time are more apt to drop out of exercise programs than those who are physically active (e.g., Andrew et al., 1981; Oldridge, 1982). In addition, nearly every study reviewed by Willis and Campbell (1992, p. 24) found a link between smoking and dropping out of exercise programs. Smokers were much more likely to drop out in the first few weeks of an exercise program than were nonsmokers, and they were 2.6 times more likely to be overall program dropouts than nonsmokers (Oldridge, Wicks, Hanley, Sutton, & Jones, 1978).

Surprisingly, some of the factors that do not seem to play a role are age, gender, and marital status. Social and economic factors such as educational background, occupation, and income have not been systematically investigated to any significant degree. Personality traits of exercisers versus dropouts as predictors of exercise adherence tend to be conflicting or inconclusive (Willis & Campbell, 1992, p. 27). Measures of self-motivation, Type A behavior, internal/external locus of control, and self-reporting personality inventories such as the Profile of Mood States (POMS) have yielded inconclusive evidence of particular personality factors being significantly related to exercise adherence. As Box 2.2 shows encouragement by health professionals is helpful to get people to exercise more.

Box 2.2
A Research Tidbit: The Influence of the Physician on Exercise

Lewis and Lynch (1993) examined patients over a two-month baseline period who were visiting their family physician and were 18 years old or older. The researchers asked whether their physicians had discussed exercise with them. During the following two-month experimental phase, the researchers continued to ask the patients for the same exercise information. However, half of the physicians whom the patients were seeing were trained to give brief exercise advice during the experimental phase. The physicians were trained to:

1. Ask about physical activity in the past month.
2. Assess whether the patient was walking about 2 hours a week or expending about 500 calories a week.
3. Advise the patient to begin exercising if the patient was not already fulfilling the exercise requirement.

   This protocol took about 2–3 minutes of the physicians' time, and the physicians could cancel the activity if they were too busy. The patients were followed for one month, and changes in patient exercise frequency and duration were the dependent variables.
   The results showed that even though half of the physicians did not receive training, they also gave exercise advice. However, the trained physicians gave advice twice as often. Patients who received this advice showed significant increases in the length of time they exercised. This study suggests that even brief advice from physicians to exercise can significantly increase patients' exercise time.

Promoting Exercise Adherence

Some of the factors that increase exercise adherence summarized by Willis and Campbell (1992, p. 37) are:

- An exercise program should be scheduled as conveniently as possible.
- The closer the exercise facility to work or home, the better.
- Social support from family and other program members is important.
- A program should contain enough variety to meet the different motor skills and interests of the exercisers.
- Emphasis should be placed on enjoying the exercise experience.
- The level of intensity should not be so high that clients will experience physical discomfort.
- An educational program should be part of the program, including injury prevention and various benefits of exercise, time management, and priority setting.

• An exercise program should be coordinated with other aspects of a wellness or lifestyle management program.

Epstein, Koeske, and Wing (1984) noted that there is generalization from an exercise program to other areas; that is, there is a general improvement in lifestyle in the exercisers.

EXERCISE AND AGING

The percentage of older people in the U.S. population is increasing. At the beginning of the twentieth century, only 4 percent of the U.S. population was over 65, but it rose to over 11 percent in the 1980s (U.S. Department of Health and Human Services, 1984). By the year 2030, about 20 percent of the U.S. population will be in this age group (U.S. Senate Special Committee on Aging, 1988). Increasingly so, more people will be living longer. For example, by 2030, 13 percent of Americans over 65 will be 85 or older (U.S. Bureau of the Census, 1984). With this aging population, more and more of us will be picking up a chronic disease or two such as arthritis, hypertension, hearing loss, coronary heart disease, or diabetes (U.S. Department of Health and Human Services, 1984). With the higher number of older Americans with chronic diseases, there will be an increase in the number of people with reduced ability to take care of their activities of daily living, and the consequent reduction in the quality of life. Efforts will be increasingly focused on improving quality of life and helping older Americans to live independently rather than attempting to extend life that shows less chance of significant success (e.g., World Health Organization, 1987).

Research is leading to the conclusion that regular exercise is especially beneficial for older Americans (King, Haskell, Taylor, Kraemer, & DeBusk, 1991). It is associated with reduced occurrences of coronary heart disease, hypertension, adult onset (type 2) diabetes, osteoporosis and the bone fractures that accompany it, obesity, colon cancer, and psychological difficulties, as well as diminishing the effects of chronic diseases once they take hold of the individual (King et al., 1991).

In women, the available evidence indicates that they report less exercise of all types than men, and exercise participation drops significantly with age (e.g., Caspersen, Christenson, & Pollard, 1986). The majority of older women belong to the most sedentary population group, and thus they would have the most to gain from an exercise program (Lee, 1993; Powell, Spain, Christenson, & Mollencamp, 1986). According to Lee (1993), although the evidence is limited, it seems that middle-aged and older women do have positive attitudes toward exercise, but many seem unwilling or unable to initiate an exercise program. Lee reports that she does not see any clear-cut answers in the relevant literature as to why this is so. She calls for more research on the environmental and social experiences of men and women to determine why older women exercise so little.

Exercise and Psychological Functioning in Older Adults

Tomporowski and Ellis (1986) have suggested that exercise may improve cognitive functioning such as short-and long-term memory, psychomotor capability, attention span, and problem solving. In a study by Hill, Storandt, and Malley (1993), 87 sedentary Caucasian adults, aged 60 to 73 and evenly mixed between men and women who engaged in a year-long endurance exercise program, were compared to a matched nonexercising control group. Cognitive testing and baseline physiological measures were obtained prior to the exercise procedures. Each individual participated in an individually prescribed exercise program based on his or her initial fitness level determined by maximum oxygen uptake ($VO_{2\ max}$) obtained during baseline physiological testing. Subjects engaged primarily in walking, which included uphill treadmill walking, and running on an indoor track. Individual exercise programs were updated weekly.

Results indicated that the exercising subjects improved their cardiovascular fitness and had an improvement in self-reported morale as measured by the Philadelphia Geriatric Center Morale Scale. Cognitively, there was a statistically significant effect noted on scores for the Wechsler Memory Scale Logical Memory Subtest comparing the exercising group to the nonexercising controls. However, this effect was caused by a decline in performance from pre-to post-testing in the control group. According to the researchers, their long-term endurance exercise training program had little, if any, effect on improving cognitive function in the exercising group. Note, however, that the exercisers' performance did not decline as did that of the nonexercise control group. The researchers believe that the results, though difficult to interpret, do not rule out the possibility that exercise training may help to prevent the so-called normal memory declines associated with aging.

Research on whether exercise improves mood in older people has been inconsistent (Emery & Blumenthal, 1991). Needed are more exacting measures of psychological changes in the elderly and more large-scale prospective longitudinal studies (Emery & Blumenthal, 1991). Currently, there are insufficient studies on older people to draw any definitive conclusions on whether exercise produces positive mood changes. Certainly, studies of younger people have shown that exercise does improve mood (Griest et al., 1981; Young, 1979), so there is reason to suspect that the same results are applicable to older people.

SUMMARY

Exercise seems important to people, but only a small segment of the U.S. population gets enough exercise to be aerobically fit. People exercise for the social experience, for health and fitness, as a way to handle stress and negative emotional states, and as a way to challenge oneself. Exercise has many benefits including weight control, preservation of muscle, prevention of heart disease, reduction and control of blood fats, prevention of adult onset diabetes, and improvement of quality of life, and it may also help to extend life.

Reasons for not exercising include lack of time, feelings of fatigue, and lack of exercise facilities. Upon closer examination, these reasons generally do not appear valid.

Exercise seems to have a positive effect on mood-states such as anxiety and depression. Improvements in depression may occur from changes in neural transmitters, increased feelings of mastery and self-control, and improvements in body image and self-concept.

In the 1970s, a controversy raged regarding whether long-distance running such as running a marathon protects absolutely against heart disease. More recent evidence indicates that marathoning does not protect absolutely, but it does improve quality of life.

Adherence to exercise programs is not good, with about half dropping out after several weeks. However, steps can be taken to increase adherence such as increasing convenience of scheduling and location, and increasing social support and variety.

As we age, exercise takes on increasing importance in maintaining quality of life. Exercise has a variety of physiological benefits, but it may have positive effects on cognitive and emotional functions as well.

Food for Thought

1. Why do you think the American populace is getting heavier, but large numbers of people are reporting that they are getting "plenty of exercise?"
2. How would you respond to people who say they do not exercise because they do not have enough time? Wouldn't an additional demand to exercise increase stress levels in an already time-starved population?
3. What are some of the ways in which exercise may improve psychological states? What might be some of the mechanisms?
4. Why don't older people exercise more than they do? What are some of the positive effects of exercise as we age?

GLOSSARY

adherence: persisting in a given pattern of behavior in order to reach agreed-upon goals.

aerobic: exercising at a level that will not put muscles in oxygen debt as in anaerobic.

cross-train: exercising different muscle groups on different days so muscles will not become injured and antagonist muscles will not become unbalanced.

muscle-to-fat ratios: the ratio of fat to muscle in the body; more fat lowers metabolic rate, more muscle raises it.

runner's high: feelings of euphoria in some aerobic exercisers, possibly from internal physiological changes such as internal opioid levels.

running addiction: feelings of discomfort, fatigue, and depression from missing a running day.

toughness: more efficient adrenal gland responses in more fit individuals.

CHAPTER 3

Obesity and Weight Control

In this chapter we will consider the following subjects:

- Various models of obesity
- Health problems associated with obesity
- Ways to control your weight
- Maladaptive behaviors associated with food
- Eating disorders among athletes

John was an extremely obese 28-year-old man who was referred by a vocational services agency for a psychological evaluation to direct him in some manner to a more productive life. He weighed well over 300 pounds. He had been raised in a relatively normal manner, but a grandparent had doted on him and provided for his every need. As he went through elementary school and high school, he gained more and more weight. He was constantly teased and harassed by the other students. Eventually, unable to take anymore, he quit school before finishing high school and lived at home. He was in his twenties when he presented himself for evaluation, and he was engaged in no productive work outside of the house. His parents had moved away, and he was provided for by an inheritance. John was not interested in much outside of the house. He stated that he had a very hard time getting jobs and that his problems were the result of not being very interested in the jobs that he could get. Even though he did not finish high school, he tested in the very bright range on the Wechsler Adult Intelligence Scale, a well-standardized intelligence test. It was obvious that most, if not all, of his problems stemmed from his excessive obesity. He knew that it was a problem, but he did not see it as a major obstacle. The need for therapy was clear. Specifically, he was urged to pursue a program of weight reduction, preferably medically supervised, with behavioral modification components. After he went on the program and his weight was reduced to more normal levels, his job opportunities seemed to improve. He was able to move around more easily, and his previous lack of motivation for work outside of his home changed.

Obese people face major obstacles in our society. They are made fun of, talked about, humiliated, provided with unwanted advice, and discriminated against both occupationally and personally.

OBESITY

Obesity is a national obsession. Based on self-reports from four federal studies of health practices, 33 percent to 40 percent of adult women and 20 percent to 24 percent of adult men are presently trying to lose weight, and an additional 28 percent of both men and women are trying not to gain (National Institutes of Health Technology Assessment Conference Statement, 1992, p. 7), making dieting "normal" eating for millions. Chronic dieting and food restrictions seem to have become normative aspects of white women's lives in middle- and upper-middle-class groups (Bowen, Tomoyasu, & Cauce, 1991; Polivy & Herman, 1987). However, the lifestyle of poor women does not permit chronic dieting and exercise, as it does with middle-class women, and so obesity is more of a problem among the poor (e.g., Bowen et al., 1991; Ross & Mirowski, 1983) (see Box 3.1).

Concern about weight was not always the case among middle-class women. Prior to this century, for both women and men being robust was a sign of affluence and wealth. Being fat even as an infant or a child was a positive, rather than a negative, attribute. Heavier women, in particular, were thought attractive possibly because a heavier woman could more easily support nursing children. In contemporary times, "thin is in" especially with women. As the modern adage goes, "you can never be too thin or too rich."

It has not always been a bad thing to store fat. If food was scarce, as it still is in many countries of the world at present, the ability to store fat allows one to get through the hard times when no food is available. This can lead to higher survival rates. However, many people who need to lose weight for health reasons have a much harder time losing and maintaining a lower weight than do others. Individual differences in the ability to store and retain fat could account for this difficulty.

Differences in basal metabolism may explain why some individuals gain weight by storing and maintaining fat supplies more efficiently than

Box 3.1
A Research Tidbit: Weight and Ethnicity

Black women are more likely to be overweight than white women. In a study involving the first Health and Nutrition Survey (1971–1975) of women in the 25–44 age range weighed at the beginning and end of a ten-year interval, black women gained more weight than did white women (Kahn, Williamson, & Stevens, 1991). This result can be viewed as a tendency among black women to be less likely to lose weight. The researchers suggested that the black race is independently associated with a reduced likelihood of major weight loss. In this study, women with the greatest risk of weight gain were those who did not have a college education, were just entering marriage, and had very low family income. In a later study by Burke et al. (1992), black women had a higher age-adjusted mean Body Mass Index and subscapular skinfold thickness than did white women. The results could not be completely explained by a more sedentary lifestyle, a higher energy intake, and other obvious factors. The authors call for further study to develop intervention strategies for weight problems among black women. In a study by Fetzer, Solt, and McKinney (1985) among women in Philadelphia, black women made up only 6 percent of dieters who preferred low-calorie items, whereas white women made up 94 percent. Among blacks in this country, it is possible that there is less concern for obesity and a more relaxed attitude toward weight, which contributes to the higher incidence of obesity.

others on the same amount of food. Because of these differences, one person will gain a significant amount of weight, while another, eating significantly more food, will not. In addition, there may be biological differences in insulin secretion; some secrete higher levels of insulin than others (Rodin, 1985). One purpose of insulin is to promote excessive food energy storage as fat. With this higher level of insulin, fat is more easily stored. Other individuals with more normal levels of insulin store less fat and thus gain less weight.

By eating more calories, there is a higher probability of gaining weight. It is a simple equation: if more calories are taken in than are burned up, the individual will gain weight. Given that people differ in their basal metabolism and insulin levels, it is necessary to do either or both of two things: reduce calories by diet changes and/or increase calorie expenditure by exercise. Researchers now believe that dieting may be the least efficient method (Brownell & Wadden, 1992; Polivy & Herman, 1983). Exercise may work better, and the combination of the two is the best (Brownell & Kaye, 1982; Brownell & Wadden, 1992). Some research suggests that lowering the amount of fat in the diet and increasing complex carbohydrates may be the most effective diet manipulation for long-term weight reduction maintenance (Brownell & Wadden, 1992).

People who repeatedly lose and gain weight are sometimes called "yo-

yo" dieters (Brownell, 1988). It was earlier thought that it was harder and harder to lose weight with each loss–gain cycle. This may be true in some situations or with some individuals, but there has been no consistent demonstration of this idea (Brownell & Rodin, 1994). In any case for most of our evolutionary history, a period of excessive food intake in the presence of an available and perishable food source was likely followed by a period of famine until the next food source was found. It was adaptive to eat all that one could of a food supply because the next meal was not guaranteed to come about soon. If the food was rich in fat and protein, all the better. We have probably evolved with strong desires to eat as much of a rich food source as possible. Thus, when food is more freely available as it is in affluent societies, there are no natural biological stop mechanisms that have been tempered in the self-preservation fires of natural selection.

Animal and human studies (Brownell, Greenwood, Stellar, & Schrager, 1986; Keys, Brozek, Henschel, Michelson, & Taylor, 1950; Sims & Horton, 1968) have indicated for quite some time that deviations from a predetermined weight by either artificially increasing it or decreasing it can be maintained only with extreme difficulty. When weight is lost, the body becomes more efficient in its metabolism so that fewer calories are required to maintain a given weight. The body interprets the reduction in calories as a famine and acts to restore homeostasis. Also, human subjects who are chronically hungry, have a continual preoccupation with food and a desire for high-calorie foods (Keys et al., 1950).

Some animal (Hoebel & Tietelbaum, 1966) and human evidence (Sims & Horton, 1968) suggests that the body also attempts to reduce weight when it has gained weight above its set point. A form of adipose tissue known as brown fat, the amount of which is inherited, also plays a role in weight maintenance. Apparently, brown fat increases body metabolism so that not as much weight is gained as would be expected by caloric intake (Trayburn & James, 1981). There does seem to be a complex interaction of environmental and biological variables that play a role in weight control. This complexity has given rise to several theories that attempt to explain at least some of the issues in weight control. They can be sorted into the general categories; psychoanalytic, social/environmental, and physiological.

THEORETICAL MODELS OF OBESITY

Psychoanalytic Model

The psychoanalytic model, stemming from the medical tradition, was the earliest model that dealt with eating behavior, and it was the dominant paradigm in the field of psychology in the early part of this century. In general, subsequent research has not supported the psycho-analytic model. However, some evidence exists that as a person becomes more functional in psychoanalytic psychotherapy, the individual may lose weight in the process, although that may not have been the primary goal of the therapy (Rand & Stunkard, 1983). The psychoanalytic approach assumes that some unconscious conflict is causing an individual to deal with the anxiety generated by the conflict by overeating. The goal of psychotherapy is to point out the unconscious conflicts and thereby eliminate the reasons for overeating.

Following the psychoanalytic model of searching for clues to behavior by looking at childhood experiences that could be buried in the unconscious, early research by Hilde Bruch (1973) suggested that inexperienced mothers were at fault. Infants who would become fat in adulthood had mothers who could not distinguish between infants' states of hunger and other motivational and emotional states that caused discomfort. The evidence was procured by case study, as is the nature of psychoanalytic studies, and so was not solid experimental evidence. However, it did initiate a program of solid experimental research following the social learning model. This model investigates not unconscious and childhood forces controlling present behavior, but social and environmental forces that act on an individual.

Social Learning Model

Eating may or may not be affected by unconscious motivations, but it is certainly often done in the company of other people and in the presence of pervasive food cues in the environment. The social learning model has been very helpful in more completely understanding eating behavior, but it does not adequately consider genetic and biological factors that play strong roles in obesity. There have also been some methodological difficulties in some of the conclusions, to which we will now turn.

After reading the earlier research by Bruch and some early research by Stunkard and Koch (1964) in which obese subjects were found to be less aware of internal hunger sensations than normal-weight individuals, Stanley Schachter and his colleagues (Schachter, Goldman, & Gordon, 1968) launched a long series of studies suggesting that social factors rather than unconscious motivation, early childhood experiences, and biological factors were primary contributors to obesity. Schachter and his colleagues found that external, social factors were more important for the obese than those of normal weight. In one experiment, Schachter found that if a large amount of food was placed in front of obese subjects, they would eat it, and if a smaller amount of food was placed in front of them, they would eat it. In both cases, however, with some physical effort, they had the opportunity to get more food. But they did not do so, regardless of whether they had eaten the smaller or the larger amount. In contrast, subjects of normal weight did not eat all of the larger amount of food, but they exerted the physical effort to get more food when the smaller amount of food was placed before them.

In another experiment, Schachter jimmied a clock to show 12 noon when it was really 11:30 A.M. Obese people ate more than the normal controls. If the opposite was done (clock set to 11:30 A.M. when it was really 12 noon), obese people ate less than controls of normal weight. Schachter's colleagues showed that if all of the social cues surrounding food are taken away, obese people lose weight. For example, if obese subjects are not allowed to watch TV, listen to a radio, read a newspaper, converse and eat with others, and are given nutritious but rather bland food, they seem to drop weight rapidly. However, when they are allowed their freely chosen environment again, they gain their lost weight back. In yet another study, it was found that if food was adulterated by a bitter-tasting substance (quinine), obese people, were much less likely to eat the food than were normal-weight people even though both groups were food-deprived.

All of these studies suggest that internal cues such as stomach contractions and feelings of fullness were of less importance to the obese than to the nonobese. The environment, their social situation, the taste of the food, and the amount of physical effort involved in procuring food seemed to be more important to them. Now, whether Bruch was correct in suggesting that the mothers of these obese subjects were at fault in preventing them from learning to use internal, biological cues to hunger as others do (thus changing the obese individual's focus to other cues for eating as demonstrated by Schachter and his co-workers) cannot be answered by experimental evidence at this time.

Judith Rodin (1980), who had worked with Schachter early in her career, found flaws in Schacter's social and external model of obesity. Some of her research showed that obese people do not always overreact to external stimuli and that some people of normal weight do. In addition, many of Schachter's subjects were extremely overweight women. Many obese individuals do not eat breakfast in the morning (showing what Stunkard calls morning anorexia), which could have differentiated them from people of normal weight. Thus, the normal-weight individuals used in the control groups may have been different from the obese in their experience of hunger when deprived of breakfast. Also, the relationships that the very obese have with food may be very different from the eating behavior of the more common experiences of individuals who gain weight slowly over the years.

The social, cultural, and biological factors to which males are subjected could also differentiate them from the subjects of Schachter's research.

For example, the distribution of body fat on males and females seems to be different. Males tend to get big bellies, whereas women are more likely to gain weight on the hips and thighs. This pattern is strongly influenced by genetics and may represent the balance between the hormones estrogen and testosterone in the human body.

Rodin (1985) has suggested that the obese may have exaggerated insulin responses to the sights, smells, and thoughts of food. Insulin promotes the storage of fat in the body. A high level of insulin increases the likelihood of weight gain. There may be something to the complaint heard from some people trying to lose weight that they get fat just looking at food. So, they restrict their food intake to lose weight. However, as the saying goes, "You're damned if you do, and you're damned if you don't."

Research by Polivy and Herman (1983) showed a difference between those who are constantly restricting their eating and those who are not. Replicating and extending Schachter's research, they found that those who are restricting their diets are hyperresponsive to external cues and taste, whereas those who are not on a diet are not as responsive to these cues. Polivy and Herman preloaded those who were dieting and those who were not with milk shakes. Contrary to what one would expect, if the subjects restraining their appetites were extensively preloaded with the milk shakes, they ate more (in this case, ice cream) than did the dieters who were not preloaded. It appears that after dieters see that they have eaten more than they normally allow themselves, they figure "what the hell" and so they drop their inhibitions completely (Polivy & Herman, 1983). Their inability to control themselves may make it difficult for them to believe that they can adhere to a weight-loss diet in the long run. Self-concept also seems to play a role in whether or not loss of inhibition occurs. Apparently, those dieters who have a better view of themselves are less likely to lose their inhibitions and overeat than those who think less of themselves (Polivy, Heatherton, & Herman, 1988). However, as Schachter had found earlier with the obese, the food must taste good or dieters will not show this loss of inhibition effect; that is, they are less likely than nondieters to continue to eat in the presence of perceived aversive food cues.

Since a large number of individuals seem to be on diets at any one time, it seems that this phenomenon is a prescription for eating disasters. The more restrained the eating, the higher the probability of losing one's eating inhibition and overeating. This seems to be most true for those who have low self-esteem. The lack of success in dieting likely leads to a lack of self-esteem leading to a vicious cycle. The National Institutes of Health (National Institutes of Health Assessment Conference Statement, 1992) has recently concluded that most people on formal diet plans are likely to gain the lost weight back within five years, so many people on diets are bound to fail, with a concomitant loss in self-esteem. Some of these individuals (mostly young women at this time) on diets may be setting themselves up for the eating disorders of bulimia and the more serious *anorexia nervosa*, which is lethal in some cases.

Physiological Models

One of the earlier biological models to gain popularity was the set-point theory of weight. This theory states that different people have different set points, and so the body is going to resist any variation in this set point (Bennett & Gurin, 1982; Keesey, 1980; Nisbett, 1970). People may be born with this set point, or they may develop it in the very early part of life. Men and women differ in the amount of fat that they retain, which may be hormonally based. Also, these hormones may induce a different distribution of fat in males and females. (Males gain weight around the midsection, whereas females gain weight around the buttocks and thighs.) It seems that the female weight distribution pattern may be the healthier of the two. Males with the "apple" shape of fat distribution are more likely to develop heart disease than females with the "pear" shape. However, 80 to 90 percent of the people found in weight control programs are women. These differences may be culturally based, with males equating size with masculinity (e.g., football players, basketball players, weight lifters,) and females equating thinness with beauty (e.g., female models on TV, high fashion models). Twin studies (Bouchard et al., 1990; Stunkard, Harris, Pedersen, & McLearn, 1990) also strongly indicate that fat distribution is genetically based. In adoption studies, it was found (Stunkard et al., 1986) that adopted children much more closely resemble their biological parents in weight than their adoptive ones.

It is suspected, however, that the environment also plays a role. Excessive eating very early in life (perhaps the first two years) may determine to a large extent the number of fat cells that an individual may have the rest of his or her life. The more fat cells that are developed, the harder it is to control the amount of weight that an individual gains in his or her life. Given the genetic predisposition to be fat and a conducive environment, obesity becomes extremely likely.

If an individual has a set point for weight that is determined genetically and very early in life, then it is quite a struggle to modify it. Some authors (e.g., Herman & Mack, 1975) suggest that many obese are actually restrained eaters. That is, they spend much of their time trying not to eat. They are, therefore, in an almost constant state of hunger. When these restrained eaters experience emotional turmoil of any sort, they respond by overeating. The attempts at restraint become weakened when they are upset, and so they eat to make themselves feel better.

Apparently, restrained eaters are more likely to continue to eat once they decide to eat.

Much early physiological work focused on the hypothalamus as the critical area in the regulation of body weight. It had been known for many years that tumors in the hypothalamus produced overeating and obesity. However, with the advent of stereotaxic surgery and the ability to make relatively discrete lesions in the hypothalamus, specific areas in the hypothalamus could be identified (Stellar, 1954). If the lesions (damage) were done in the lateral hypothalamus (LH), the animal (in most cases, a rat) would stop eating and would have to be artificially fed for a period of time until it recovered some of its ability to eat. If the lesions were done in the ventromedial hypothalamus (VMH), the animal would gain in a short period of time, up to 300 percent over its base weight. At this point the animal would stabilize and resist further changes in its weight. If force-fed, it would lose weight, going back to its original heavy weight, and if starved, it would gain weight, returning to its new heavy weight if provided free access to food.

A strong case has been made that this dual-center set-point theory of eating is too simplistic and not correct (e.g., Pinel, 1993). A more modern approach is that the ventromedial hypothalamus (VMH) regulates metabolism rather than directly controls eating. That is, the VMH primarily increases the body's tendency to produce fat and decreases its tendency to release fat into the bloodstream. In this scenario, organisms do not get fat because they eat too much, but they eat too much because they are getting fat. This is done by the body's regulation of insulin. Insulin facilitates the conversion of glucose to fat and thereby promotes the production of fat. It also hinders the breakdown of fat for metabolic requirements. Possibly because of the increased insulin observed in these animals (e.g., Powley, Opsahl, Cox, & Wengarten, 1980), more fat is stored and is therefore less available for ongoing energy requirements in the animal. The animal must then eat more than normal amounts in order to have enough energy to carry on its biological activities. Humans can even be conditioned to show an insulin response to the sight and even the thought of food. Those who show this kind of response are more likely to gain weight than those who do not (Rodin, 1985). Based on evidence cited in Pinel (1993), the VMH may not even be intimately involved with the regulation of eating. Evidence suggests that nerve fibers that course near the VMH were damaged in the early lesion studies. These fibers travel to a nearby collection of neural cell bodies called the paraventricular nucleus of the hypothalamus, which may be much more important in the regulation of eating.

The last several years have witnessed a flurry of research on a fat cell-derived protein called the OB protein, or leptin, which is part of a complex hormonal and neural link between adipose tissue and the central nervous system (Kennedy et al., 1997). Leptin appears to regulate body weight through receptors possibly in the VMH area. When obese mice were injected with leptin, they lost a significant amount of weight, but they regained weight after the leptin injections were stopped (Campfield, Smith, Guisez, Devos, & Burn, 1995). These results show that leptin is a satiety factor and may work in the area of the VMH. According to Rohner-Jeanrenaud & Jeanrenaud (1997), leptin may be offset by neuropeptide Y, which facilitates eating. It is tempting to suggest that this neuropeptide works on receptors in the LH. Obese people, through some metabolic mechanism, become insensitive to high levels of leptin and remain obese (Rohner-Jeanrenaud & Jeanrenaud, 1996). Recently, Kristensen et al. (1998) showed that a brain-located peptide called CART (cocaine- and amphetamine-regulated transcript) is closely connected to leptin and neuropeptide Y. CART may be the mechanism by which leptin blocks eating induced by neuropeptide Y. Although obesity is a devilishly complex behavioral and medical problem to treat, within the next few years research may allow leptin to be used in some form to aid in regulating of weight in humans.

The role of the LH is still not clear. The area is a complicated one, and many other behaviors are affected when the area is damaged (see Valenstein, 1973). Also, there is significant variation in the responses in different subjects (Schallert, Whishaw, & Flannigan, 1977).

The more modern interpretation is that eating is an interaction of internal and external factors. There is a strong attraction (incentive value) to food, which varies with level of deprivation. When one has eaten a high caloric meal, the incentive properties of all food decline. However, when presented with a highly palatable food such as a favorite dessert after a rich meal, it is likely to be consumed. If provided unlimited amounts of even a favorite food, satiety seems to develop for that substance but not other dissimilar foods. Given the fact that people in Western industrialized countries rarely experience real hunger, the incentive properties of the varieties of food to which we are exposed probably play a greater role in eating than internal mechanisms.

Given the many internal and external factors that play a role in eating behavior, it is easy to see why so many people have problems with their weight. But along with weight problems come health problems.

HEALTH RISKS OF OBESITY

It appears that being a little over the ideal weight (less than 20 percent) as indicated by the Metropolitan Life Insurance Company Height and Weight Charts is not related to increased health risks (e.g., Bray, 1976; Sorlie, Gordon, & Kannel, 1980). However, when weight is over 20 percent above the ideal weight, problems ensue. Over 40 percent above ideal body weight causes another significant jump in the risk factors, and obesity is considered morbid when an individual is 100 percent over ideal body weight. At this level, individuals become candidates for surgical interventions such as stomach stapling, intestinal shortening, and other invasive measures.

Not everyone who exceeds ideal weight, however, is fat. For example, many professional football players are larger than normal but have a relatively low fat to muscle ratio. That is, most of their excess weight is muscle and not fat. Muscle is heavier than fat and is more metabolically active. Paradoxically, one of the best ways to lose weight permanently is to increase muscle weight. Fat/muscle ratios, number of fat cells, and the distribution of fat on the body are formidable physiological variables that are only partly under voluntary control and partly under genetic control. An extensive series of studies done in Denmark by Sorensen, Holst, Stunkard, and Skovgaard (1992) found that genetics plays a large role in determining fatness in adults.

The Genetics of Fat

In one large-scale study using the extensive and accurate records on adoption that are kept by the Danish government (Sorensen, Holst, Stunkard, & Skovgaard, 1992), the researchers looked at adoptees between 1924 and 1947 who were separated from their biological families shortly after birth and placed in adoptive homes very early in life (90 percent within the first year). The researchers used the Body Mass Index (BMI), (see Box 3.2.) a measure that is now commonplace in obesity research. (As noted in Box 3.2, you can calculate your own BMI and waist-to-hip ratio to determine if you are overweight, and if you are, whether or not your weight is distributed in a healthy pattern. A BMI above 25 is considered above desirable, and a waist-to hip ratio greater than .95 in males and .80 in females is considered above desirable.) Results of the Sorensen et al. study indicated that there was no correlation in fatness between the adoptees and their adoptive parents. Significant correlations were found between their biological mothers, fathers, and full siblings. The study concluded that shared genetics seems to fully account for the family resemblance in BMI in natural families. Stunkard et al. (1986) reached the same conclusions in an earlier study and found that the family environment alone has no apparent effect across a large range of weight classes. However, when Lissau-Lund-Sorensen and Sorensen (1992) used a longitudinal approach by measuring children at 9–10 years of age and ten years later, they found that although parental education and occupation had no effect on whether children would be overweight in adulthood, quality of dwelling where they were raised did have an effect. That is, a poor quality of dwellings increased the risk of being over-

Box 3.2
Is Your Weight Bad for Your Health?

While being overweight can raise the risk of disease, especially cardiovascular disease, your risk is only partially determined by the number you see on the scale. The following is an approach devised by Dr. George Bray of the Pennington Biomedical Research Center at Louisiana State University and psychologist Thomas A. Wadden of Syracuse University to more accurately judge risk of disease. To find your Body Mass Index, multiply your weight in pounds by 700, divide by your height in inches, then divide by your height again.

BMI _____

Another crucial factor in health, particularly to distinguish those who are more prone to cardiovascular disease, is the waist-to-hip ratio. This measurement is done by taking a tape measure and finding the circumference of your waist at its narrowest point when your stomach is relaxed.

Waist _____ in.

Next, measure the circumference of your hips at their widest (where your buttocks protrude the most).

Hips _____ in.

Finally, divide your waist measurement by your hip measurement.

Waist/hip = _____ Waist-to-hip ratio

Source: Copyright 1993 by Consumers Union of U.S., Inc., Yonkers, NY 10703-1057. Reprinted by permission from CONSUMER REPORTS, June 1993.

weight in adulthood in these children. This result is presumably related to the idea that lower socioeconomic groups living in these dwellings are less focused on the importance of food and nutrition in health and disease, and are more likely to make cheap and easily available food choices that promote obesity.

These studies used an indirect form of measurement of body fat (BMI). This ratio does not account for the contributions of muscle mass and bone to the ratio. Thus, individuals with more muscle and bone mass because of height differences, for example, could produce misleading BMIs. Bouchard, Perusse, Leblanc, Tremblay, and Theriault (1988) used more direct fat measures, which involve weighing an individual in water for a more accurate determination of fat mass (hydrostatic weighing) and measuring subcutaneous fat through skinfold measurements. As you may know, the more fat you have, the more likely you are to float compared to someone the same weight but with more muscle mass. Thus, the difference between what you weigh dry and what you weigh submerged in water will be greater. This is the basis for the hydrostatic weighing method. Bouchard et al. found that the genetic effect for variation in total fat mass was 25 percent. This effect suggests that the genetic contribution to the BMI is not nearly as large as Stunkard and his colleagues claim. Thus, with more accurate methods of measuring body fat, the relative contribution of environment to obesity may be more than what has been indicated in the earlier studies.

Teasdale, Sorensen, and Stunkard (1992) investigated the relationship of the BMI index of obesity to intelligence test scores and educational level throughout the full range of body weight in a population of young adult males. Although the relationships were small and other interpretations are possible, the researchers suggested that there may be a relationship between intelligence and obesity, with reductions in intelligence at progressively higher levels of weight.

Although the amount and interaction of heredity with environment in determining intelligence is subject to debate (even the definition of intelligence itself is subject to debate), some researchers believe that intelligence as defined by scores on standardized intelligence tests has a significant genetic component to it. If intelligence and obesity have genetic components, and they are inversely correlated, Teasdale et al. (1992) are suggesting that an inverse relationship may exist between the genetics of intelligence and the genetics of obesity, especially at the more extreme levels of obesity. This work will need to be replicated and extended with family and longitudinal studies before any firm conclusions can be drawn. There is also the chicken-and-egg problem again. Do the special experiences that the obese face every day have an effect on their intelligence, or does their level of intelligence in some way promote obesity? As you can see, we must be careful in drawing strong conclusions from studies such as these so as not to add more fuel to the fire of discrimination against the overweight in our society. Being overweight is the result of inherited, psychological, social, cultural, and socioeconomic factors. However, the evidence points to a significant, inherited component to obesity at this time, although the size of this component is in dispute.

Although we inherit a certain predisposition for a certain body weight, it would seem that the nonbiological factors affecting weight could be manipulated so that we could acquire some control over what Pinel (1993) implies is a "settling point" rather than a set point. Settling implies that the body does not actively defend against weight variation, but that weight is more of a passive response to both internal biological factors and external factors such as the incentive value of easily available food.

WEIGHT CONTROL

Since huge numbers of people in our society are interested in gaining control over their weight, and environmental factors play a role, it would seem that there would be some clear-cut ways to manipulate these environmental factors. However, since the problem is multifaceted with a genetic component to it, solutions to weight control are not so clear-cut. It is even possible that the focus on weight loss is wrong. For example, is the necessity for weight loss more important than the development of lifestyle patterns that will enhance health and well being (Brownell & Wadden, 1992)? Maybe the answers to questions concerning the necessity of weight loss and a healthy lifestyle are complementary, or maybe carrying out plans to succeed in one of these areas precludes success in the other. For example, the drive to lose weight can precipitate eating disorders such as anorexia nervosa where life-threatening losses of weight occur which decrease health and well being. Exercise and the absence of dieting with its all-too-often concomitant failures may enhance health and well being but may preclude loss of significant amounts of weight.

With these conundrums and many others with which to deal in tow, the National Institutes of Health (NIH) Nutrition Coordinating Committee and the NIH Office of Medical Applications of Research (cited earlier) held a technology assessment conference in the Spring of 1992. They assembled a panel of experts that attempted to answer the following questions: (1) How often and in what ways do Americans try to lose weight, (2) how successful are various methods of weight loss and control? (3) what are the short-and long-term benefits and adverse effects of weight loss, (4) what fundamental issues should be used to select a personal weight loss and control strategy, and (5) what should be the future directions for research on weight loss and control?

According to the NIH, four federal surveys showed that 33 to 40 percent of adult women and 20 to 24 percent of adult men were as of the time of the surveys trying to lose weight, with an additional 28 percent in each group trying to maintain weight. On the average, women attempted to lose weight 2.5 times in a two-year span, and men tried twice. The gender factor was more disparate in the high school years. Forty-four percent of high school females and 15 percent of high school males were trying to lose weight in a two-year span. This gender disparity could have to do with high school males being more concerned with developing large muscles to show their strength, virility, and athletic ability. Also, females in this age group generally are going through growth spurts earlier than boys and may be uneasy about their sudden weight gains.

Among women trying to lose weight, 84 percent were eating fewer calories, whereas slightly fewer men were (76 to 78 percent). Slightly more than 60 percent of both genders were trying to lose weight by increasing their physical activity. Diet and exercise were the most frequent ways to lose weight, with vitamins, meal replacements, over-the-counter products, weight-loss programs, and diet supplements cited by both sexes in decreasing order. In students, exercise was the dominant method tried at one time or another, but almost twice as many females used this method as did males (80 percent and 44 percent, respectively). Diet pills and self-induced vomiting followed at much lower levels, with higher rates for females than males. One technique used to control weight was smoking (Weekley, Klesges, & Reylea, 1992). Many people know that smoking seems to keep weight off. They also know that when they stop smoking, many people put on weight. Thus, a large percentage of women and men use smoking to control weight. Klesges and Klesges (1988) assessed a large sample of college students and found that 39 percent of the females and 25 percent of the males reported that they smoked to keep their weight under control; overweight females were much more likely than females of normal weight to start smoking to control their weight. It is obvious that the primary motivation in controlling weight by smoking is appearance to the detriment of health. One young woman in one of my classes told me that she would rather have cancer and be thin than be healthy and fat.

In the adult population, diet restraint is the most popular method of weight loss. This method ranges from total calorie reduction to changing the proportions of carbohydrates, proteins, and fats. People can lose a large amount of weight in a relatively short period of time. However, the NIH report indicates that there is a strong possibility that they will gain much of the weight back. Although there are not a lot of data on five-year followups of weight-loss plans, available evidence indicates that only a small percentage maintain their weight loss beyond five years. Varying the composition of the diet in terms of carbohydrates, proteins, and fats apparently has a limited effect on weight loss in comparison to caloric restriction (National Institutes of Health Statement, p. 10).

The next most popular type of weight control is exercising. The NIH report stated that the weight loss by exercise programs alone is limited. However, the report refers to studies which have shown that the weight loss is not large because the body builds muscle while it is losing fat during the exercise program. Since muscle is heavier than fat, the individual may feel that he or she is not losing fast enough. However, increasing muscle mass raises metabolism and makes it easier to maintain the weight losses that are attained. Some weight-loss programs, especially the very low calorie diet programs, cause the loss of both fat and muscle. In fact, it is possible that the significant losses in the first weeks of a very low calorie diet plan are muscle tissue and water rather than adipose stores. As the NIH report states, exercise tends to increase lean body mass, and if people persist at it, they are less likely to regain the lost weight. Research shows that the amount of weight lost by the combination of diet and exercise is more than diet alone by a margin of about 4 to 7 pounds (Epstein, Wing, Penner, & Kress, 1985; National Institutes of Health Statement, 1992). Exercise has a large number of other physiological and mental health benefits that are discussed in Chapter 2.

Behavior Modification Techniques

Most programs that use behavior modification techniques approach weight control by (1) identifying (targeting) the eating and other behaviors that need to be modified, (2) setting clear and specific behavioral goals for modifying these behaviors, (3) modifying the antecedents and consequences of the behaviors that are to be changed, (4) recording and analyzing the behavioral changes that are made, and (5) further modifying the antecedents and consequences of the targeted behaviors until the stated goals are reached.

Some of the strategies include (1) self-monitoring, which entails keeping close records of the type and amount of food eaten during the day and the internal and external circumstances surrounding the behaviors, (2) maintaining stimulus control, which entails keeping food out of sight, (3) making it inconvenient to eat large amounts of food by putting smaller amounts of food on the table, (4) eating in only one place with the minimum of other stimuli present such as reading material, the TV, and even other people who tend to overeat (this last situation is usually extremely difficult to modify without major upheaval in the family and friendships), and (5) carrying out some form of contingency contracting where rewards for sticking to the diet and punishments for not sticking to the diet are instituted. For example, regarding this last point, a significant amount of money could be laid aside at the beginning of the diet and certain amounts returned with successive weight loss. If weight loss was not achieved in a reasonable amount of time, the holder of the money could keep a certain amount of the money.

A cognitive behavioral strategy for weight control is the use of cognitive restructuring where the focus of change is the system of beliefs about dieting and weight. People may believe that they have little control over their weight. They may believe that since everyone in their family is fat, there is little they can do regarding their weight. They may have feelings of helplessness and hopelessness regarding their weight control abilities, or even about their lives in general. Psychologists and others who work with these problems may use counterarguments and dispute the defeatist thought processes. More hopeful and helpful thought pat-

Table 3.1
Methods for Enhancing Maintenance of Weight Loss Based on Research and Clinical Experience

1. Better apply theory in treatment research.
2. Utilize concept of reasonable weight.
3. Match treatments to individuals.
4. Extend length of treatment.
5. Assess dieting readiness before treatment.
6. Integrate exercise adherence techniques.
7. Teach crisis intervention and relapse prevention techniques.
8. Build coping skills to match dynamics of relapse crises.
9. Integrate treatment of negative body image.
10. Evaluate and intervene with binge eating.
11. Emphasize low-fat diet.
12. Explore technological developments (e.g., computer-assisted programs).

Source: Brownell, K. D., & Wadden, T. A. (1992). Etiology and treatment of obesity: Understanding a serious, prevalent, and refractory disorder. *Journal of Consulting and Clinical Psychology, 60*, 512. Copyright © 1992 by the American Psychological Association. Reprinted with permission.

terns can then be substituted for the more malevolent ones such as, "I can do something about my weight; I can succeed in losing weight."

Brownell and Wadden (1992) observe that concentrating on a certain amount of weight loss which conforms to some cultural ideal may be self-defeating. Weight-loss programs, whether they be behavioral modification, psychoanalytic, or pharmacological procedures, should be tailored to the individual. There should be less attention paid to the so-called best weight-loss program and more attention to the program that best fits each individual.

As Table 3.1 shows, the strategies for weight loss indicated by Brownell and Wadden are multifaceted. For example, treatment needs to be extended to at least 25 to 40 weeks to improve maintenance. There should be an increased focus on exercise for weight-loss maintenance. Brownell and Wadden point to research indicating that the largest reductions in risk from being overweight come from moving from very low to moderate levels of exercise, not from exceedingly strenuous exercise regimes (e.g., Blair, Kohl, Gordon, & Paffenbarger, 1992). Brownell and Wadden note that there is little programmatic research to test theory, and this may be part of the reason why so little is known about why treatments do or do not work. (This is the first point made in Table 3.1.)

According to the NIH report (1992), whatever the weight loss, one-third of the weight will be regained at the end of the first year and most of the weight will be regained at the end of five years. Only a small percentage of individuals maintain the weight loss they achieve, and we have no clear ideas on how they succeed. Thus, many individuals may have to settle on a "reasonable weight" for them. A reasonable weight is more likely to come about by focusing on healthy lifestyle changes such as the following: getting enough sleep, reducing and managing stress, eliminating smoking, reducing alcohol intake to two drinks a day or less, reducing fat in the diet, and getting regular exercise of sufficient intensity and duration to improve cardiovascular and musculoskeletal health. Less emphasis should be placed on weight loss per se. Brownell (1993) has recently posed a caveat to the general understanding that dieting approaches for the most part do not work. He indicates that data showing high rates of failure have been based on university-based programs that make up about 5 percent of all diet programs attempted by the general population. These people tend to be heavier, are more likely to be binge eaters, and have higher levels of psychopathology. All of these factors predict higher failure rates. We have little evidence on those who have attempted to lose weight on their own. Diets used by most people may or may not work, but we do not have enough broad-based data as yet.

The NIH report suggests that phenylpropanolamine, which can be purchased without a prescription, has had some success in weight loss. However, the longitudinal studies required to determine the effectiveness of this drug and other drugs have not been done. At one time amphetamines, which are stimulants, were prescribed routinely to help people lose weight. However, when these drugs worked, they were often only temporary, with the lost weight being regained in a matter of weeks or months. Cocaine, which also stimulates neurotransmitters in the brain that suppress eating, may sometimes be used to control weight.

As mentioned earlier, smoking and the drug it involves, nicotine, is another method used for weight control. People who smoke tend, on the average, to weigh less than nonsmokers. This effect has not been lost on people who have had trouble controlling their weight and may account for at least some of the new cases of smoking found predominantly in adolescent girls.

Recently, it has been discovered (e.g., Meyerowitz & Jaramillo, 1992) that loss of weight is one of the side effects of the second-generation antidepressant, fluoxetine (Prozac). Earlier antidepressants seemed to induce weight gain. Prozac inhibits the re-uptake of serotonin, a neural transmitter, back into the secreting neurons to be deactivated, thus making it more freely available at the synapses. It is possible that we may see more use of this drug and other second-generation antidepressants as medical treatment for weight control, especially in individuals who have associated depression.

A unidimensional approach such as employing only drugs to the complex and very individualistic problem of obesity probably will not be effective in the long run. We will be more likely to see success with a multidimensional approach to weight control such as is recommended by Brownell and Wadden (1992). In this approach, cognitive restructuring of how we think about eating, maintaining behavior modification of eating habits such as type of food eaten and speed of eating, exercising to increase the ratio of muscle to fat and to increase metabolism, imposing positive social support for weight control, and countering other habits that do not promote health as well as using pharmaceutical agents in an appropriate and well-thought-out manner to effectuate permanent fat loss rather than rapid weight loss will prove to be most effective for enhancing quality of life. Failure to control our weight gains by a multidimensional approach emphasizing factors within our control can be costly.

Costs and Benefits of Weight Loss

There is an abundant amount of research that being obese increases the risk of hypertension, diabetes, cardiovascular disease, and other illnesses (e.g., Bray, 1986; Pi-Sunyer, 1991). Fat found primarily in the upper body is more likely to cause health problems than fat in the lower body; upper body fat is more likely found in males (Bjorntorp, 1985; Sjorstrom, 1992). As Brownell and Wadden (1992) point out, weight loss in men should be given special attention because of this male pattern of obesity. Most of the treatment studies have been on women, however, perhaps because of researchers' more ready access to the female population and the higher level of concern among females regarding their weight.

Being obese carries not only biological risks, especially with the male pattern of obesity, but psychosocial risks as well. The obese are more likely than the nonobese to suffer discrimination in gaining admission to college, promotion at work, and satisfaction in interpersonal relationships (Stunkard & Wadden, 1992; Wadden & Stunkard, 1985). Brownell and Wadden (1992) propose that the psychosocial problems associated with obesity may be more significant than the biological ones. In addition, shame, anger, and frustration are often associated with the cycles of weight loss and regain. This weight cycling is a high-rate occurrence in dieters (Brownell & Rodin, 1994). However, these adverse psychological effects have not been found universally. A recent prospective study of weight cycling by Foster and his colleagues (Foster, Kendall, Wadden,

Stunkard, & Vogt, 1996) found no adverse psychological effects in 117 women treated for obesity at the University of Pennsylvania's Weight and Eating Disorders Program.

People who are not significantly obese but try to lose weight by stringent dieting alone suffer a disproportionate loss of muscle mass. Studies over the short term indicate that weight loss in lean persons leads to a greater proportional loss of muscle to fat and increased feelings of fatigue than that experienced by the morbidly obese when losing weight (National Institutes of Health Statement, 1992). The NIH report was also concerned about the possibility of an increase in binge eating and *bulimia nervosa* (overeating and self-induced purging) in moderately overweight women who are dieting. The report also states that there is no solid evidence that mortality decreases with weight loss.

Epidemiological studies employing longitudinal designs are now showing that large weight fluctuations both up and down are associated with increased morbidity (coronary heart disease) and mortality (e.g., Hamm, Shekelle, & Stamler, 1989; Lissner et al., 1991). There is no experimental way to determine cause-effect relationships, which would be ideal, from these large-scale epidemiological studies. However, statistical control is the next best thing. Lissner et al. (1991) statistically controlled for obvious confounding variables such as smoking and high blood pressure in showing increased morbidity and mortality from large weight fluctuations.

The fluctuations in weight found in these studies are most likely the result of yo-yo dieting. Most dieting Americans initiate a weight-loss program without effective long-term maintenance of the weight loss. This should not be considered a "can't hurt, might help" situation. Dieting is serious business indeed! However, the benefits of weight loss in the morbidly obese probably outweigh any benefits of not losing weight, and a focus on weight loss may be appropriate here. It is debatable whether a focus on weight loss per se is healthy for the rest of the population. However, weight loss in those who are fatter than the norm does improve cultural acceptance at this time and reduces some of the discrimination they suffer. Their problem then becomes one of maintaining the weight loss, a daunting task to be sure.

Controversy: Fasting

Is fasting good for you, and does it cleanse the body of toxins? Not according to Joanne Larsen (1998), registered dietitian at Johns Hopkins University. She reported that since the body burns proteins, vitamins, and minerals 24 hours a day, fasting does not provide food that the body needs for fuel. Fasting tricks the body into thinking that a famine has occurred, and so metabolism slows down. The body burns fewer calories and will burn muscle tissue as well as stored fat for energy. According to Larsen, protein and fat are expensive fuels. Seventy percent of protein and only 30 percent of fat can be converted to glucose. This leaves no protein for repair of muscles and organs. If glucose is not available for fuel, stored fat is incompletely broken down into ketones which are used as a fuel source for muscles and organs. However, the brain needs glucose. Glucose is obtained from breaking down muscle tissue to supply the brain. Therefore, prolonged fasts bring about loss of muscle tissue that contributes to metabolic slowdown. The reason for this is that muscle increases metabolic rate, so the less muscle the slower the metabolic rate becomes.

There is also no evidence that fasting cleanses the body of toxins. Instead, the body is depleted of essential elements from food that would be normally available. There are no good health reasons for fasting except for medical procedures.

Selecting a Program of Weight Loss and Maintenance

So, what to do? According to the NIH report, a fundamental principle of weight loss and control is a lifelong commitment to a change in lifestyle and dietary practices. It is clear that at least some who believe they should lose weight should not do so. Individuals with medical conditions or pregnant or lactating women should not. Young women who are normal in weight but believe they "should lose a few pounds" by dieting alone should not. It is always a good idea to be assessed by a trained physician or other health professional before weight loss is attempted. Certainly, rapid loss programs with very low caloric intake (800 calories a day or less) should be undertaken only under close medical supervision because of side effects such as vitamin deficiencies and electrolyte imbalances. In addition, the programs pose the risk of producing binge eating and purging, anorexia nervosa (symptoms include excessive loss of weight), and psychological stress from not being able to achieve permanent weight loss.

According to Brownell and Wadden (1992), weight-loss programs should concentrate on a "reasonable weight" for each individual, and not the ideal weight indicated by our culture. Some individuals, owing to their resting metabolic rate, their number of fat cells, and other genetic factors that affect both physical and psychological attributes, will never be able to achieve and maintain the cultural ideal body shape and size. Weight-loss programs should be tailored to the individual. The NIH report suggests that no matter what, modest goals of weight loss and a slow weight-loss program sparing lean body mass will most likely lead to success in losing the weight and maintaining the weight loss. Brownell and Wadden (1992) advocate a compassionate approach by health professionals who are treating individuals trying to lose weight: they advocate incorporating empathy and understanding in treating individuals reaching sticking points in losing weight later in the weight loss process. They should be alert to the possible occurrences of binge eating and to the feelings of frustration, helplessness, and sometimes anger that ensue from the failures. It would be optimal if the social support system of the individual who was trying to lose weight understood these problems as well.

In general, it is best to avoid weight-loss methods that provide rapid weight loss with little followup and supervision and with little instruction on a lifetime of healthy eating and physical activity. Some diet plans may also contribute to the beginning of eating abnormalities, such as binge eating, bulimia nervosa, and anorexia nervosa.

Controversy: Spot Reducing

Many among the general public believe that exercising a particular body part will reduce the fat associated with it. Hence we find ab (for abdominal) machines on the market produced by a variety of front-line companies. One company, though aware that spot-reducing exercises did not work, realized that a lot of money could be made on them. Fearful of losing out to its competitors, it entered the ab machine market as well. The principle of the ab machines is to produce a "six-pack" of abdominal muscles and a flat stomach. However, no exercises will reduce the fat around a particular body part without also reducing body fat from the entire body. In terms of fat distribution, we tend to look like our biological relatives no matter what we do. Furthermore, genetics conspires against many of us and refuses to reduce fat in particular body parts no matter what we do.

For example, males tend to accumulate weight around the trunk, particularly the stomach, and females tend to gain their weight around the thighs and buttocks. The best method to reduce body fat anywhere on the body continues to be to eat less and to exercise large muscle groups through aerobic exercise and strength training.

EATING DISORDERS

Karen began dieting when she was about 13 years old because she noticed that she was gaining weight. She started to be obsessed with her weight and refused to eat most foods that her family ate. After several months, her weight dropped to below 90 pounds (which was less than 85 percent of her normal weight), and her family, only worried before, now became alarmed. Her physician recommended inpatient treatment at a facility that specializes in the care of individuals diagnosed with anorexia nervosa. Karen remained in this institution for six weeks. Following her inpatient treatment, she was seen by a psychotherapist on an outpatient basis for 30 individual psychotherapy sessions. In the early stages of the outpatient treatment, Karen struggled with periods of depression, problems of self-esteem, and conflicts with her family and friends. Later, she also began to overeat excessively and then get rid of the food by self-induced vomiting and laxatives (bulimia nervosa) to help control her weight. She had a relapse with bulimia nervosa while an outpatient and was abusing laxatives so severely that she needed to be seen in the Emergency Room of the local hospital for loss of essential minerals and dehydration (electrolyte imbalance). Following this episode, she has made slow, steady progress with both her anorexia and bulimia. Though she continues to diet, she has maintained her weight and reports that she is not binging or using laxatives. Her conflict with her family, especially with her mother, seems to have abated. She successfully finished high school and is now in college participating in a college eating disorders group and is doing well.

Karen was suffering from a combination of two eating disorders; anorexia nervosa and bulimia nervosa. (*Nervosa* is an old medical term that refers to "nervous" or psychological causes.) The combination of the two disorders is often seen in clinical practice. Real-life disorders often do not neatly fit the somewhat exclusive categories that we set up for them. And sometimes they do not have happy endings; many people struggle with the disorders for years, occasionally, as in the case of anorexia, with fatal results. Of people admitted to university hospitals, the long-term mortality is over 10 percent usually from starving to death, committing suicide, or electrolyte imbalance (American Psychiatric Association, 1994, p. 543).

Although eating disorders have been around for many years, they have shown an increase in incidence, prevalence, and notoriety. The report of Karen Carpenter, the noted singer, dying in the early 1970s of anorexia nervosa and by misusing Ipecac (a drug that induces vomiting—its use indicating she was suffering from bulimia nervosa as well), the struggle that Tracy Gold in the sitcom "Growing Pains" has had with anorexia, the prevalence of anorexia and bulimia in the modeling industry and the entertainment industry which place a premium on physical appearance, and revelations in the sports world of eating disorders have brought these disorders to public attention. Box 3.3 illustrates the problems that one female gymnast had.

Anorexia nervosa and bulimia nervosa have been established psychological disorders for quite some time. However, in the latest version (1994) of the Diagnostic and Statistical Manual used by mental health professionals (DSM-IV), the term *bulimia* has been added for those individuals who binge but do not purge themselves regularly as in bulimia

---

Box 3.3
In the News

Christy Henrich was a ferocious competitor whose nickname was E.T. (for Extra Tough). However, because of her eating disorder, she stopped competing in 1990 because she was too weak. Christy Henrich was a victim of both anorexia nervosa and bulimia nervosa. She died in 1994 of multiple organ system failure after more than two weeks in the hospital. She was confronted by her coach, Al Fong, about her eating disorders, and subsequently became alienated from the family. Apparently, the coach threw her out of the gym after repeated attempts to set her up with nutritionists and failing. He stated that the gymnast was "throwing herself into the equipment because she could not do the routines." The coach thought that the gymnast would kill herself if she did not get help.

Source: The Press of Atlantic City, August 9, 1994. Copyright by the Associated Press. Reproduced by permission.

---

nervosa. No matter how many categories mental health professionals ultimately settle upon, categories overly simplify a complex and interacting continuum of eating disorders.

It is not even entirely clear what some of the terms mean. For example, to some bulimia may mean simply overeating, whereas to others it may mean excessively large amounts of high-fat and high-carbohydrate food intake followed by extreme feelings of guilt and depression and loss of control. In addition, some bulimics do not purge themselves with laxatives or by vomiting, which has given rise to the consideration of bulimia as a new category; others purge themselves occasionally; and still others perform these functions all of the time. There are even isolated cases of individuals who eat so much that their stomachs burst and they die of peritonitis and infection. Because approximately 30 percent of individuals attending hospital-affiliated weight control programs tend to binge without routine purging, a group of investigators (Spitzer et al., 1992) have suggested a new category entitled "Binge Eating Disorder," which is now included in DSM-IV. It is associated with a history of obesity and marked weight fluctuations. However, anorexia nervosa is the more extreme of the two disorders and is also more rare. In this disorder individuals develop a morbid fear of becoming fat. They do not seem to see themselves as thin, even though they lose enough weight so that they appear as bony skeletons to other people. If this disease progresses without professional help, there is a significant minority that will die. Hsu (1990) has indicated that about 50 percent of anorexics relapse after being discharged from treatment programs and need further treatment.

Although more research is necessary, the anorexic and bulimic categories may ultimately be biologically separable. Anorexia seems to develop at an earlier age than bulimia. Anorexics develop their disorder when they see themselves gaining weight at puberty or as their bodies mature. This weight gain frightens them, and they seem to go to any means to arrest this process. Husain et al. (1992) looked at 24 women undergoing treatment at the Duke University Medical Center Eating Disorders Unit who had received the diagnosis of anorexia nervosa (12) or bulimia nervosa (12). The subjects were subjected to Magnetic Resonance Imaging (MRI). The researchers found that anorexics had smaller thalamic and midbrain areas when compared to bulimics. The researchers report that earlier studies have shown a decrease in brain volume in both anorexics and bulimics, which is at least partly reversible with enhanced nutritional status. However, the authors also point out the resolution problems and lack of precision in the earlier anatomic studies. Husain et al. suggest that the thalamus, which is smaller than normal in anorexics, is part of a metabolic circuit that has been identified in earlier anatomic studies. They further hypothesize that the dopamine circuit of the midbrain may be involved in anorexia. As evidence, these researchers cite an earlier study by Sato, Igarashi, Miyagawa, Nakajima, and Katayoma (1988), which indicated a marked reduction in dopamine secretion in anorexia nervosa. There also seems to be a different role for serotonin in comparing the two eating disorders; the neurotransmitter may operate in opposite directions (Oliveros, Iruela, Caballero, & Baca, 1992).

The upshot of this biological research is that there are promising leads that the bulimic and anorexic disorders may be anatomically and neurochemically separable. However, the research requires replication, and caution should be exercised regarding conclusions from these results at present. If biological differences do hold up, treatment plans may have to include some different approaches to the disorders. For example, different classes of psychotropic drugs may have different effects in each disorder. Some of these possibilities will be discussed later in the chapter.

If an individual is unfortunate enough to have a combination of bulimia and anorexia, researchers have found that they also have the highest prevalence of personality disorders, most commonly the borderline personality disorder (Herzog, Keller, Lavori, Kenny, & Sacks (1992). They are also more likely to have the eating disorder for a longer period and difficulties such as anxiety and depression. Given the complexities of these eating disorders, the various subtypes that are now being developed, and the various environmental and physiological factors that interact with these disorders, it may be a while before the conclusions from research are clear and consistent.

Anorexia Nervosa

General Symptoms

The most severe of the eating disorders, anorexia nervosa, is an extreme eating disorder characterized by intentionally starving oneself sometimes to the point of dying. Other characteristics include loss of body weight sometimes to skeletal-like proportions, intense fear of gaining weight, preoccupation with food and its preparation, and distorted body image. In order to maintain extremely low body weight, sometimes the individual engages in excessive exercises up to six hours a day, self-induced vomiting with medication such as Ipecac or gagging oneself, and laxative abuse. Sometimes the disorder is a mixed disorder with bulimia also involved. Anorexics typically see themselves as fat, even though they are of extremely low body weight. This distorted self-image is extremely difficult to change. With the reduction of body fat, women sometimes develop a failure to menstruate. This can increase the likelihood of osteoporosis (brittle bones) later in life.

Social and Psychological Influences

Previously, anorexia seemed to be a disorder of the affluent. However, this disorder now seems to be shifting to individuals in the middle and lower classes. According to Witaker et al. (1989), this social class distinction may no longer be a reliable predictor of anorexia. Age categories for the disorder are also shifting. There is some evidence that anorexic symptoms are developing at younger and younger ages. Mothers may encourage dieting in their offspring if they notice that their daughters are becoming heavier than normal. Also, if the mother has weight and diet problems of her own, she may have greater concern and worry about these problems for her children. Young girls arriving at puberty may also have problems of their own with their sexuality, and this anorexic behavior allows them to stop the advent of menstruation and mature feminine characteristics in general.

Szmukler (1987), maintains that the families of anorexics are high achievers and controlling. This influences the young girl to take control of something in her life that she can manage (i.e., her weight). Compounding this problem is the socioeconomic possibility that this generation of adolescents will not achieve the same socioeconomic success as their immediate ancestors did, and therefore achievement and control in other realms besides body weight become less viable possibilities for them. Anger, frustration, and perceived lack of control over their lives, along with a preoccupation with physical appearance in our society, may precipitate undo emphasis on controlling body weight.

Physiological Influences

Physiological hypotheses include abnormalities in the hypothalamic-pituitary-adrenal axis. Fluctuations in hormonal output and irregular menstruation cycles may contribute to this disorder. For example, some research indicates that irregular menstruation may precede anorexia rather than follow it (Neuman & Halvorson, 1983). Other suggestions include an immature pituitary gland, which through hormonal imbalances and possible interactions with neural transmitters in the brain could cause the onset of anorexia nervosa. Some preliminary evidence points to the efficacy of cyproheptadine in helping anorexics who are not simultaneously bulimic (Walsh & Devlin, 1992). Anorexics who are receiving standard behavioral treatment do not appear to derive additional improvement with a variety of different classes of *antidepressants*.

Treatment

The prime objective in anorexia treatment is to bring the individual's weight back to a more normal range. Techniques include hospitalization with medical supervision and use of behavioral therapy and cognitive behavioral therapy. In the realm of behavioral therapy, operant conditioning can be used where individuals will be reinforced with visits or social events in return for eating more normally. However, as with other behavioral treatments, there is sometimes a problem in generalizing the training in a hospital to the home environment. When individuals return to the same family and environment, they tend to resume the same behavioral patterns. Cognitive behavioral therapy focuses on the false belief systems that anorexics develop such as "everything that I eat will turn to fat" and "people will hate me if I gain any weight." No matter what the therapy, however, the results are mixed. Even if the anorexic has succeeded in gaining sufficient weight under supervision, this does not mean that she will keep her weight on after returning to her social environment (Hsu, 1990). For example, behavioral principles may sabotage the therapists. Knowing that she is going to get out of the hospital if she gains weight, she does so, and then she promptly reverts to her old patterns of behavior once she is home (Agras & Werne, 1977). Ongoing psychotherapy is probably necessary in order to enhance self-esteem and to allay any depression that may be occurring. Family therapy is sometimes advised to aid in working out family dynamics that may be contributing to the problem. Anorexics remain very difficult problems to treat. Some research (Hsu, 1990) indicates a 50 percent relapse rate, and about 11 to 20 percent remain under normal weight. If the disorder persists for four years or more, a lethal outcome is more and more possible.

BULIMIA

At the present time, bulimia is defined as an eating disorder characterized by repeated cycles of eating great quantities of food (binging)
followed by purging in a variety of different ways. There is still some
confusion regarding what binging is. For example, a discrepancy seems
to exist between the lay and technical uses of the term. Beglin and Fairburn (1992) found that young women placed more emphasis on loss of
control and less on the quantity eaten. Others regarded binge eating as
a form of overeating with a large amount of food eaten, loss of control,
and subsequent fullness and dysphoria (unhappiness). Wilson (1992)
found that no data bear on the requirement that a binge requires rapid
eating and relatively few studies bear on the requirement that a binge
involves a large amount of food. In addition, there are few data on the
frequency of overeating which would qualify for a classification of bulimia. Also, as mentioned earlier, some people do not purge following
binge eating. This phenomenon represents the new DSM-IV category,
Binge Eating Disorder (American Psychiatric Association, 1994 p. 729).
According to Devlin, Walsh, Spitzer, and Hasin (1992), significant numbers of obese and nonobese young women have this overeating problem,
but more research is needed.

In many cases, dieting itself is apparently sufficient to cause bulimia.
Usually, a stress or some difficulty in the individual life is sufficient to
set off the binge aspect of the binge/purge cycle. This is followed by
feelings of guilt, frustration, and loss of control. Some subset of these
bulimics then purge by the use of various methods. Whereas the anorexic's weight tends to be at least 20 percent less than normal, bulimics
tend to be of normal weight or overweight. Apparently, the more obese
one is, the more likely one is to engage in bulimic behavior (Telch, Agras,
& Rossiter, 1988).

Treatment

Bulimics, as well as anorexics, seem to respond to behavioral and cognitive behavioral therapy. However, a behavioral technique called exposure and response prevention has been attempted with bulimics. In
this technique the individual eats a large amount of food and then is
prevented from purging. According to Hsu (1990), this is an effective
technique, but other researchers believe that it adds nothing to the behavioral treatments (Agras, Schneider, Arnow, Raeburn, & Telch, 1989).
As with anorexics, family and group therapy is helpful in treating this
disorder. However, long-term longitudinal studies will be useful in determining psychological therapies of choice.

Bulimics also seem to respond to a class of pharmacological agents used to counter depression called antidepressants. A variety of chemically different antidepressant medications seem to be useful in the short-term treatment of bulimia nervosa (Walsh & Devlin, 1992). Anorexics do not appear to benefit from these drugs as do bulimics.

EATING DISORDERS IN ATHLETES

In a book edited by Brownell, Rodin, and Wilmore (1992), a discussion of research on eating disorders among athletes is collected under one cover for the first time. Given their drive to excellence, many of our top athletes are likely to employ anything that will give them an extra edge. This extra edge ranges anywhere from anabolic steroids to losing weight in order to perform better in endurance activities and activities that require low body weight. In some activities where fractions of a second can determine the winner, any extra edge is important. All of this comes about at a time when the athletes are at prime age for eating disorders, as witnessed by these disorders in the general population. Brownell, Rodin, and Wilmore report that dealing with this problem is far more prevalent than was previously recognized and that it lacks sufficient well-controlled studies. The authors report that athletes are being hospitalized, attempting suicide, and developing various psychological problems relating to eating and weight control. Brownell and Rodin (1992) note that the athletes themselves often underreport the prevalence of eating disorders. The athletes are afraid of reporting their problems to their coaches and to the school because of embarrassment from their peer group and the loss of the privilege of competing at the college level. Underreporting is also a problem in the general population (Beglin & Fairburn, 1992) but is likely to be much worse with athletes because of the additional concerns and pressures of giving one's best. The premier athlete walks a very fine line: to reduce fatty mass to a bare minimum while keeping lean body mass intact. Athletes who have eating disorders often do not spare lean body mass, and thus their performances suffer as a consequence. As Brownell et al. (1992) point out, the problem of weight control and eating behavior has cultural, psychological, and physiological bases.

Young women who are athletes seem to be most prone to this disorder at present. Culturally, young women are faced with pressure to be thin and to have a physically attractive body shape. In addition, if they are interested in performing at peak levels, their body fat mass must be at a minimum while they remain physically strong. Our culture has reinforced the idea of being physically fit as well as being increasingly lean. The cultural body ideal of women began to become thinner in the mid-1960s when the waiflike body shape as epitomized by the model Twiggy became desirable. The prevailing cultural belief is that with proper discipline over eating behaviors and exercise, one can lose all of the weight that one wants to and develop Adonis-like proportions in body appearance. Brownell et al. maintain that there are biological limits to how much the body can be molded and changed. For example, as mentioned earlier, to a large extent inherited characteristics determine ultimate weight and body shape distribution. Research is discovering how difficult it is to change these basic parameters.

As Brownell, Rodin, and Wilmore (1992) point out, the problems with eating and weight control occur at a time when biological changes are forcing young women to gain weight. Following puberty, body fat increases in females in order to biologically prepare them for reproductive activities. Trying to restrict food intake and keeping weight down work against this natural biological process. Some professional female gymnasts keep their body weight inordinately low and therefore delay onset of menstruation. This delay of menarche may have all sorts of biopsychosocial effects later in life. However, the longitudinal studies have not yet been done to determine exactly what these effects may be. The authors point out that by restricting caloric intake, highly trained females may require fewer calories than a normal female nonathlete would require. That is, the body reacts to the stress of weight loss produced by intense training in the same way that it would to severe fasting. It thus becomes harder and harder to keep weight down even by reducing calories in the diet. This difficulty in weight control does not seem by any means limited to female athletes. Professional heavyweight fighters are frequently reported to be significantly heavier when they are not training for a fight, and they seem to have more and more difficulty in making weight for each succeeding fight. Witness the metamorphosis of George Foreman from his early days of boxing to the present. Increasingly stringent demands to control diet to keep weight down seem to be important ingredients in developing eating disorders that limit vitamin, mineral, protein, and fluid intake to dangerous levels in athletes. With further attention and research in this area, it is hoped that something can be done about our culture's preoccupation with "win at any cost" to the detriment of many people in the prime of their physical powers.

EATING DISORDERS IN MALES

Although most of the eating disorders have been reported in young women, a number of males also exhibit these problems. Men with eating disorders seem to experience, along with a gradual decrease in testosterone, decreased libido and sexual performance. Brownell et al. (1992) have also found an increased incidence of HIV positive males with bulimia, which is not the case in the larger number of females with this eating disorder. Research suggests that males with eating disorders have a two- to fivefold incidence of homosexual orientation above the general population (Anderson, 1992). There is likely to be a greater concern for physical appearance among this subset of males consonant with their female counterparts (Anderson, 1992). Anderson identifies several other reasons for dieting in men: (1) An actual past obesity history in males, (2) teasing or being criticized for their weight, (3) dieting in relation to sports activities, and (4) defensive dieting in order to prevent weight increases that they feel will occur as a result of an injury from a sports activity. One study by Anderson, Barlett, Morgan, and Brownell (1995) indicated that many male competitive body builders show severe dieting practices, including binge eating, particularly during the week before competition. With more research on eating patterns in males, we may see greater incidence of eating disorders.

All in all, there is a complex intertwining of biopsychosocial factors in determining type, onset, and duration of particular eating disorders in young women, and to a lesser extent in young men.

WHAT'S A BODY TO DO?

Weight control and eating disorders is a complex and highly active research area. There are no clear answers and simple solutions to the problems of weight control and dealing with eating disorders. The best advice is to pay less attention to the problems of weight and eating per se, and more attention to leading a healthy lifestyle. To be more specific, we should do as many of the following as possible: (1) reduce the amount of fat in our diet to somewhere below 30 percent as recommended by the American Heart Association, (2) exercise moderately and consistently at least three to four times a week, concentrating on aerobic fitness and muscle tone, (3) reduce alcohol intake to no more than two drinks a day, (4) stop smoking, (5) learn stress management and how to prioritize your time, (5) get enough sleep, and (6) think about your physical appearance in a realistic way, based on your body shape and size rather than often unattainable cultural ideals. These suggestions are more within our control than some aspects of weight management that are strongly resisted by inherited characteristics. Some of the benefits are increased physical and mental health and quality of life in general.

SUMMARY

Many people in this country are dieting, but we are not getting thinner as a nation. The availability of high-fat and convenient food sources, coupled with the many energy-saving conveniences available in our society, have conspired against us. Also, there are significant individual differences in the ability to store fat based on differences in individual metabolic rates and insulin levels. In order to lose weight, evidence suggests that the most inefficient method may be caloric restriction. One of the most effective methods is exercise.

Several theories have been proposed to account for the difficulty in varying our weight to any significant degree. The earliest theory was the psychoanalytic. In general, research has not supported this theory of obesity. However, it gave rise to the social learning theory, which proposes that many of the causes of obesity arise not from early childhood conflicts but from factors to which the individual is exposed in the social environment. This theory has had some successes and some failures.

Early work in physiological theory centered around the concept of a set point for each individual. This set point was set by heredity and early in life. Fat distribution tends to vary with the gender of the individual; males are more likely to gain around the middle, and females around the hips and thighs. The gains around the middle are more predictive of atherosclerosis and heart disease than gains around the hips and thighs. The set-point theory is too simplistic, and more recent physiological evidence indicates that multiple biological factors both within the central nervous system and outside of it determine body weight.

Behavior modification techniques have enjoyed some success in terms of permanent weight loss, but weight-loss programs of any type should be tailored to the individual rather than to a particular approach. Losing weight may not even be appropriate for many people except for the very obese. Studies show that weight variation, whether up or down, may have negative effects on health. If the decision is made to lose weight, a slow weight loss that spares muscle will aid in maintaining the loss. Rapid weight-loss programs also increase the chances of developing eating disorders.

Although eating disorders do not come in neat categories in the real world, several have been seen consistently enough that they have names: anorexia nervosa and bulimia nervosa. More categories may be added, and many sufferers have a combination of these disorders.

Athletes are a special category of individuals who may suffer from eating disorders. With the tremendous pressure to outperform competitors in our society, every little edge pays off in accolades and in money. This pressure is producing more athletes who are showing eating disorders. At the present time, these disorders are showing up in predominantly female athletes. Highly trained athletes may also find it harder and harder to lose weight because of weight loss from training in the past. This win at any cost philosophy may be extremely detrimental to the overall health of people who should be in the prime of their lives.

Food for Thought

1. Describe the theoretical models of obesity. Which one makes the most sense to you? See if you can come up with an integrative model that considers in some way all of the factors in the traditional models. Can you describe why obesity is multifaceted based on your integrative model?

2. Describe the Body Mass Index (BMI) measure. Is it sufficient to determine obesity? What other measures would you use? Describe methods that are more effective than simple dieting to prevent obesity.

3. What are the differences between anorexia nervosa and bulimia? What are some of the effects of the two disorders? How would you deal with someone you knew well that had an eating disorder?

4. Do you think the "win at any cost" mentality is justified in this country? Are eating disorders an unfortunate, but reasonable, cost to pay for high-level success in sports where weight is an issue? What changes in sports would you make if you thought weight was overemphasized?

GLOSSARY

anorexia nervosa: an eating disorder characterized by excessive dieting, excessive exercising, and purging resulting in a body weight that may be 20 percent or more below optimum weight and is life-threatening.

antidepressants: pharmacological agents that affect certain brain neurotransmitters in such a way that these neurotransmitters become more available at neural receptor sites with the consequent relief of symptoms of depression.

Body Mass Index: a method used by many researchers to measure the amount of fat in an individual. It is obtained by a formula using the height and weight of an individual.

brown fat: fat that seems to have a higher metabolic rate than other fat. Organisms with more brown fat are less likely to gain weight.

bulimia: a new category in the Diagnostic and Statistical Manual IV for psychological disorders which describes an eating disorder with repeated cycles of overeating and dieting but without regular purging.

bulimia nervosa: an eating disorder characterized by repeated cycles of extreme dieting and overeating followed by purging by vomiting or laxatives.

cognitive restructuring: a method of therapy whereby individuals are taught to change negative self-statements to more constructive ones so that they can better adapt.

dual-center set-point theory: the theory that the ventromedial hypothalamus inhibits eating and the lateral hypothalamus facilitates eating.

incentive value of food: a motivational concept that suggests people overeat because of the immediate positive reinforcement property of food.

MRI: Magnetic Resonance Imaging, which allows for detailed pictures of anatomical structures without invasive procedures.

physiological model of obesity: a model that suggests that biological factors such as a set point in the brain, number and size of fat cells, and other neural and hormonal influences determine obesity. Twin studies and adoptive studies suggest that much of these biological factors are inherited.

psychoanalytic model of obesity: a model that suggests that much obesity stems from early childhood conflicts.

reasonable weight: a weight at which an individual would be most healthy, but not necessarily a weight at which the culture defines as a most ideal weight.

social learning model of obesity: a model that suggests obesity stems from social and environmental cues that induce overeating such as the family, peer groups, the media, and cultural influences.

yo-yo dieting: repeatedly alternating between dieting and regular eating, which leads to repeated weight gains and losses. Some evidence suggests that this practice increases morbidity and mortality rates.

CHAPTER 4

Unhealthy Behavior

In this chapter we will consider the following subjects:

- The causes and effects of alcoholism, treatments for alcoholism, and controversy in the field of alcohol research
- Some of the reasons why we smoke and ways to treat it
- The effects of drugs such as cocaine, heroin, inhalants, and marijuana
- Why athletes and others are using steroids and how they affect the human body

In a *New York Times Magazine* article (January 29, 1995, pp. 40–41) entitled "It's Drugs, Stupid," former Secretary of Health, Education and Welfare Joseph A. Califano, Jr., stated that neither the Republicans nor the Democrats get the message that alcohol and drug abuse are at the root of crime, poverty, and health care costs in this country. Califano indicated that the National Institutes of Health spend about $4 billion for research on cancer, cardiovascular disease, and AIDS, but "less than 15 percent of that amount for research on substance abuse and addiction, the largest single cause and exacerbator of those diseases." He also argued that if "mainstream" diseases such as diabetes and cancer had as much of a negative impact on people in the United States as alcohol and drug abuse, this country would "mount an effort on the scale of the Manhattan Project to deal with it."

Granted that people do not sufficiently understand the great costs to this country of drug and alcohol abuse, there are also problems in clearly understanding the causes of these disorders. What we implicitly believe as causes may affect our willingness to pay for research and treatment. Is drug and alcohol abuse in the genes and therefore a biological problem, or is it a moral and spiritual failing, or a personality defect, or just learning the wrong behaviors? Does the movie actor, Robert Downey, Jr. have a moral weakness, an inherited predisposition for drugs and alcohol, or has he just been in the wrong company? You may recall that this actor was found incoherent in someone else's house and bed in 1996, and that he walked away from a drug and alcohol treatment facility where he was being treated. He then ended up in jail.

A second very popular addicting substance (notwithstanding Bob Dole waffling on this issue during the 1992 presidential race) is nicotine. As of 1998, even several tobacco company chief executive officers were admitting (even though they denied it under oath in the past) that nicotine can be addictive. Through the process of evolution, the tobacco plant has developed nicotine that wards off insect predators. However, humans have learned to exploit this substance for their own pleasure. The use of nicotine by inhaling it into the body has also been around for quite some time, and it has become legitimized for different reasons than alcohol. Most notably, it does not have the same observable behavioral effects as alcohol, and for quite a number of years it was not considered a health risk. Only since the 1960s and the Surgeon General's report in 1964, have we begun to realize what a health threat smoking is. As a result, cigarette smoking is declining in the American population (European countries such as France are also beginning to take note), but smoking in some segments of society is declining more slowly than in others.

Cocaine and marijuana have become illegal in our society, although for reasons that are more historical accident than the notion that they pose greater danger to our mental and physical health than alcohol and nicotine. Research has shown that cocaine is addictive, detrimental to our mental and physical health, and potentially lethal. Marijuana has also been shown to produce detrimental health effects, although positive health uses have been found for it as well, such as reducing intraocular pressure in the eye (glaucoma) and pain relief in terminally ill patients. Treatment programs for cocaine addiction are in their infancy but will probably contain many of the elements used to reduce other addictions.

Finally, we will discuss a rising phenomenon of drug abuse in this country (and elsewhere): the use of anabolic steroids. Continuous accusations from various sources that top professional and amateur athletes are using anabolic steroid drugs in ways that are difficult to detect by standard drug testing are constantly being reported by the press. For example, at the 1996 Atlanta Summer Olympics, great suspicion surrounded the Irish swimmer, Michelle Smith, and her remarkable increase in swimming speed to gold medal status in a matter of two years. Her husband had been previously suspended for the use of steroids. However, she was tested repeatedly and found to be negative for performance-enhancing drugs. The Chinese swimming team had remarkable performances in the 1992 Barcelona Summer Olympics, and several tested positively for anabolic steroids. However, the Chinese team did not fare so well at the Atlanta 1996 games where they tested negative. Gail Devers, a gold metalist at the Atlanta games, and other runners have been accused of using performance-enhancing drugs, most notably by another well-known runner, Gwen Torrence. These drugs seem to give the user extra strength, size, and speed. These drugs are said to produce improvements in athletic performance that are not the direct result of training. Winning then becomes a matter of chemistry rather than dedication, talent, and training. Not only premier athletes may be using these drugs, but many adolescents and young men are reportedly using them to improve their strength and physical appearance for a variety of reasons.

ALCOHOL

Use of alcohol is thousands of years old. Most of the ancient cultures used it in some form or another. Although drinking and drunkenness are tolerated in various degrees in many cultures throughout the world, Muslim countries and Mormon societies prohibit alcohol.

Per capita alcohol consumption in the United States was significantly higher in the 1700s and 1800s prior to Prohibition than it is now. As a rule, drunkenness has never been publicly condoned in this country except at various celebrations such as weddings, birthdays, and holidays (depending, of course, on social and ethnic traditions). For most of present-day society, it is not socially acceptable to be publicly drunk. However, because of its longevity, acceptability, and legal accessibility in our culture, alcohol is the most widely used *psychoactive* drug. In the United States, about 13 percent of all adults have had a diagnosable problem with alcohol at some time in their lives (Kendall & Hammen, 1995). A survey by Presley and Meilman (1992) found an inverse relationship between the amount of alcohol drunk by college students and their grades; D and F students averaged 11 drinks a week, and A students averaged less than three. Also, 43 percent of the students surveyed reported an alcohol binge at least once in the last two weeks (Presley & Meilman, 1992). In a recent informal survey of one of my classes in Abnormal Psychology, 63 percent of the students reported that they had had, or now had, a close friend or relative with "a drinking problem." Young and middle-age adults drink more than either people over 60 or adolescents. About 20 percent of the men between the ages of 18 and 29 report some problems related to alcohol consumption. Women show much lower rates of alcohol dependence and problems related to alcohol consumption (5 to 6 percent), which become almost nonexistent after the age of 60. However, there appears to be an increase in binge drinking among college women, which could increase alcohol dependence rates for women in the future. Not all ethnic and racial groups drink at the same levels. Asian Americans, Hispanics, and African Americans have lower rates of alcohol dependence than are found in the majority culture (U.S. Department of Health and Human Services, 1990).

The number of alcohol-related automobile fatalities decreased from 43.6 percent in 1986 to 37.4 percent in 1992. These results are probably due to increased sanctions for driving while intoxicated, less public tolerance for drinking and driving, and increased attempts to stop underage drinking and driving (National Institute on Alcohol Abuse and Alcoholism, 1996). However, alcohol also significantly increases the chances of injury and death in recreational pursuits and on the job. For example, alcohol increases the risk of accidental drownings, falls, burns, fatal snowmobile accidents, and, of course, boating accidents. For example, in 1993 three professional baseball players were riding in a boat when they smashed into a dock and the driver of the boat was killed. The blood alcohol level of the driver of the boat was well above the legal limit of intoxication.

The heaviest drinkers tend to be young people between the ages of 21 and 34. Also, males are more likely to be classified as alcohol abusers than females. Females tend to be less tolerant physiologically of the effects of alcohol. Given that women are on the average smaller than men, less alcohol is needed for a systemic effect. In addition, women seem less likely to metabolize alcohol as effectively as men in part because women have less of the stomach enzyme, alcohol dehydrogenase, which breaks down alcohol in the stomach before it has a chance to affect the central nervous system. In a study by McGue, Pickins, and Svikis (1992) male *monozygotic* twins of *probands* (the subjects identified by the researchers) that were alcohol dependent or alcohol abusers were more likely than male same-sex *dizygotic* twins to report alcohol, drug, and conduct disorder problems. Since monozygotic twins are 100 percent related (they have 100 percent of their genetic material in common) and dizygotic twins have only 50 percent of their genetic material in common, results suggest a genetic basis for some forms of alcoholism in males. However, the research dilemma remains: male monozygotic twins may be treated more similarly by society because they usually look more alike than male dizygotic twins, confounding the demonstration of any genetic cause-effect relationship. For women, the rates of alcohol, drug, and conduct disorder problems did not differ between monozygotic and same-sex dizygotic twins. The opposite-sex male twins of a dizygotic twin showed more alcohol, drug, and behavioral problems than the female twins did. Furthermore, when the proband had an early rather than a late onset of alcohol abuse or dependence, the statistical evidence for a genetic relationship was stronger. In women there was no such effect of age of onset. The authors conclude by suggesting that genetic effects may be strong only in early-onset male alcoholism.

One of the most devastating effects of drinking excessive amounts of alcohol occurs in pregnant women. The result is often a child with mental retardation and characteristic facial features called fetal alcohol syndrome. A large number of additional children have some of the effects of fetal alcohol syndrome but do not have the full-blown syndrome. It is the leading cause of mental retardation in this country. The clear message is that if a woman is pregnant, she should not drink.

It has been estimated that 14 percent of adults (ages 15–54 years) had "alcohol dependence at some time in their lives, with approximately 7 percent having had dependence in the last year" (American Psychiatric Association, 1994, p. 202). Abuse and dependence can be separated (American Psychiatric Association, 1994, p. 196). Abuse is defined as a maladaptive pattern of alcohol abuse even though there are persistent or reoccurring social, occupational, psychological, or physical problems caused or exacerbated by the use of the alcohol, or reoccurring use of the alcohol in situations that may be physically hazardous (i.e., driving heavy equipment or automobile driving) within a twelve-month period.

The criteria for alcohol dependence are much more elaborate. Several of the criteria, in addition to abuse, are a great deal of time spent in activities necessary to try to get the substance, frequent intoxication, or withdrawal symptoms when expected to fulfill major role obligations, and social occupational and recreational activities given up or reduced because of the use of alcohol, and more tolerance developing over a period of time (American Psychiatric Association, 1994, pp. 195–196).

Inherited Factors

Studies in the early 1980s by Bohman, Sigvardsson, and Cloninger (1981), and Cloninger, Bohman, and Sigvardsson (1981) suggest that alcoholism is inherited in at least one of two ways. Type One alcoholism seems to affect both men and women. When there is significant environmental stress, then the tendency for alcoholism increases. Stress in this case activates the genetic susceptibility to alcoholism. In Type Two alcoholism, there appears to be a highly significant genetic component. The alcoholic tendency is passed from father to son in about 90 percent of cases. Type Two begins earlier than Type One, often originating in adolescence and becoming progressively worse. Type One may begin in later adulthood, and symptoms are usually not as severe. Type One alcoholics often do not develop severe personality disorders, and they manage to adapt quietly to their environments. Type Two alcoholics tend to be involved in brawling, have difficulty inhibiting impulsive thoughts, tend to drink and drive in a reckless manner, and are more likely to be involved in criminal behavior in general. Buydens-Branchey, Branchey, and Noumair (1989) suggest that Type Two alcoholics may be prone to depression and suicide. Often not concerned about the effects of their actions on others, they may engage in high-risk behaviors that cause them to be classified as criminals. A combination of high-risk behavior, lack of consideration of others, compulsiveness, and aggressiveness are symptoms of the antisocial personality disorder (DSM-IV, 1994). Further research is necessary to determine whether this personality disorder is a cause or a result of Type Two alcoholism.

Genetic effects of susceptibility to alcoholism seem to show up even before the alcoholism manifests itself. Schuckit and Gold (1988) compared nonalcoholic children of alcoholics to nonalcoholic individuals with no family history of alcoholism. Following ingestion of alcohol, both of these groups were given tests to determine responses to alcohol. Children of alcoholics showed less of a subjective reaction to the alcohol than children of nonalcoholics, suggesting that they have a higher tolerance even before they are exposed to regular intake of alcohol.

It is also known that when subjects are given a task such as discriminating between visual stimuli, a positive brain wave (termed the P300 wave) occurs about 300 milliseconds after visual stimuli are presented. Alcoholics tend to show a lowering of this P300 wave. Children of alcoholics also show this dampening effect, which rules out an effect of chronic alcohol exposure per se. For example, Begleiter, Porgesz, Bihari, and Kissin (1984) showed this dampening effect in boys as young as seven years old, none of whom had been exposed to alcohol. There is also indication that some alcoholics and their sons experience increased *alpha wave* activity after consuming alcohol (Pollock et al., 1983). This increase in alpha waves is correlated with feelings of relaxation and reduction in tension. Apparently, some people respond in a more positive manner to alcohol's positive reinforcing effects. Also because of the buildup of physiological tolerance (ability to drink more and more alcohol) and the seeming absence of breaks in the drinking behavior, some people are more predisposed to develop alcoholism.

We have collaborative evidence in animals other than human. Murphy, et al. (1986) have been able to breed alcoholic rats. These alcohol-preferring rats will choose alcohol to water and will become intoxicated. Over time they will develop alcoholic tolerance. That researchers can selectively breed alcoholic animals buttresses the argument that genetic factors may be involved in human alcoholism as well.

Blum and Payne (1991) argue that alcoholism is largely the result of deficiencies or imbalances in brain chemistry that are perhaps genetic in origin. These abnormalities, they state, are represented in the "reward centers" in the brain. Certain chemicals in the brain, they assert, are undersupplied or in improper balance and may produce a range of unpleasant feelings such as anxiety, anger, depression, and cravings for relief from these feelings. The solution to the problem, they believe, will probably be biochemical and corrected by physicians with appropriate medications. According to these researchers, psychologists have ignored the vast body of research findings over the past four decades and have unjustly rejected the disease concept. This leads to misleading hypotheses such as the controlled drinking controversy. In particular, the authors strongly disagree with the Sobel and Sobel reports and the Rand Corporation Reports in 1976 and in 1981 which suggested controlled drinking was possible (Blum & Payne, 1991, pp. 240–241). It is generally conceded that these earlier studies were methodologically flawed. However, more recent evidence (e.g., Miller & Sanchez, 1994) reveals that some problem drinkers may be able to learn to drink in moderation with new approaches such as brief motivational counseling (which is described in more detail in the treatment section of this chapter). Controlled drinking may be a more appropriate strategy for individuals who cannot escape social environments that encourage drinking. Long-term longitudinal studies are needed in this area to resolve this issue.

Blum and Payne (1991) believe that pharmacological intervention for alcoholism is the way to go. Specifically, drugs like alcohol and other drugs like morphine and cocaine temporarily offset or overcome genetic abnormalities, which produce deficiencies in the reward systems of the brain. These deficiencies cause what the authors term "compulsive diseases." The alcoholic may have a deficiency of *opioid peptides*, which are related to reward, the structure and function of the *dopamine receptors* may be distorted, and the number of dopamine receptor sites in the brain may be reduced. Alcohol, morphine, and cocaine can overcome these defects by enhancing the release of abnormal amounts of dopamine. Furthermore, the metabolism of alcohol in the body produces opiate-like substances, and possibly substances that act as opiate antagonists (oppose the effect of opiates) can block the effects of alcohol. Blum and Payne postulate the "link hypothesis," which states that when alcohol metabolizes it produces TIQs ([tetrahydroisoquinolines], natural alkaloids that resemble opiates) that act on opiate receptors. Basically, this hypothesis states that because of a genetic deficiency, alcoholics can turn a higher percentage of alcohol into TIQs than do nonalcoholics. According to Blum and Payne, a root cause of a compulsive disease such as alcoholism may be a defect in a gene or genes which regulate the function of the neurotransmitter dopamine receptor labeled D2, a critical reward receptor. This genetic defect may be involved in individuals seeking alcohol, cocaine, morphine, and even glucose to enhance the availability of dopamine to these reward receptors. Blum and Payne call their biomedical approach to alcoholism, *the neurogenetic theory of compulsive disease.*

A new drug for alcohol dependency recently approved by the Food and Drug Administration lends support to this biomedical theory. In January 1995, DuPont Merck Pharmaceutical Company announced that it would sell the opiate antagonist, naltrexone, under the trade name, ReVia. ReVia is the first new drug since Antabuse was marketed over 45 years ago to fight alcohol dependency. ReVia decreases an alcoholic's craving for the drug, whereas Antabuse makes alcoholics nauseous when they drink. As a consequence, many patients do not take Antabuse as they should.

Psychosocial and Cultural Factors

Evidence shows that environmental factors interact with biological predispositions to produce alcoholism. Zucker and Gomberg (1986) noted from a review of long-term longitudinal studies that individuals most likely to become alcohol dependent in adulthood were prone to childhood problems such as aggressive and sadistic behavior, trouble with the law, rebelliousness, lower achievement in school, and greater truancy. They were sometimes hyperactive as children and had other indications of possible early neural difficulties. Interaction of these social and biological effects may promote the transition from using alcohol in a socially responsible way to alcohol dependence.

Vaillant (1983) also reported evidence of cultural influences on alcoholism. Although Irish Americans are seven times more likely to be alcoholics than most other ethnic groups, a large proportion of them are also total abstainers. This group therefore seems to hold no middle ground about alcohol; that is, one is either alcohol dependent or one abstains. Both Native Americans and Chinese Americans are of oriental heritage, and many members of both groups seem to have an exaggerated reaction to alcohol called a skin-flushing response which causes skin warming and nausea (Peel, 1992). However, some Native American tribes have the highest rate of alcoholism of any cultural group in the United States, whereas Chinese Americans have a very low rate. African-Americans have higher rates of abstinence from alcohol, but they also have the highest rate of mortality from alcohol-induced illnesses (Herd, 1989; Sutocky, Shultz, & Kizer, 1993). Thus, fewer African Americans indulge, but when they do, they are more subject to the adverse effects of alcohol. Many factors could contribute to this outcome, such as poor access to health care and low socioeconomic status. In addition, a study done by McGue, Pickens, and Svikis (1992) examined identical and fraternal twins. They found that genetic factors were minimal influences on alcoholism in women of all ages and men who were alcoholic after adolescence. However, genetics was a strong factor in men who became alcoholics early in adolescence.

In general, these studies indicate that certain overriding psychosocial and cultural influences can inhibit or facilitate any natural genetic predispositions to alcoholism.

Treatment

The treatment used for alcoholism often depends on how it is defined. For example, following the medical model, alcoholism can be considered a disease. A study reported in Vaillant (1983) by Campbell, Scadding, and Roberts (1979) indicates that 85 percent of general medical practitioners agree that alcoholism is a disease, which is approximately the same number who believe that hypertension, coronary artery disease, thrombosis, and epilepsy are diseases. However, only 50 percent of the medical academicians surveyed agree that these disorders are diseases. More of the academicians believe that malaria and diabetes are diseases. The medical community exhibits a real uncertainty regarding what is a disease and what is not. However, Vaillant reports that the deeper one looks at any particular disorder as a disease, the more likely one is to find that lifestyle, life stress, cross-cultural variables, and interpersonal variables play significant roles in the disorder. Vaillant does not believe that the medical model is without value, however. Alcohol abuse reflects a multidetermined continuum of drinking which is affected by one's culture, peer group, habits, learning history, and heredity. As Vaillant points out, this is also true of diseases like hypertension. As the drinking abuse continues over time, the individual increasingly behaves as if his problem was a disease rather than a problem of choice and habit. Just as one could possibly control hypertension in the early stages by diet, loss of weight, and exercise, the choice to drink or not to drink might be relatively easier in the earlier stages of alcohol dependence than in the later stages.

Calling alcoholism a medical disease also allows one to dichotomize the world. For example, one is either an alcoholic or one is not. This thinking may be simplistic (Ellis, McInerney, DiGuiseppe, & Yeager, 1988; Vaillant, 1983). Thinking of alcoholism on a continuum rather than as a dichotomous variable (i.e., yes, the disease is present, or no, it is not) may be more effective in developing treatment strategies against it. Even severe intake of alcohol involves more than just a biological disorder; it is also a behavior disorder. One must engage in the behavior of drinking in order to abuse alcohol. However, calling alcoholism a disease puts a label on it and allows people to feel they have something that is not their fault, rather than feeling they are bad people. If it is a disease, then it can be more easily treated by health care professionals. If it is a morality issue or a bad habit, then it is more the person's responsibility and a failing of character.

Controversy: Abstinence versus Controlled Drinking

A sometimes acrimonious debate develops between those who propose the medical model and those who propose a social learning or behavioral model of alcoholism. The contention of some who propose the social learning/behavioral model is that individuals can learn to be responsible in their drinking behavior. On the other hand, medical model proponents and Alcoholics Anonymous (AA) maintain that drinking even a little bit renders one powerless over alcohol.

Alcoholics Anonymous

Alcoholics Anonymous is a widely used treatment program founded in 1935 by two former alcoholics. Individuals who join AA are told that they must maintain complete abstinence because they have no power over the alcohol once they start drinking again. According to this model, alcoholics are always in the process of recovering and are never fully recovered. That is, they are alcoholics for a lifetime. Individuals are encouraged to attend as many meetings as possible over the course of their recovery. Some people attend three, four, and even five meetings a week.

Little information is available on how effective AA is. It is difficult to do research on AA members because they belong to an organization that provides anonymity. For example, we have no real information on dropout rates, recovery rates, and AA's effectiveness in relation to such treatments as behavioral psychotherapy, psychoanalytic psychotherapy, and multimodal therapy. Miller and Hester (1980) suggest that AA may work best with individuals who function well in organizations with a clear hierarchy, tight structure, and social involvement. Some data seem to contrast with AA's insistence on abstinence for recovery from alcohol dependence. Vaillant (1983) followed alcoholics over the 40-year span of the studies and found that some alcoholics spontaneously remit and return to asymptomatic drinking. According to Miller and Hester (1980), this remission rate is about 19 percent.

Controlled Drinking

The most famous studies on *controlled drinking* employing experimental and control groups were done by Sobel and Sobel during the late 1960s and 1970s (e.g., Sobel & Sobel, 1973, 1976). Subjects were male inpatients whose drinking problems had gotten successively worse over the years. (These are sometimes called *gamma alcoholics*.) The goal of one group was controlled drinking, and that of the other group was abstinence. They were not randomly assigned but had expressed some preference for one or the other of the groups. The controlled drinking group was further subdivided into two. One group of the two received behavioral therapy, and the other received conventional AA-oriented treatment. After two years, approximately 85 percent of the behavioral therapy subgroup was functioning well as compared to the conventional AA-oriented group (approximately 42 percent). These studies have been both criticized (e.g., Pendry, Multsman, & West, 1982) and supported (e.g., Heather & Robertson, 1983). Carey and Maisto (1985) point to the need for further research but also suggest that self-control treatments may have the potential for early intervention in alcoholic-related problems. However, the long-term effects of these self-control treatment programs remain to be determined. Controlled drinking may be indicated for people who are younger, do not have a long history of heavy drinking, are married rather than single, and believe that environmental rather than biological conditions contribute to their drinking. Ellis, McInerney, DiGiuseppe, and Yeager (1988) believe that the individual who is experiencing long-term alcohol-related problems and drinks five or more drinks at a sitting may require the more radical approach of total abstinence from alcohol.

A group of drinkers that fall between moderate drinkers and heavy drinkers is a group called problem drinkers (see Box 4.1).

Another controlled drinking approach that emphasizes psychological variables is taken by Miller and Sanchez (1994). They have summarized this approach with the acronym, FRAMES, which has the following meaning:

- FEEDBACK of personal assessment results
- Emphasis on personal RESPONSIBILITY for change
- ADVICE to change use
- Description of a MENU of options for change
- Therapeutic EMPATHY as a predominant counseling style
- Support for client SELF-EFFICACY and optimism

This approach is subsumed under work Miller and his colleagues have called "brief motivational counseling." Using the FRAMES method in their motivational counseling, they state, produces the highest evidence of efficacy at the lowest cost. The FRAMES approach also has exciting possibilities for treating other addictive behaviors. Their method of treatment usually requires only one to three sessions. The personal assessment, which can be quite extensive and which includes both psychological and medical assessment, is the most expensive part of the FRAMES approach. This cost is offset by the approach's brevity.

Box 4.1
Problem Drinkers: A Unique Category of Drinkers

In their book, *Problem Drinkers: A Self-Change Treatment* (1993), the Sobells contend that a large population does not fall into the category of alcohol dependence, but nonetheless has problems with its drinking patterns. They report studies that show that the population of problem drinkers is much larger than the population of alcohol-dependent drinkers (possibly 4:1). Estimates of alcohol-dependent drinkers run about 10 percent of the population in this country. Summarizing research, the Sobells state that:

- Problem drinkers do not have a history of severe alcohol withdrawal symptoms.
- Problem drinkers tend to have a shorter problem drinking history, typically around five years, and seldom over ten years.
- Problem drinkers tend to have greater social and economic stability.
- Problem drinkers tend to have greater personal, social, and economic resources to call upon in treatment (i.e., they have greater opportunity to help themselves).
- Problem drinkers are not likely to view themselves as different from persons who do not have drinking problems (i.e., they do not self-identify as alcoholic, and their self-esteem is usually higher than that of persons with more severe histories).
- Problem drinkers can become caught in a motivational dilemma, knowing that they still have a great deal to lose but also feeling that conditions in their lives are not so bad as to justify extensive life changes or sacrifices to deal with their drinking.

The Sobells describe a brief intervention program (assessment of drinking, two homework assignments, and two 90-minute treatment sessions) that is designed to facilitate self-change by identifying reasons for changing, by providing assistance in changing, and by capitalizing on individuals' own strengths. The program does not require intensive intrusions into individuals' lifestyle such as direct confrontation methods and hospitalization, and it emphasizes self-help.

The Sobells report that in the year following the treatment, the total number of drinks reported by the clients was reduced by 54 percent. They noted a significant increase in the number of abstinent days and a significant decrease in the number of heavy drinking days. Their work indicates that problem drinkers can gain better control over their drinking habits without the use of more traditional approaches such as complete abstinence.

Source: Sobell, M. B., & Sobell, L. C. (1993). *Problem drinkers: Guided self-change treatment.* New York: Guilford Press, pp. 21–22. Reproduced by permission.

SMOKING

Years ago I was in training to become a registered nurse on an internal medicine ward in Buffalo, New York. I was caring for a man in an iron lung, which was a popular treatment for individuals with severe respiratory problems in those days. The man whom I was caring for spent 23½ hours in the iron lung, allowed only half an hour's reprieve from the iron lung each day. He was able to breathe on his own for approximately that amount of time; then his skin, lips, and fingernails would start to turn blue. The man for whom I was caring spent most of the time out of the iron lung intensely smoking one cigarette after another locked away in the men's bathroom. He and his visitors had stashed cigarettes in various places that were difficult for others to find. Following his cigarette smoking orgy, he would resume his time in the iron lung. I was flabbergasted at the time (and still am) regarding the addictive qualities of cigarettes. I did not care for the individual long enough to find out what happened to him after I was transferred from the floor. However, I suspect his stay in the hospital was a short one.

According to the U.S. Department of Health and Human Services (1988), the percentage of smokers in the United States has declined since the 1960s, with approximately 26 percent of Americans still continuing to smoke. Women appear to be stopping smoking at a slower rate than men (Fiore et al., 1989). According to the Surgeon General's report, smoking is directly related to 390,000 deaths annually in the United States (Novello, 1990, p. VIII). In addition to this statistic, many people are suffering from chronic bronchitis and emphysema; babies are born with low birth weight; and sidestream smoke affects millions of others. Cigarette smokers also do not appear to be as concerned about healthy lifestyle behavior as nonsmokers are. For example, smokers tend to drink more alcohol (e.g., Fehily, Phillips, & Yarnell, 1984; Gordon, Kannel, Dawber, & McGee, 1975); they tend to take in more caffeine (e.g., Istvan & Matarazzo, 1984; Morabia & Wynder, 1990), smokers have been found to consume more saturated fats (Cade & Margetts, 1989; Morabia & Wynder, 1990), and more fried foods (Whichelow, Golding, & Treasure, 1988) but less fiber (Klesges, Eck, Clark, Meyers, & Hanson, 1990; Subar, Harlan, & Mattson, 1990), fewer fruits and vegetables (Whichelow et al., 1988; Morabia & Wynder, 1990; Subar et al., 1990), and less minerals and vitamins (Fehily et al., 1984; Haste et al., 1990). Since there is a clustering of unhealthy patterns of nutrition along with smoking, this complicates attempts to determine smoking by itself as a causative agent and many of the diseases and health hazards associated with it. To complicate matters even further, smokers may differ from nonsmokers in terms of education and income (Pierce, Fiore, Novotny, Hatziandreu, & Davis, 1989) and personality factors (Eysenck, 1973). In general, smokers have fewer positive lifestyle behaviors to balance against negative lifestyle behaviors than do nonsmokers.

Why We Do It

Individuals start smoking for many reasons. Lichtenstein and Brown (1980) suggest that the availability of cigarettes, the natural curiosity of teenagers, rebelliousness against authority, models such as peers and siblings and parents, and the ability of cigarettes to provide perceived social confidence all interact to initiate smoking activity.

In addition to the social and environmental pressures to start smoking, a genetic predisposition may influence addiction to smoking (Epstein, Grunberg, Lichtenstein, & Evans, 1989). Along with the genetic effects are physiological factors that become important after beginning to smoke. Nicotine is highly addictive to smokers and thus extremely positively reinforcing. Pomerleau and Pomerleau (1984) point out that nicotine increases the release of the neural transmitters acetylcholine, norepinephrine, and dopamine, increases cortisol (an adrenal gland hormone), and increases natural opiates in the brain. All of these chemicals improve mental alertness; acetylcholine has been associated with sharpening memory, and the opiates reduce tension and anxiety. Smokers have to deal not only with the positively reinforcing effects of nicotine but also with the punishing effects of withdrawal, which may last several weeks and make the individual feel tired, lethargic, drowsy, and distractible. The individual is negatively reinforced by the relief of tension when he or she again resumes the cigarette habit. The punishing effects of a cigarette habit such as heart and lung disease are usually long delayed. A tried and true fact in learning theory, with some exceptions, is the idea that immediate reinforcement is more powerful in affecting behavior than long-delayed punishment. The immediate physiological effects of nicotine rushing to the brain outweigh the long-delayed effects of health hazards down the line. There are also immediate punishments for not smoking in a confirmed smoker: for example, reduced concentration, feelings of anxiety, tension, irritability, and a generally bad feeling occur with the loss of nicotine from the body. No wonder it is so difficult to stop smoking.

It has long been assumed that smoking helps control body weight. I recall instances of dancers in some of my classes stating that they smoked to keep their body weight down. Body weight control in our culture could be a very powerful motivator to start smoking, return to smoking when one's weight goes up, and not attempting to quit. Klesges, Meyers, Klesges, and Lavasque (1989) report in their review of the literature that cross-sectional and longitudinal studies indicate that as a group smokers weigh less than nonsmokers and they tend to gain weight when they do stop smoking. In a survey determining intentional use of smoking for weight control, Klesges and Klesges (1988) found that 32.5 percent of smoking college students in a sample of 1,076 endorsed the deliberate use of smoking to control weight. They also found that overweight females were more likely than normal weight females to report that they started smoking to control their weight. Weekley, Klesges, and Reylea (1992) found that weight control smokers were more likely to gain weight after they had previously quit, had less formal education, reported higher weight among their biological parents (and were thus more at risk for obesity), and were more likely to be chronic dieters. Weekly et al. (1992) believed that weight control was a significant factor in whether or not individuals smoked. Based on this research, weight control issues should be given high priority in any attempt to change individual smoking habits.

An hypothesis involving body weight *set point* advanced by Kenneth Perkins (1992) at Western Psychiatric Institute may help in dealing with these weight control problems. Perkins has reviewed the effects of tobacco smoking on caloric intake and has found in cross-sectional studies that despite smokers' lower body weights they do not eat less than nonsmokers or ex-smokers. In fact they may tend to eat slightly more. Perkins reports that longitudinal studies have shown that eating consistently increases immediately following an individual's cessation of smoking, but food intake may regress to pre-cessation levels with continuing of abstinence from smoking. If an individual begins to smoke again, this is followed by a reduction in eating. Perkins points out that changes in eating behavior are noted with changes in whether an individual stops or begins to smoke again. Perkins notes that smoking and the nicotine it provides does not necessarily decrease caloric intake in smokers. When a smoker stops, however, caloric intake increases, at least in the short run, and may decrease again if the individual resumes smoking. This pattern of results seems to parallel the effects of smoking on self-reported desire for sweet, high-fat food. That is, when a smoker stops smoking, there is a reported increase in desire for sweet, high-fat food.

Another theory is that smokers become tolerant to the effects of nicotine. This theory may explain why chronic smokers eat as much, if not more, than nonsmokers as they become tolerant to the effects of nicotine. That is, the *anorectic* characteristics of the nicotine have less and less of an effect on the nervous system the longer the nervous system is exposed to the nicotine. Nicotine is less and less effective in suppressing the appetite. However, without additional assumptions, this theory does not easily explain why people have an increased desire for sweet, fatty food when they stop smoking. If tolerance to nicotine has developed by long-term smoking, then it should have no effect when the nicotine is removed. That is, if it was not working (not effective in suppressing the appetite) while the smoker smoked, why should it all of a sudden work (affect the appetite in the opposite direction) when the smoker stops smoking? However, this theory can be strengthened by adding the additional assumption of the presence of a rebound, *opponent process* to explain the increased desire for sweet, fatty food (Solomon & Corbit, 1973). Solomon and Corbit proposed that many addictive processes produce slow-growing opponent processes, which they theorized might operate in the nervous system in the opposite direction to the original processes.

These are theoretical constructs and as yet have no identifiable neural substrates. They are like the ancient Chinese female-male opposing principles of yin and yang. For example, if the original process produces pleasure from the stimulation of an addictive agent (e.g., opiates, alcohol, nicotine, etc.), then the opponent process produces pain and misery by the removal and absence of the addictive agent. The longer the addictive agent has been used, the more severe the opponent process will be when the agent is removed. In heroin addiction, for example, it accounts for the withdrawal symptoms that the addicts experience when they go "cold turkey." In the case of nicotine and eating, the pleasurable effects of the long-term use of nicotine and its anorectic properties could develop a strong anti-anorectic opponent process, which when released during nonsmoking produces a strong eating drive. As the effects of the opponent process wear off, as Solomon and Corbit predict, the eating behavior of the ex-smoker should return to smoking pre-cessation levels. This is exactly what Perkins reports as happening. Solid experimental evidence for this hypothesis remains to be determined.

Another alternative hypothesis is that smoking alters the reinforcing value of food (especially sweet-tasting food), so that the removal of nicotine, a powerful reinforcer, increases the reinforcement value of food possibly by a reinforcement contrast effect. Removal of one type of reinforcement enhances the value of other types of reinforcement. When the reinforcing qualities of nicotine are gone, other biological reinforcers such as the distinctive qualities of sweet-tasting food become more salient. This hypothesis does not easily explain why ex-smokers later reduce their caloric intake to smoking pre-cessation levels, unless one posits some sort of habituation of salience effect that takes place with continued exposure to the food.

Perkins also indicates that it is not immediately clear why eating would be suppressed at all in smokers since initial exposure to nicotine is usually reported as aversive. If anthing, eating should be enhanced on the basis of either the opponent process theory or reinforcement contrast effects. Indeed, cross-sectional studies summarized by Perkins do indicate that the caloric intake of chronic smokers is not significantly different from that of nonsmokers.

Perkins observes that the best hypothesis for explaining eating behavior and weight changes related to smoking is that smoking alters the body weight set point. Perkins points out several deductions that are confirmed if nicotine alters the set point. They are: (1) regular smoking is associated with a lower body weight but does not have a clear effect on eating, (2) smoking cessation leads to an increase in weight up to the level of nonsmokers as the new set point is reached, and (3) resumption of smoking decreases body weight back to the level when the individual was smoking, with a short-term decrease in eating until the new lower set point is reached.

This set-point hypothesis has several implications according to Perkins. First the sharp change in eating following changes in smoking status may strongly reinforce the idea that smoking is a general anorectic; thus, people will not want to stop smoking because of the fear of gaining weight. Second, if removal of nicotine causes an increase in body set point, it may be very difficult to prevent this weight gain. Dieting strategies and increases in exercise as well as the use of nicotine gum or patches can all delay the weight gain. Cognitive behavioral strategies may be implemented. Third, it might help ex-smokers to realize that their weight increases are simply weight increases they would have had if they had not smoked in the first place. Perkins mentions that fenfluramine (a nonamphetamine appetite suppressant drug that increases levels of serotonin and blocks its reuptake in the brain, and the major problem in the infamous Fen-Phen diet medication associated with heart valve problems) may help to reduce the *dysphoria*, or unpleasant feelings, that is associated with smoking withdrawal in some ex-smokers. I doubt whether anyone will want to use this medication because of the heart valve problems it may produce. Other selective serotonergic reuptake inhibitors such as Prozac may also reduce dysphoria. However, as mentioned previously, nicotine gum or patches and increased exercise may also do the same thing. The ex-smoker should be informed that even an increase in body weight is healthier than continuing to smoke.

Controversy: Smoking in Restaurants

In New Jersey, as in several other states, smoking is allowed in restaurants that seat fewer than 50 people and in bars and taverns. Larger restaurants are required by law to have smoking and no smoking sections. Restaurant and bar owners argue that outlawing smoking will drive trade away, and their businesses will go down the tubes. Others who wish a smoke-free eating environment argue that second-hand smoke is as dangerous to the innocent bystander as it is to the smoker. People who wish a smoke-free eating (and drinking) environment should patronize smoke-free restaurants, and these businesses will not only survive but thrive. Parenthetically, some of the casinos in Atlantic City have

---

Box 4.2
Personality and Smoking

Besides family, peer, and mass media pressures to smoke, personality factors
may also play a role. Lipkus, Barefoot, Williams, and Siegler (1994) collected
data from the Minnesota Multiphasic Inventory on 3,810 men and 836 women
in 1964–1967 to predict smoking initiation and cessation over a 20-year follow-up period. The researchers found that people who subsequently began
smoking were more rebellious, impulsive, sensation seeking, and hostile, were
less likely to present a positive self-image, and were more extroverted in college. Of the personality variables measured, hostility seemed to be the most
significant factor in separating ex-smokers from current smokers. The authors
note that hostility is linked to coronary disease and that smoking has the same
link. The research provides further evidence of links among personality factors such as hostility and smoking and heart disease.

Source: Lipkus, I. M., Barefoot, J. C., Williams, R. B., & Siegler, I. C. (1994). Personality
    measures as predictors of smoking initiation and cessation in the UNC Alumni
    Heart Study. *Health Psychology, 13*, 149–155.

---

initiated smoke-free areas with no reported dropoff in business. However, powerful lobbying forces in New Jersey have prevented significant
changes there so far.

Box 4.2 illustrates that personality factors such as hostility may also
play a role in smoking.

Treatment

If smoking changes the set point, and rapid weight gains and losses
follow cessation and resumption of cigarette smoking, short-term diet,
exercise, and cognitive behavioral techniques may reduce the perceived
immediately reinforcing effects of weight loss by nicotine and the punishing effects of weight gain on cessation. According to Lichtenstein and
Brown (1980), prior to the 1980s many different cessation methods were
developed to help people stop smoking. One of these older techniques
is hypnosis, which many perceive to be an effortless way to change behavior. I occasionally hear in classes of an individual who has stopped
smoking through hypnosis, and I know of relatives who have stopped
and have not resumed their smoking habit. If hypnosis is used correctly
by associating unpleasant images with smoking, using relaxation techniques of various sorts, and using self statements, then it works like
many other behavioral interventions and may have some success. However, solid research confirming this hypothesis is limited (e.g., Frank,
Umlauf, Wonderlich, & Ashkanazi, 1986).

A behavioral therapy called *aversion therapy* has been used with some success. Initially in this therapy, electric shock was used as an aversive stimulus (punisher) after each puff of a cigarette. Cigarette packages were also wired to deliver a shock every time the individual reached into it to obtain a cigarette. In one type of aversion therapy, individuals puff a cigarette every six seconds until they can smoke no more (*hypersatiation*). Even a positive stimulus such as cigarette smoking can become aversive if it is used over and over again (Rimm & Masters, 1979). As one can imagine, symptoms of nicotine overdose can develop as well as an increase in carbon monoxide in the blood, which increases heart rate and in blood pressure changes.

Focused smoking (Hackett & Horan, 1979) is a technique that seems to eliminate some of the problems of hypersatiation. In focused smoking, the person is told to concentrate on negative feelings and sensations associated with smoking while smoking at a more regular pace.

Another aversive procedure used is smoke holding. This technique consists of holding smoke in the mouth until the flavor of the smoke becomes aversive. This may be a more effective strategy than focused smoking (Walker & Franzini, 1985).

Drugs are another method that at first blush appears to be a fairly simple way to get individuals to stop smoking. Tranquilizing drugs are sometimes used to ease withdrawal from the nicotine in smoking, but there seems to be little evidence of their efficacy. In fact, sedatives, antianxiety agents, and most other psychotropics (mind-altering drugs) appear to be relatively ineffective in smoking satiation. Nicotine chewing has been used more recently to get individuals to stop smoking. Apparently, many people using nicotine gum report side effects such as nausea, gastrointestinal distress, soreness and injury to the mouth, and headaches (Fortmann, Killen, Telch, & Newman, 1988). However, nicotine gum is not meant to be used in conjunction with cutting down on smoking. It is to be used when individuals have stopped and are dealing with some of the withdrawal symptoms of nicotine loss. Nicotine in forms other than cigarettes does not contain some of the tars and gases that have severe health consequences. Nicotine gum must be used in combination with behavioral treatments. In the short term it may be effective, but in the long run it does not seem to improve the probability of success in quitting smoking (Hall, Tunstall, Rugg, Jones, & Benowitz, 1985).

Nicotine patches were introduced in 1992 and soon became very popular. In this procedure, nicotine is absorbed from the patches through the skin in declining doses over a period of a few weeks. Initially, manufacturers could not keep up with the demand. Following the tremendous initial interest, however, demand has waned somewhat. They certainly seem to eliminate the mouth soreness and ulcers sometimes associated with chewing nicotine gum. A prospective quasi-experimental study by Kupecz and Prochazka (1996) showed that the nicotine patch produced a higher short-term quit rate, fewer adverse side effects, and a longer time to relapse than nicotine gum. From time to time, however, there are reports of individuals continuing to smoke while they are using the patch, with the possibility of toxic consequences.

Hypnosis and acupuncture were extremely popular in the 1980s as aids to smoking cessation and are still successful commercially, even though the scientific evidence for their effectiveness is scant. For example, West, Fellows, and Easton (1995) and Spanos, Mondoux, and Burgess (1995) found hypnosis had no significant effect on smoking cessation, whereas Baillie, Mattick, Hall, and Webster (1994) found acupuncture had no effect.

So far, there is no "magic bullet" to smoking cessation that works without a comprehensive and multimodal approach. As Schelling (1992) points out, the environmental, social, and physiological factors involved in smoking must also be addressed. For example, individuals may smoke when they feel distressed, when they are happy, when they have a cup of coffee, when they have a drink, after eating, and other social and environmental situations that evoke emotional responses. Peer and social pressure may also induce individuals to start smoking when they have stopped. Cigarettes are among the easiest of the addicting drugs to obtain; they are also among the cheapest, they do not produce lethargy, slurring of speech, or cognitive changes to any great degree, and they allow the individual to remain productive and in tune with reality.

The first step of a multimodal plan to stop smoking proposed by Lichtenstein and Brown (1980) is preparing to quit. The key objective of this preparation is to establish a target quit date that allows an individual to mentally prepare to quit smoking. Second, individuals should self-monitor their smoking in order to establish how much they smoke at baseline, and they should identify the antecedent and consequent conditions of their smoking behavior. Third, the motivation to quit must be reviewed and strengthened. Of the three steps the last one, motivation, is critical according to these authors and determines whether an individual will be successful in quitting. Individuals should be educated on the hazards of cigarette smoking, but most people are well aware of these hazards. According to these authors, a better approach is to focus on health benefits and the positive reinforcement that accrue to an individual if he or she stops smoking. This would certainly involve a discussion of the weight gain that many individuals experience, with the statement that it is temporary and that an individual can increase his or her metabolic rates by exercise and controlling the amount of fat and calories in the diet. Brownell, Marlatt, Lichtenstein, and Wilson (1986) suggest that physical exercise may be very helpful in smoking cessation. It is very difficult to effectively engage in aerobic exercise while continuing smoking. Smoking behavior will usually cease if the individual continues in the aerobic activity. Supportive social pressure is important here, as well as emphasizing the physiological improvements in energy and the ability to move around without being winded. A written contract involving attendance at the treatment program, keeping careful records, and doing homework assignments is helpful in motivating people to stop smoking. An individual could even forfeit money that would be given back as the person progressed through the program successfully.

A cognitive behavioral relapse prevention procedure proposed by Marlatt and his colleagues (Cummings, Gordon, & Marlatt, 1980) attempts to increase subjects' feelings of control over their smoking behavior by teaching them to cope with specific problem situations and what they are thinking at the time. DeClemente (1981) found that feelings of self-efficacy were better predictors of smoking cessation than other factors, and that the belief that one can continue to abstain from smoking is a good predictor of successful quitting.

The Marlatt and Gordon Relapse Prevention Program consists of five parts: (1) lifestyle balancing, (2) identification of risk situations, (3) relapse rehearsal, (4) dealing with a cognitive affective reaction called the Abstinence Violation Effect (AVE), and (5) self rewards. Lifestyle balancing based on helping individuals deals with balance in their lifestyles between "shoulds" and "wants." Shoulds are activities that are unpleasant or under our obligation to perform, and wants are activities that are fun and pleasurable. Lifestyle imbalance occurs when activities have too many shoulds and not enough wants. Lifestyle balancing suggests that a negative addiction like smoking which we should not do can be replaced with a positive "addiction" such as meditation, jogging, yoga, relaxation, or some sort of exercise program that we will eventually want to do. In risk identification, an individual is asked to identify the relapse situation in detail. These experiences will serve as stimuli that will allow the individual to rehearse strategies to prevent the perceived relapse situation. When the individual experiences AVE, individuals are encouraged to think of relapse as a slip rather than a relapse. A slip is considered a learning experience to analyze why the individual resumed smoking so that the slip can be prevented the next time. Individuals add in their own rewards as they persist in their cigarette abstinence. These rewards should not be destructive; rather, they should be health-enhancing wants and other identifiable individualistic rewards.

Finally, Marlatt and Gordon recommend a buddy system comparable to that used in Alcoholics Anonymous and Weight Watchers.

OTHER DRUGS

Cocaine

Cocaine is a stimulant drug derived from coca leaves. It can be sniffed as a powder, injected intravenously, or smoked in the form of crack. It produces a strong euphoric feeling that occurs rapidly but lasts no more than 15 to 30 minutes. Following the rush of euphoria there is a crash marked by anxiety, agitation, some depression, and a craving for more of the drug to end these negative feelings (Gawin, 1991). Over time, the individual does not feel reward except through use of the drug. The world becomes gray and unpleasant unless the individual has cocaine in the system (Gawin & Ellenwood, 1988). Estroff and Gold (1985–1986) report that cocaine dries out the mucous membranes so that they crack and bleed easily. Individuals develop runny noses, hoarseness, and sometimes dull headaches. Heavy snorting can destroy the cartilage between the nostrils. Cocaine has a variety of physiological effects such as constricted blood vessels, elevated blood pressure, increased heart rate, and sometimes epileptic seizures (Pascual-Leone, Dhuna, & Allafullah, 1990). Cocaine can even kill. As many basketball sports fans know, Len Bias, the professional basketball player, died from an overdose of cocaine. Crack cocaine, which is cheaper than cocaine, is also more dangerous, with dependencies developing in a matter of weeks. The term "crack" comes from the cracking sound it makes when heated (Julien, 1995). "Crack," a more concentrated form of cocaine, is made by boiling cocaine in a solution of baking soda and water until the water evaporates. This base form (from the baking soda) can then be inhaled with a heated pipe.

Heroin

Heroin is produced from an opium derivative, morphine, through an alteration of morphine's chemical structure. It is about three times as powerful as morphine (Julien, 1995). It passes through the blood-brain barrier faster than morphine, and it leads to a "rush" or feeling of euphoria when it is smoked or injected intravenously (Julien, 1995). Heroin and other derivatives of morphine such as Demerol and Dilaudid access the reinforcement areas of the brain that may be akin to engaging in survival behaviors such as eating, drinking, and sex (Gold, 1993). These substances along with codeine, which is also derived from opium, are extremely addicting.

Marijuana

Marijuana is the most commonly used illegal drug in the United States, with about 20 million people in the United States using it regularly. Marijuana is made up of leaves, flowers, and branches of the cannabis sativa found almost everywhere. The active ingredient in marijuana is tetrahydrocannibinol (THC). The THC in marijuana tends to produce a feeling of well being, relaxes some people, and relieves anxiety and inhibitions. It sometimes produces an increased sensitivity to sight, sounds, and touch, some perceptual distortion, and a slowing of time. There are reports of increased sexual responsiveness in experienced users. On the down side, marijuana can interfere with concentration, logical thinking, and the ability to form new memories and to remember what is said (Hooker & Jones, 1987). Chronic use of marijuana has been associated with what is called the *amotivational syndrome*. This is a general apathy and lack of interest in doing most anything productive. Smoking marijuana can cause respiratory damage even more rapidly than cigarette smoking (Ray & Ksir, 1993). Studies with male and female smokers have reported a reduction in sperm count and activity, as well as irregular and abnormal ovulation (Hembree, Nahas, Zeidenberg, & Huang, 1974; Nahas, 1984).

Recently, it has been postulated that marijuana interacts with brain reward systems, making this substance fundamentally similar to other abused drugs (Gardner & Lowinson, 1991). Gardner and Lowinson proposed that marijuana enhances electrical brain stimulation in THC-sensitive rats by preventing the reuptake of dopamine by neurons and enhancing dopamine release in reward circuitry. They also proposed that it modulates the brain's opioid receptors and is blocked by an opiate antagonist, *naloxone*. However, these studies were done with laboratory rats, and whether they generalize to humans at this time is not known. Interestingly, just as other abused drugs seem to affect different individuals differently, several strains of rats do not respond to THC at all. These animal studies would predict that at least some individuals would become physiologically addicted to marijuana and that naloxone may reduce the withdrawal effects. According to Grilly (1989, p. 248), studies have determined that cessation of heavy chronic marijuana use can precipitate an abstinence syndrome that may produce irritability, restlessness, decreased appetite, sweating, tremors, nausea, and vomiting. However, chronic THC exposure likely does not produce dependence of the opiate variety.

Inhalant Abuse

Inhalant abuse is the inhaling of volatile (breathable) substances that alter the mind, usually producing a temporary euphoria. Solvent abuse is alternatively known as glue sniffing, sniffing, and huffing. These volatile substances can be ingested by sniffing or "snorting" through the nose, by "bagging" (inhaling fumes from a plastic bag), and by stuffing an inhalant-soaked rag into the mouth. These inhalants are depressants like the closely related compounds, the anesthetic gases, but they initially produce feelings of stimulation. Some of the effects of inhalants are giddiness, dizziness, slurred speech, staggering, and impulsiveness along with euphoria. The National Institute on Drug Abuse (1994) reported that the use of inhalants is as common as the use of stimulants and is only less popular than the use of marijuana, alcohol, and cigarettes. A frightening statistic by the National Institute on Drug Abuse (1994), on the basis of a multisite survey, indicated that close to 20 percent of surveyed eighth and tenth graders and high school seniors had had previous experiences with inhalants. Mainly because other substances are not readily available to them, younger students are more likely to use inhalants. Students who chronically use inhalants show poor academic achievement, delinquency, and dysfunctional social relationships (Chadwick, Yule, & Anderson, 1990). According to Kerner (1988), the most effective strategy is early education. The earlier discussion is initiated with children about the dangers of inhalant use the better, because inhalant use begins with children as young as 7 years of age. Kerner (1988) also suggests that exposure to positive role models and reinforcement of alternative constructive activities (possibly sports and physical activity) are important strategies in trying to decrease inhalant use.

Anabolic Steroids

Initially, anabolic steroids were developed for medical use and are now used in, for example, the treatment of male reproductive dysfunctions. They are also being used in ways that were not originally intended, such as for performance-enhancement and muscle building in sports and body building. Terry Todd, an expert in sports history, states that the spread of anabolic steroids began with Bob Hoffman's York Barbell Club team when they began using *Dianabol*, a synthetic anabolic steroid (Todd, 1987). Hoffman reported a little known training technique called isometric contraction to which he attributed the rise of three of his weightlifters to national championships. However, he did not mention the use of anabolic steroids as part of this package. Apparently, information on steroids came to the York Barbell Club by way of Dr. John Ziegler, who was the U.S. team physician at the world weight-lifting championships in Vienna in 1954. The Soviet team physician reportedly told him that the successful Soviet team was using testosterone, an anabolic steroid (Yesalis, Courson, & Wright, 1993, p. 38).

Information spread on anabolic steroids and their remarkable effects on the human body. Todd reported that the hammer thrower Howard Connelly testified at the U.S. Subcommittee hearings on drugs in athletics that he became hooked on steroids in 1964. In 1968, Dr. Tom Waddell, who placed sixth in the decathlon that year, estimated that a full third of the U.S. track and field team had used steroids prior to the Mexico City games in 1968. According to a personal interview conducted in 1986 as reported by Todd, a woman power lifter reported that she had been off steroids for two years but still had to shave every day.

Controversy: To Win or Just Play the Game?

Is it more important to win at any cost or just participate in a sport that you enjoy? Many people say that they enjoy the camaraderie and exercise they get in playing a sport and that winning is only secondary. However, Dr. Gabe Mirkin, the talk show sports adviser, stated that he once asked more than a hundred competitive runners if they would take a magic pill that would guarantee them an Olympic gold medal but also would kill them within the year. He found that more than one-half of the athletes answered that they would take the magic pill.

Since the 1960s, use of anabolic steroids has apparently increased, and there has been a continuing technologizing of sport in general. Various drugs that enhance performance have been developed to keep one step ahead of the drug testers. Recently, athletes have begun using human growth hormone (HGH), which cannot yet be detected by drug tests (see Box 4.3). According to Todd (1994), athletes are looking to other techniques such as implants of electrodes and computer chips placed inside the body to generate super physiological doses of natural hormones, especially testosterone, to improve strength and appearance. A computer chip might be able to stimulate the natural neural transmitters of the brain to increase athletic prowess and enhance the body's appearance.

Without question, anabolic steroids of various types increase the size and number of muscle cells, increase strength, and add to an overall muscular appearance. It is not just Olympic athletes and professional athletes who seem captivated with these effects. A national study (Buckley, Yesalis, & Bennell, 1993) found that about 6.6 percent of high school senior boys have used anabolic steroids. A later survey (National Institute on Drug Abuse, 1991) found that 5 percent of high school senior boys and 0.5 percent of high school senior girls reported using steroids at some time. A survey done by DuRant, Ashworth, Newman, and Rickert (1994) showed ninth-grade steroid users were also more likely to be polydrug users. Some of the other drugs used by steroid users were marijuana, cocaine, smokeless tobacco, and alcohol. According to Todd, one can walk into almost any gym in the country and within a short time make a contact to buy these anabolic steroids.

Psychological changes seem to go along with anabolic steroid use. Taylor (1982) interviewed 100 body builders and other athletes who used steroids. Ninety of the 100 subjects admitted that while using steroids they experienced episodes of extremely aggressive or violent behavior. Pope and Katz (1988) studied steroid-using athletes and found that nine subjects displayed full affective disorders such as depression and mania

Box 4.3
Fountain of Youth?

Todd (1994) reports in *Texas Monthly* magazine on a businessman from Houston who was so influenced by research on human growth hormone that he began injecting himself with the hormone regularly. He claims that since January 1991, when he began his injections, his waistline has dropped from 42 to 32 inches, his muscles have hardened, his eyesight has improved, his skin has thickened, his palsy-like tremor has vanished, and his sex drive is where it was when he was in his twenties. This man also convinced his physician to begin injections. This physician reportedly experienced many of the same effects from the injections that his patient had. In 1992, the two men set up the Rejuvenation and Longevity Institute in Mexico. Things did not go so smoothly for the two men, however. The physician apparently underwent mood changes on the growth hormone and testosterone that he was taking. His colleague, who shared an office with the physician, reported that he was obsessed with his physique, started an affair, and brought his pistol to his office with him. Reportedly, one night he had a fight with his girlfriend, drank a large amount of vodka, passed out, and choked to death.

The market for the possible anti-aging effects of growth hormone is huge, and would be a godsend to those experiencing the infirmities of age. However, it will necessitate prospective and long-term studies, which are now being supported by the National Institute on Aging. The drug does seem to burn fat and build muscle, but scientifically reliable information on the drug's effects is not yet available. Meanwhile, people such as those running the Rejuvenation and Longevity Institute in Mexico continue to pass their literature out, promising great improvement in physical well being with minimum discussion of side effects, and possibly targeting the enormous anti-aging and fat-loss market. Let the buyer beware!

Source: Todd, T. (1994). Growing young. *Texas Monthly, 22,* pp. 46–50. Reproduced by permission of the author.

while on steroids and five experienced classic psychotic symptoms. They had not experienced such symptoms prior to using the steroids. Other studies indicate that anabolic steroids produce psychological dependence (Brower, 1993). Steroid users sometimes feel they cannot live without the drug. As Bahrke (1993) points out, however, many of these studies suffer from methodological flaws such as biased samples, lack of control groups, and use of a variety of methods to assess the psychological outcomes.

Many physical disabilities resulting from anabolic steroid use have been reported (Friedl, 1993, p. 112), but solid scientific evidence as to the accuracy of some of these reports is still lacking. For example, some of the reported physical problems may be the result of impurities, composition, and methods of administering of drugs obtained on the black market. Nonetheless, there are reports of increased infections, increased risk of cardiovascular disease and stroke, increased susceptibility to colon cancer, prostatic enlargement and cancer, and liver dysfunction (Friedl, 1993, p. 112). Treatment programs for steroid use are not available, and even if they were, they would be destined for little success in our present sports culture where a win-at-any-cost attitude prevails.

There may even be a parallel between this desire to look better and the phenomenon of anorexia nervosa. Mostly young males in gyms throughout the country seem to take these anabolic steroids to increase their physical appearance and strength among their peers. Losing touch with how they look, they continually desire to look bigger and to be stronger. Similarly, many young women desire to look thinner and thinner and lose touch with how thin they really are. In both cases, the goals are lost in the process of getting to them.

SUMMARY

Alcohol has been around a long time. Because of its long history, acceptance, and legal accessibility, it is the most widely used psychoactive drug. However, alcohol-related problems cost the American economy and our health care system vast amounts of money. There is evidence that alcohol dependence may be inherited, but biological sexual identity, environmental, ethnic, and cultural forces interact with this genetic predisposition in complex and, as yet, unknown ways. Treatments depend on how alcoholism is defined. If it is defined primarily as a disease, then abstinence and pharmacological cures are possible. If it is seen primarily as a habit and a product of social, ethnic, and cultural learning, then various learning and behavioral modification strategies should be able to stop or change the destructive habit. If alcoholism is more susceptible to treatment strategies involving learning early in the development of the disorder, and abstinence, medical, and pharmacological treatments later in the disorder, then it helps to know the time course of the alcoholism disorder so that it may be treated.

Rational emotive therapy is a useful example of a learning approach to treating alcoholism, and the neurogenetic theory of compulsive disease model postulates biomedical and pharmacological approaches to alcoholism treatment emphasizing alcohol abstinence. Interwoven in the debate of cause and treatment is the lack of clear definitions of the terms disease and habit.

Smoking also has a long history, but only recently have we become aware of the tremendous threat this behavior has on health in the long term. The number of smokers has declined in this country, but some segments of the population are quitting at slower rates than others. Women, for example, seem to be stopping at slower rates than men.

Smoking is connected to a generally less-than-healthy lifestyle, and treatment programs that are moderately successful seek to balance the lifestyle of smokers with health-promoting behaviors such as exercise, meditation, and relaxation procedures. Some people use smoking for weight control, but losing weight in this manner does more to destroy than promote general health.

Cocaine in powder form or as "crack" cocaine is addictive; it is dangerous to mental and physical health, and can occasionally be lethal. Cocaine treatment programs are in their infancy, but successful regimens will probably contain elements from treatment used to treat other addictions.

Anabolic steroids are drugs that promote muscle size, strength, and quickness. They are a problem both in American sports at the top and with everyday gym users. Properly conducted research is needed to show what long-term effects the chronic use of anabolic steroids may have on body and mind.

Food for Thought

1. What do you think are the reasons why some people drink more than others? Are there ways to deal with them? What advice would you give your friends if they asked you how to deal with someone who drank too much?

2. When do you think the best time would be to start educating someone about the dangers of smoking? What would you tell them? What influences determine whether someone starts to smoke? Do you think smoking is a gateway drug to other drugs? How would you go about proving it?

3. Can you think of some of the reasons why the use of inhalants is more popular than alcohol among preteens? What would you tell your younger brother or sister about the effects of inhalants if you caught them "huffing"?

4. Imagine that you had a chance to participate in the Olympics. Would you use steroids to enhance your performance? What are some of the reasons for the use of steroids in competition? What are some of the reasons that would prevent you from using them?

GLOSSARY

alpha waves: slow 8–12 per second brain wave patterns signaling relaxed wakefulness.

amotivational syndrome: reduction in desire to carry on the activities of daily living stemming from chronic marijuana use.

anorectic: loss of 80 percent of normal body weight from lack of eating and other forms of caloric reduction, and excessive exercise.

aversion therapy: use of stimuli eliciting unpleasant responses and pairing these stimuli with stimuli normally eliciting pleasant responses.

controlled drinking: not drinking to excess in situations where excessive drinking had taken place.

Dianabol: a synthetic steroid used by athletes.

dizygotic: from different eggs. Twins that are dizygotic have 50 percent of their genetic material in common, as do nontwin brothers and sisters.

dopamine receptors: receptors on neural cell bodies that respond exclusively to the neurotransmitter, dopamine.

dysphoria: unpleasant feelings that may come from withdrawal from an addictive substance.

gamma alcoholics: alcoholics who increase alcohol abuse over the years.

hypersatiation: an aversive technique in which an individual smokes an excessive number of cigarettes to change the pleasant experiences of smoking to unpleasant ones.

monozygotic: from the same egg. Twins that are monozygotic have 100 percent of their genetic material in common.

naloxone: a drug that opposes the effects of opiates in the central nervous system.

neurogenetic theory of compulsive disease: a biomedical theory stating that alcoholics have a genetic deficiency in a subset of dopamine receptors; this deficiency produces a craving for drugs which stimulate these receptors and enhance positive feelings.

opioid peptides: short-chain amino acids that function as opiates in the central nervous system.

opponent processes: balancing forces in the central nervous system that pull hedonic experiences in opposite directions.

probands: the index case or case of record.

psychoactive: drugs that induce changes in consciousness.

set point: a point set by genetics or early experiences which the body will actively defend to maintain.

PART III

Stress

CHAPTER 5

Stress Theory

In this chapter we will consider the following subjects:

- Purposes of stress
- General Adaptation Syndrome
- Criticisms of the General Adaptation Syndrome
- Effects of adrenal gland glucocorticoids
- Effects of gonadosteroids produced by the gonads and adrenals
- Behavioral and physiological effects of the Type A personality (Type A behavioral pattern)
- Short-term and long-term effects of post-traumatic stress disorder

Jim had a great job, considering his eighth-grade education. He worked as a clammer on a clam boat, and he would go out on the ocean in almost any kind of weather. One day in October when the seas were particularly rough, he was working alone on the back of the boat. The piece of equipment that controls the clam rakes swung in the bad weather and knocked him off the back of the boat. Since he was working alone in the back, against regulations, a period of time went by before he was missed from the ship. When he was finally missed, he had been in the cold water for about a half hour. The boat then retraced its route by a zigzag method that is regulation for "man overboard." He was finally spotted as a "small speck in the water," difficult to sort out from all the other specks in the water. By then he had been in the water for about an hour. He was very lucky to be rescued and alive. Following that event, Jim developed a number of symptoms, including flashbacks of the episode, difficulty remembering recent events, diminished concentration, jumpiness, and mood swings. He stated that during his ordeal he had little doubt that he was going to die, but he kept treading water while his body and mind became numb. He reported that even fear left him while he was in the water.

Jim experienced an extreme and unusual stressful experience, which produced a psychological residual that often takes months or years to go away. The formal name of the disorder is *post-traumatic stress disorder*.

A SHORT HISTORY OF STRESS

Stress has been with us since the beginning of human existence. In order to survive, individuals had to fight each other, withstand the elements, and obtain food through struggle. Those who were successful in handling stress lived; those who were not successful died off. Charles Darwin (1859) understood that stressful experiences affect different individuals in different ways. Some live and pass on their genetic potential to their offspring, whereas others become genetic failures. In the latter part of the nineteenth century, Claude Bernard (1957, english translation) argued that life is dependent on well-coordinated physiological regulatory mechanisms. He laid some of the groundwork for later researchers in the early part of this century. Another pioneer in this area, Walter B. Cannon, was a highly respected physiologist who became interested in how we balance our physiological systems in the manner which he called *homeostasis* (1939). When an individual becomes stressed, systems in homeostasis (e.g., blood pressure, heart rate, hormonal systems) become unbalanced. The individual prepares for "fight or flight." At this time, the individual can either fight back or flee from danger. Another survival response that frightened organisms can make is freezing, or staying very still (e.g., playing oppossum). In Michael Crichton's book *Jurassic Park* some of the humans used this freezing response to avoid being seen by *Tyrannosaurus rex* (even though the coexistence of the two species is an impossible event in natural history). These survival responses involve activation of the sympathetic portion (SNS) of the *autonomic nervous system* and SNS stimulation of the interior of the adrenal gland called the medulla. The medulla secretes the hormones epinephrine (adrenalin) and norepinephrine (noradrenalin) (see Figure 5.1).

Following Cannon's development of the concepts of fight or flight and homeostasis, Hans Selye (1946), the father of modern stress theory, initiated a series of experiments in which he developed stress as a modern research topic. Selye (1973) considered stress to be a general response to any demand. He believed that even though stress-producing stimuli (he called them *stressors*) can be varied and diverse, they produce somewhat the same biological stress responses by the organism. He drew this con-

Figure 5.1
The Major Endocrine Glands, with the Heart and Kidneys as Reference Points

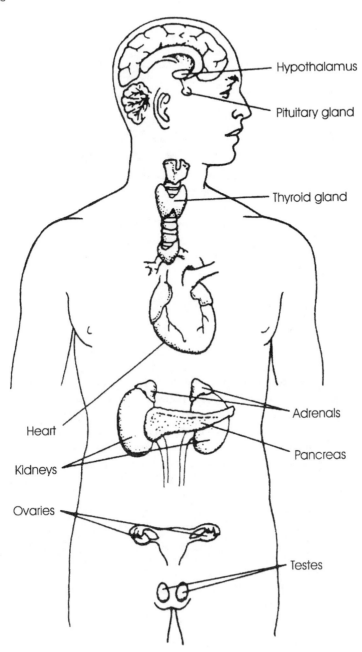

- Hypothalamus
- Pituitary gland
- Thyroid gland
- Adrenals
- Pancreas
- Heart
- Kidneys
- Ovaries
- Testes

Source: Smith, J. C. (1993). *Understanding stress and coping*. New York: Macmillan, p. 40. Copyright © 1993. Reprinted by permission of Prentice-Hall, Inc., Upper Saddle River, NJ.

clusion based on experiments in which he subjected rats to severe aversive stimuli such as bitter cold, extreme heat, fractures, wounds, and toxins. Stress seems to be taken from terms used in mechanics and in physics, although Selye (English was not his native language) presumably meant *strain*, which is a force's effect on the object, rather than stress, which is the force applied to the object. The internal state of stress produces a syndrome that consists of all of the nonspecifically induced changes within the biological systems of the organism (Selye, 1936).

CONTROVERSY ABOUT THE STRESS CONCEPT

According to Weiner (1992), the stress-producing factors that Selye used were severely damaging to the organism (e.g., wounds, cold, toxins). The research rats were prevented from making any of the appropriate behavioral responses that they would make to cope with the stressors in their natural environment. Therefore, it is difficult to tell what the animals' natural coping strategies were. Selye believed that the corticosteroids mediated the anatomical damage that he observed based on his findings of enlargement of adrenal cortical tissue. Weiner (1992, pp. 23–27) discussed Mason's (1971) hypothesis that no organism would survive if its behavioral and physiological responses were not attuned to the type of environmental and physical challenges that it experienced. That is, different types of physiological responses, rather than the nonspecific responses described by Selye, may be more in tune with survival of the organism. Weiner does not accept the idea that stress should be considered as a circumscribed, nonspecific response to an independent stressor from the environment (or from internal sources) in some sort of antecedent-consequent linear fashion. Rather, he believes that we should consider processes that co-vary in a parallel fashion in rhythmically organized systems that are intimately related to each other through communication signals. That is, many different types of biological systems which are connected vary in an organism and may run in parallel, but they may not in fact be directly connected cause-and-effect relationships. Weiner argues for a nonlinear non-cause-effect description of stress. Stress is a complex pattern of physiological changes. Because of the nature of the research enterprise which concentrates on a few isolated variables, research may mislead us into believing that relatively simple responses occur to stressors. For example, in his early research Selye indicated that a small number (triad) of nonspecific changes occur as a result of any stressor, be it disease, predation, pain, or any other. That triad was: (1) atrophy of the thymus gland and lymphatic structures, (2) hypertrophy of the adrenal glands, and (3) gastrointestinal lesions.

According to Weiner, modern research has shown stress responses to

Figure 5.2
The Stages of the General Adaptation Syndrome

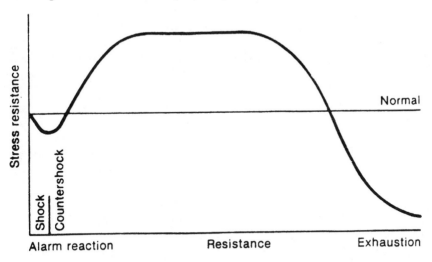

Source: Smith, J. C. (1993). *Understanding stress and coping*. New York: Macmillan, p. 44. Copyright © 1993. Reprinted by permission of Prentice-Hall, Inc., Upper Saddle River, NJ.

be much more complex, sometimes specific to the type of stressor, and sometimes modulated and nondamaging to the organism.

GENERAL ADAPTATION SYNDROME

In 1951, Hans Selye postulated the *General Adaptation Syndrome (GAS)*, which has been a popular concept in stress theory and research for many years. The GAS is used to describe a three-part series of neural and endocrine gland changes that take place when an individual organism is under chronic stress (see Figure 5.2). Stage one is called the Alarm Reaction. A stressor causes an initial activation of the body's defense mechanisms. A large number of different types of stressors—such as heat, cold, wounds, and poisons—can produce this response. The alarm reaction produces an initial shock phase during which body temperature and blood pressure drop, muscles slacken, and other physiological changes take place. This phase is immediately followed by a second phase in which the hormones of the *adrenal medulla*, norepinephrine and epinephrine, are released, followed closely by *adrenocorticotrophic hormone (ACTH)* released from the pituitary gland, and then the release of the adrenal cortical (outside rind) hormones, mainly the glucocorticoid, *cortisol*, into the bloodstream. Cortisol has anti-inflammatory and other physiological effects on the biological systems of the body. This alarm reaction is part of the SNS response known in Cannon's terms as the *fight-or-flight* response.

Stage Two is the Stage of Resistance. There is a dramatic decrease in the physiological responses that occurred during the Alarm Stage, and the organism appears to be adapting rather successfully, although the stressor continues. Cortisol is elevated in the bloodstream and the body appears to be functioning fairly normally. The adrenal glands enlarge and then shrink back to normal as the stressor continues. If the stressor continues, or there is an increase in other stressors which would not normally bother the organism when not under stress, the organism proceeds to Stage Three, the Stage of Exhaustion. Here, high circulating levels of cortisol from the adrenal cortex produce changes in the digestive system and in the immune system. The thymus gland starts regressing, there is atrophy of the adrenal gland, and ulceration and other pathological changes occur in the gastrointestinal tract. Since most of the body's biological resources are depleted, the body can no longer resist, and the organism is likely to die.

According to Asterita (1985), during the GAS, the septal-hippocampal areas in the limbic system contribute emotional coloring to the stress response and transmit signals to the hypothalamus. There, the hormone-releasing factors (hormones) of the anterior hypothalamus influence the anterior pituitary gland to secrete trophic (stimulating) hormones, which induce various target organs to secrete their hormones. The target organ hormones then prolong and continue to heighten arousal until the organism is exhausted or the threat goes away, concluding the GAS (see Box 5.1 to assess your own stress level).

Problems with the General Adaptation Syndrome

According to Weiner (1992), stressful experience is not just a stress stimulus and its relationship with the stress response. This relationship is only one aspect of the experience. According to Weiner, the totality of the experience should be described and not just its linear cause-effect properties. Emotions and the physiological changes associated with stressful experiences are not of necessity causally related to each other. They may or may not occur independently of each other. However, Weiner indicates that more of the stressful experience should be described rather than just the stress stimulus leading in a linear fashion to circumscribed behavioral or physiological changes. Following stressful experiences, people do not simply collapse or fall ill but often return to homeostasis. Weiner suggests that the stressful experience is stored in the nervous system of the individual and a neural reorganization in some way occurs.

Human beings usually respond to most stressful experiences in an

Box 5.1
Assess Yourself: Student Stress Questionnaire

Following are events that occur in the life of a college student. Place a check in the left-hand column for each of those events that has happened to you during the last twelve months.

Life Event	Point Values
___ Death of a close family member	100
___ Jail term	80
___ Final year or first year in college	63
___ Pregnancy (to you or caused by you)	60
___ Severe personal illness or injury	53
___ Marriage	50
___ Any interpersonal problems	45
___ Financial difficulties	40
___ Death of a close friend	40
___ Arguments with your roommate (more than every other day)	40
___ Major disagreements with your family	40
___ Major change in personal habits	30
___ Change in living environment	30
___ Beginning or ending a job	30
___ Problems with your boss or professor	25
___ Outstanding personal achievement	25
___ Failure in some course	25
___ Final exams	20
___ Increased or decreased dating	20
___ Change in working conditions	20
___ Change in your major	20
___ Change in your sleeping habits	18
___ Several-day vacation	15
___ Change in eating habits	15
___ Family reunion	15
___ Change in recreational activities	15
___ Major illness or injury	15
___ Minor violations of the law	11
	Score ___

Add up the point values of the items you checked. If your score is under 150 points, your stress level is low; if your score is between 150 and 300, your stress level is moderate to borderline high; and if your score is over 300, your stress level is high.

Source: Girdano, D. A., Everly, G. S., & Dusek, D. E. (1990). *Controlling stress and tension* (3rd ed.). Englewood Cliffs, NJ: Prentice-Hall, pp. 66–67. Copyright © 1990 by Allyn and Bacon. Reprinted by permision.

integrated and specific way that is appropriate for the individual. Only the most overwhelming and traumatic experiences cause nonspecific physiological responses. In addition, in the past stress theories neglected interpersonal relationships and their importance to the health and longevity of humans (House, Landis, & Umberson, 1988). This oversight is easy to understand since most of the early stress research was done on nonhuman animals, particularly rats. Biologically based theories describing more permanent response characteristics may seem appropriate when dealing with rats in controlled experimental conditions, but they may be much less appropriate in the everyday lives of humans. When observing humans going about their daily lives, it is easier to appreciate stress as an ever-evolving and changing process in response to the environment and to danger (Appley & Trumbull, 1967; Lazarus, 1971).

According to Weiner, stressful experiences consist of selective pressures that come from the physical and social environment such as Darwin described in his formulation of natural selection. Organisms meet these selection pressures through integrated behavioral and physiological responses that are appropriate to the task. If the responses are not effective, however, then the organism and its ability to contribute to the gene pool dies out. Organisms are exposed to natural disasters, human-made disasters, and personal experiences that are traumatic. Where humans are concerned, much depends on cognitive appraisal of the event. Some individuals may see it as a challenge, whereas others may view it as a horrible, traumatic experience. If the individual has a sense of control over the traumatic event, then the event is more likely to be mastered. If not, there can be deterioration towards hopelessness, depression, and even suicide (Seligman, 1975). See Box 5.2 to assess your own sense of control.

A large amount of individual variability can be found in responses to stressful experiences. They are determined by (1) appraisal of external signals and correlated internal ones, (2) genetic factors, (3) coping skills, (4) social support, (5) particular meaning of the stressful event to the individuals, (6) individual personality characteristics, and (7) the age of the individual (Weiner, 1992).

According to Weiner, the study of disease has been obscured by measuring only single variables in stress rather than patterns of change. An individual starts to feel ill when the normal rhythms of some biological subsystem change (e.g., cardiac arrhythmias produced by stressful experiences). If this rhythmic disturbance is already present, stressful experiences may increase the problem leading to full-blown cardiac failure. In addition, the stressful experience may interact with a structural change that has already occurred such as cardiac muscle damage in the organism. These complex interactions are still not clearly understood. New conceptualizations of stress theory such as Weiner's indicate that the

Box 5.2
Assess Yourself: What Is Your Sense of Control?

Place the letter of your response in the space to the left of each question.

____ 1. How often do you find yourself feeling helpless or hopeless?
(a) almost never   (b) seldom   (c) often   (d) almost always

____ 2. How often do you find yourself in a situation that seems out of your control?
(a) almost never   (b) seldom   (c) often   (d) almost always

____ 3. How often do you find yourself needing to have your life well planned and organized?
(a) almost never   (b) seldom   (c) often   (d) almost always

____ 4. How often do you find yourself feeling sad or depressed?
(a) almost never   (b) seldom   (c) often   (d) almost always

____ 5. How often do you find yourself fearful of losing control over your life?
(a) almost never   (b) seldom   (c) often   (d) almost always

____ 6. How often do you find yourself feeling insecure?
(a) almost never   (b) seldom   (c) often   (d) almost always

____ 7. How often do you find yourself needing to control the people around you?
(a) almost never   (b) seldom   (c) often   (d) almost always

____ 8. How often do you find yourself needing to control your environment?
(a) almost never   (b) seldom   (c) often   (d) almost always

____ 9. How often do you feel the need to have your daily activities highly structured?
(a) almost never   (b) seldom   (c) often   (d) almost always

____ 10. How often do you feel secure?
(a) almost never   (b) seldom   (c) often   (d) almost always

____   Total score

Scoring: Items 1 to 9

(a) = 1 point; (b) = 2 points; (c) = 3 points; (d) = 4 points

Item 10

(a) = 4 points; (b) = 3 points; (c) = 2 points; (d) = 1 point

Total scores in excess of 24 may indicate a sense of lack of control.

Source: Girdano, D. A., Everly, G. S., & Dusek, D. E. (1990). *Controlling stress and tension* (3rd ed.). Englewood Cliffs, NJ: Prentice-Hall, pp. 124–125. Copyright © 1990 by Allyn and Bacon. Reprinted by permission.

effects of stressful experiences on the body do not produce linear cause-effect physiological and behavioral changes. Interacting natural rhythms of the body such as sleep, appetite, secretions of hormones, neural transmitters, and various physiological systems of the body are upset by stressful experiences in complex ways that lead to perceptions of feeling ill and to clinical disease.

Starting with Hans Selye, much of the work in stress research has involved animals other than humans (mainly rats) for a variety of reasons: they are cheap, their genetic histories and personal histories can be rigorously controlled, and manipulations can be done on other animals that cannot, for obvious reasons, be done on people. The down side of animal research is the difficulty of generalizing the results obtained from one species to another . . . us.

CONTEMPORARY STUDIES ON STRESS

Animal Studies

More recent animal studies using rats have shown that even very early stressful experiences can have significant effects on the later behavior of animals. Intrauterine stressful experiences produced by shining lights into pregnant rats' eyes while they were restrained altered the later mating behavior of male rats born to these stressed mothers by biasing them toward female styles of mating (Ward, 1972). Later work indicated that the prenatal stress suppressed *androgens* in the male rat fetuses (Ward & Weisz, 1980). Neonatal separation of rhesus monkeys from their mothers produces disastrous long-term effects attributable to separation stress (Harlow & Zimmermann, 1959); these separated animals seemed incapable of effective social behavior while growing up and in adulthood. The animal's mother plays a critical role in regulating the behavior and physiology of her offspring so that the offspring develop the means to predict, control, and avoid potential sources of stress effectively. Early stressful experiences while dependent on the mother seem to lead to disruption of intricate physiological and behavioral systems necessary for normal adaptation to the environment.

The most dire consequences to an organism occur when stress is unavoidable and unpredictable and the organism can do nothing to control it (Seligman, 1975). Animals often show analgesic responses to uncontrollable painful events. They appear outwardly to be in less pain than is appropriate to the situation, and they do not show the normal avoidance responses that they would in more controllable situations. Much of the research that Seligman and his colleagues have done on other animals has been replicated with human subjects (e.g., Seligman, 1975).

Animals show various disease processes when their social hierarchies are disrupted and stressful interactions increase. For example, dominant Cynomolgus monkeys develop coronary artery atherosclerosis regardless of what they eat if their social hierarchies, normally very stable, are continuously disrupted (Clarkson, Kaplan, Adams, & Manuck, 1987; Manuck, Kaplan, & Clarkson, 1983). Social disruption causes subordinate females of another species of monkeys not to ovulate (Weiner, 1992). Many responses to stressful experiences are complex, depending on the species of the organism, its particular genetics, and its personal history.

The adrenal gland's cortical responses to stressful experiences were the central focus of Hans Selye's work. He found that all stressful experiences produced adrenal cortical hypertrophy (enlargement) with its consequent enhanced secretion of adrenal cortical steroids (*corticoids*); thus, corticoids apeared to be central to all stressful reactions. (Selye, 1936). The enhanced adrenal corticoid production, chiefly corticosterone (it is called cortisol in humans), was the result of his animals being severely traumatized and having no control over what was happening to them. On the other hand, when female rats are exposed to predictable events, ACTH and corticosterone levels decrease once the animals bring the predictable events under control (Grey, Bergfors, Levin, & Levine, 1978). Control is the ability of an organism to make an active or passive avoidant response (for which it may be rewarded) during or after a challenging, threatening, or painful experience (Weiner, 1992). Animals can even be trained to control their corticoid secretion by reducing it (Levine & Coe, 1989). Thus, control of the environment is a critical factor in determining whether corticoid secretion is appropriate and adaptive or excessive and catastrophic for the animal, as it was in Selye's research.

GLUCOCORTICOIDS

The metabolic effects of the adrenal corticoids (glucocorticoids and mineralocorticoids) are extensive and patterned but are not indiscriminate and toxic in noncatastrophic stress. They have specific effects on each tissue. For example, they have specific dual actions on the liver: inhibiting protein synthesis and promoting the breakdown of protein to glucose for energy, and enhancing urea formation and elimination (a waste product of protein breakdown).

In general, the glucocorticoids have metabolic and anti-inflammatory effects, and help regulate the immune system in acute stressful experiences. Glucocorticoid receptors are present in the pyramidal cells of the hippocampus, which suggests that there is a neural response to these steroids. This section of the brain has been implicated for many years as an essential site for transferring short-term memories into long-term ones. Short-term stress may activate a response in the glucocorticoid neural receptors in the hippocampus, which may promote learning changes.

However, Sapolsky (1992) describes research with rats indicating that excess secretion of glucocorticoids from chronic stressful experiences produces a neural destruction in the hippocampus. However, some animals seem to be less reactive to these stressful experiences than others. For example, animals that seek out novel experiences and are socially extroverted seem to secrete fewer glucocorticoids than animals that are less adventuresome and presumably are more reactive to changing environments. These more reactive animals are prone to more hippocampal damage than their less reactive counterparts.

Whether these results are true with humans remains to be seen. If they are, then chronic stress could lead to some of the memory losses and other pathological changes that occur in our brains as we age. These changes are not part of the "normal" process of aging, but occur because of special enduring stressful conditions.

GONADOSTEROIDS

Another group of steroids affected by stress are the *gonadosteroids*, which are necessary for sexual reproduction. Sexual reproduction produces genetic variation in animals, and ovulation and mating usually occur under conditions that will ensure survival of the offspring. Successful reproduction depends on minimum stress stimuli from the physical and social environments. Stressful stimuli seem to reduce the effectiveness of the gonadosteroids for reproduction. Reproduction in nonhuman animals is more strongly dependent on gonadosteroid influences than is the case with humans. Humans seem to be less dependent on these hormonal influences and more dependent on learning for mating and reproduction, but all animals, including humans, are affected reproductively by stressful stimuli.

Gonadosteroids are normally produced by the testes, ovaries, and to a lesser extent, the adrenal glands. The major gonadosteroidal hormone produced by the testes is *testosterone* (T), and the major hormones produced by the ovaries are *estrogen* and *progesterone*. The gonadosteroids are controlled by the hypothalamus and the pituitary gland in a negative feedback loop called the hypothalamic-pituitary-gonadal axis (HPG). In any case, chronic and severe stressful stimuli depress male T levels in both nonhumans and humans (e.g., see Asterita, 1985). Apparently, estrogen and progesterone (which are produced by the ovaries), and prolactin (which is produced by the anterior pituitary and controls lactation) levels are also changed by chronic and severe stress in females. Stress interferes with the menstrual cycle, sometimes producing amenorrhea. However, the stress-hormonal interrelationships are complicated and still unclear (e.g., Asterita, 1985).

The pituitary gland secretes gonadotropins called luteinizing hormone

(LH) and follicle-stimulating hormone (FSH), which control the gona-dosteroids in a negative feedback loop. In many animals, LH and FSH levels are affected by environmental temperature, sunlight, and the presence or absence of conspecifics of the same or opposite sex, all of which are potentially stressful stimuli. Even in higher vertebrates, testosterone (T) levels are raised in male animals in the presence of females and decreased in subordinate males in the presence of dominant males. Male fighting, especially when fighting for females, raises T levels in the victor, who either is or becomes the dominant male and lowers T levels in the vanquished (see Weiner, 1992, pp. 175–176). Therefore, the HPG axis is intimately affected by environmental and social events. In brief, an organism's behavioral and physiological responses to most natural stressful experiences, unless they are catastrophic, seem to be specific rather than general, patterned, and appropriate to the situation.

PEPTIDES

Peptides are also implicated in stressful experiences. Peptides are made up of amino acid chains and are a form of protein. They were discovered only over the past 20 years, and more are being discovered daily. According to Weiner (1992), as many as 1,500 peptides may operate in the nervous system. Some of these peptides seem to change from stressful experiences. Sorting out their effects on the physiological and behavioral changes that occur from stressful experiences will be an enormous task indeed. To complicate matters even further, each neuron may contain several peptides that have different short-term and long-term effects on the body. Given that there are billions of neurons in the human nervous system, one may sense the formidable work that lies ahead.

PROBLEMS OF MEASUREMENT

Conceptualizing stressful experiences as nonlinear parallel interacting changes in the normal rhythms of the body in response to external and internal signals requires new ways of measurement and new concepts. For example, these changes could be represented in terms of amount of hormonal modification, strength of hormonal responses, and frequency of changes in parallel with waxing and waning stressful stimuli, and not just in less exacting measurements of altered levels of biological substances. These measurements would require sophisticated correlational statistics and astute observations. You may see where all this is heading; someday mathematical models may be able to describe and predict the effects of stress on the body.

To make matters more difficult, altered rhythmic functions in the body may or may not show anatomical changes (e.g., sleep disorders, psychosis, major affective disorders). As a result of eating, sleeping, exercising, mating, working, and meeting threats and challenges, rhythmic activities interact with each other. They can be altered by stressful stimuli, and some are more capable of being altered than others. In some cases, these rhythms can become chaotic and characterize a diseased biological subsystem. For example, extra beats of the heart (fibrillation) could lead to total asynchrony of the heartbeat and a subsequent heart attack.

CORONARY HEART DISEASE AND STRESS

One area that has generated a lot of research is the interaction between coronary heart disease (CHD) and psychosocial stressors. It is well documented that high blood pressure, high serum cholesterol, and cigarette smoking are all related to coronary heart disease and they are each affected by behavior. One hypothesis is that a link exists between CHD and prolonged hyperreactivity of the *sympathetic nervous system* (SNS) which invariably accompanies the stress response. Sympathetic nervous system hyperreactivity may be related to endothelial damage in the arteries and veins of the body accompanied by atherosclerotic (fatty) plaque buildup. Animal studies (Manuck, Muldoon, Kaplan, Adams, & Polefron, 1989) have indicated that cardiovascular hyperreactivity is related to damage in the arteries and veins and to the severity of coronary artery disease. In addition to cardiovascular hyperreactivity affecting the progression of atherosclerosis, neuroendocrine responses to behavioral stressors have also been linked to this process. Activation of epinephrine and norepinephrine initiates an increase in lipid mobilization (Havel & Goldstein, 1959). This increase in lipid mobilization could contribute to the acceleration of atherosclerosis because of increases in serum cholesterol, especially the low-density fraction. Corticoids have been positively associated with the development of atherosclerosis, elevated serum cholesterol, and increased proportions of dead and injured endothelial cells that line the inside diameters of blood vessels (Suarez & Williams, 1992). Thus, excessive neuroendocrine and cardiovascular responses to stressful stimulation can lead to cardiovascular disease (Suarez & Williams, 1992).

One behavioral attribute that has been implicated in the development of coronary heart disease is the multidimensional Type A behavioral pattern (TABP). The link between the Type A pattern and coronary heart disease was first discovered in the Western Collaborative Group Study (Rosenman et al., 1975). In this study, data showed that Type A persons were at twice the risk for CHD as compared to their opposite counterparts, Type B persons. The TABP is a collection of behavioral, emotional, and cognitive styles that distinguish it from the Type B behavior pattern (Friedman & Rosenman, 1974). The TABP describes an individual struggling to do more and more in less and less time. The Type A person is impatient, irritable, and aggressive toward others. The Type B behavioral pattern is the opposite of the TABP. That is, Type B individuals are nonhostile, calm, relaxed, and show little time urgency. These individuals are less likely to have CHD (Friedman & Rosenman, 1974). See Box 5.3 to assess yourself for Type A behavior pattern.

Recently TABP's failure to predict coronary heart disease has led researchers to look at particular components of the pattern which may cause coronary heart disease problems. The Multiple Risk Factor Intervention Trial (MRFIT) prospective clinical research project (Dembroski, MacDougall, Costa, & Grandits, 1989) showed that a clinical rating of hostility was positively and significantly related to the incidence of CHD. The hostility dimension seems to be the factor in the TABP which produces the link to heart disease. Suarez, Williams, and their colleagues suggest that exaggerated physiological reactivity to behavioral stressors is the biological mechanism that could explain the increased risk of coronary heart disease which is associated with hostility. They suggest that social or interpersonal stressors are critical factors in these hostility and hyperreactivity differences.

Suarez and Williams report research showing that as a Type A male ages, the stress-induced SNS hyperreactivity noted in young Type A males manifests itself as a chronic elevation of plasma catecholamines such as norepinephrine (NE) and epinephrine (E). This chronic elevation of circulating epinephrine and norepinephrine in hostile Type As could be the result of decreases in the number of adrenergic receptors, called down-regulation, from prolonged and repeated exposure to high levels of circulating catecholamines. Accompanying high levels of catecholamines are elevated levels of lipids such as cholesterol with increased age in all individuals. Ordinarily in younger individuals, high levels of cholesterol seem to increase the number of a particular type of adrenergic receptor for the catecholamines (beta adrenergic receptor). However, Suarez and Williams hypothesize that by middle age, hostile Type As may exhibit the heightened circulating levels of catecholamines with down-regulation of their adrenergic receptors from chronic exposure to the catecholamines, which is characteristic of older (65 and above) individuals. Type B middle-aged men with elevated lipid levels do not typically show the elevated catecholamine levels that Type As do. According to Suarez and Williams, there is a complex relationship between elevated cholesterol, increases in circulating catecholamines, and the TABP of hostility with the underlying hyperreactivity of the sympathetic nervous system, age, and coronary heart disease.

In addition to the pathogenic effects of hyperreactivity from interpersonal psychosocial stressors and elevated blood cholesterol levels in TABP individuals, Suarez and Williams suggest that hostile Type A persons may also suffer from a deficient parasympathetic nervous system

Box 5.3
Assess Yourself: What Is Your Pace of Life?

Indicate how often each of the following applies to you in daily life. After you have checked the appropriate column, total your score using the number that appears above each column.

	3 Always or Usually	2 Some- times	1 Seldom or Never
1. Do you find yourself rushing your speech?	—	—	—
2. Do you hurry other people's speech by interrupting them with "umha, umhm" or by completing their sentences for them?	—	—	—
3. Do you hate to wait in line?	—	—	—
4. Do you seem to be short of time to get everything done?	—	—	—
5. Do you detest wasting time?	—	—	—
6. Do you eat fast?	—	—	—
7. Do you drive over the speed limit?	—	—	—
8. Do you try to do more than one thing at a time?	—	—	—
9. Do you become impatient if others do something too slowly?	—	—	—
10. Do you seem to have little time to relax and enjoy the time of day?	—	—	—
11. Do you find yourself overcommitted?	—	—	—
12. Do you jiggle your knees or tap your fingers?	—	—	—
13. Do you think about other things during conversations?	—	—	—
14. Do you walk fast?	—	—	—
15. Do you hate dawdling after a meal?	—	—	—
16. Do you become irritable if kept waiting?	—	—	—
17. Do you detest losing in sports and games?	—	—	—
18. Do you find yourself with clenched fists or tight neck and jaw muscles?	—	—	—
19. Does your concentration sometimes wander while you think about what's coming up later?	—	—	—
20. Are you a competitive person?	—	—	—

A score of 20–34 may mean low Type a behavior, 35–44 medium Type A behavior, and 45–60 high Type A behavior.

Source: Stress management for wellness, second edition by Walt Schafer. New York: Holt, Rinehart and Winston. Copyright © 1992 by Holt, Rinehart and Winston, reprinted by permission of the publisher.

antagonism of the SNS activation of the heart arising from the tenth cranial nerve (vagus nerve). Normally, the vagus nerve has a dampening effect on SNS activation of the cardiac muscle. Type As may have weaker vagus nerve protection from SNS activation of the heart than do non-Type As. Weaker vagus nerve protection of the heart against the effects of SNS stimulation could produce another way in which hostility leads to increased CHD.

POST-TRAUMATIC STRESS DISORDER (PTSD)

A psychological disorder produced by extreme stressors, *post-traumatic stress disorder*, has attracted a lot of research attention recently. The syndrome has been around for many years, known by other names such as combat fatique during World War I, but it has received a lot of notice recently because of the stressful reactions of many Vietnam War veterans. Post-traumatic stress disorder occurs in some individuals after exposure to extreme stressors. DSM-IV classifies it as an anxiety disorder, and it is sometimes related to pathological medical changes such as hypertension and heart disease. Community-based studies have placed the lifetime prevalence of this disorder at 1 to 14 percent, varying with methodology and the population sampled. Studies of at-risk individuals have placed prevalence rates between 3 and 58 percent (American Psychiatric Association, 1994).

Post-traumatic stress disorder is an unusually maladaptive response characterized by intrusive thoughts, flashbacks of the event, excessive startle responses, difficulties in recalling the event, and other maladaptive responses indicating the individual is experiencing great stress and anxiety. If you will recall, the experience that Jim went through falling off the clam boat at the beginning of this chapter had the hallmarks of PTSD. This stress response activates all of the physiological mechanisms that overwhelming stress stimuli typically do. For example, a major stress response mechanism consists of a triad of anatomical structures called the *hypothalamic-pituitary-adrenal axis (HPA)*, which control and produce all of the essential stress hormones.

The HPA response to stress has been studied extensively ever since Selye's initial characterization of this response in his General Adaptation Syndrome. The HPA response has been the most researched biological system in stress research, and it is involved in PTSD. Apparently, HPA activation by stress produces glucocorticoids from the adrenals. The brain releases corticotrophin-releasing hormones (CRH) from the hypothalamus, which stimulates the release of adrenal corticotrophin hormone (ACTH) from the pituitary and cortisol in humans from the adrenals. Cortisol and other glucocorticoids initiate the suppression of immune system functions and other metabolic and neural defense reactions. Suppression of immune system functions prevents inflammatory processes from limiting mobility in dealing with acute crises. Glucocorticoids feed back to the hypothalamus and other brain structures, and to the pituitary via hypothalamic influences to regulate the subsequent release of CRH and ACTH. Long-term discharge of cortisol and other glucocorticoids can become toxic to various parts of the brain, in particular the hippocampus, and cause neuronal death, medical diseases, and impaired emotional responses and cognitive activity (see Sapolsky, 1992). Yehuda, Giller, and Mason (1993) found that there were differences in combat veterans with PTSD as compared with other psychiatric disorders. They suggested that reduced cortisol levels were observed in chronic PTSD, which might be associated with an increase in the number of glucocorticoid receptors (GR) in neurons or lymphocytes. They found that a strong positive correlation between GR number and PTSD symptoms in combat veterans. According to these researchers, the increased number of GRs allows quicker recovery from stress and individual PTSD by providing more ports of entry for the diminished amount of glucocorticoids. Individuals with PTSD do show periods of cortisol hypersecretion when they are subjected to an acute stressful experience. However, cortisol response seems to decrease as the individual continues to suffer from the symptoms of PTSD. It is not clear why the increase in the GRs is not associated with a dissipation of PTSD symptoms if this increase is a biologically adaptive one. Clearly, further research must be done in this area.

Although much research is still needed to sort out the complexities of how stressful experiences affect our physiology and behavior, progress has also been made on managing stressful experiences so that we can lead more comfortable and productive lives. We turn to this discussion in the next chapter.

SUMMARY

Stress has always been with us, but earlier in our evolutionary history it likely was short-lived. Individuals either fought back, ran away, or remained very still until the danger passed. Those who were better at using these survival mechanisms were more likely to live and to pass on their genetic material to the next generation. Hans Selye found that all organisms under severe stress go through a triad of physiological changes called the General Adaptation Syndrome. At present there is disagreement about whether these changes are truly what happens in most cases of stress, especially when the organism copes successfully. There is also disagreement regarding whether stress ought to be considered a linear cause-effect relationship (stressor-stress-behavioral and physiological responses to stress). The stressful response may be complex, with patterned rather than all-or-nothing physiological responses, and unique to the type of stressor.

The General Adaptation Syndrome that Selye posited from his research on rats consisted of three stages: Alarm, Reaction, Resistance, and Exhaustion. As chronic stress induces initiation of each of these three stages, the organism proceeds inexorably toward pathological atrophy of the adrenal glands, regression of the thymus gland, and ulceration and other pathological changes in the gastrointestinal tract. Ill-health, disease, and death may follow. These concepts were developed by exposing rats to extreme environmental and physiological stressors, and may not effectively describe ongoing chronic stress experiences in humans. In humans, cognitive appraisal of events determine whether events are traumatic or challenging. If the individual has control over the event, it is less likely to become a stressful experience than if no control is perceived to be possible. Individual variability in response to stressful experience is determined by a multiplicity of internal and external factors.

The secretion of glucocorticoids from the cortex of the adrenal glands in response to stressful experiences produces metabolic changes that permit more effective response to the stressful event and have immunosuppressive effects by suppressing the immune system to prevent restriction of mobility. In the long run, however, there is some evidence that glucocorticoids are toxic to neural tissue.

The gonadosteroids produced by the ovaries, testes, and adrenal glands are controlled by a negative feedback loop called the hypothalamic-pituitary-gonadal (HPG) axis. This axis is controlled by environmental and social events. The HPG axis responds to stressful events, unless overwhelming, in a specific, patterned, and appropriate way.

Various disease processes and stress mutually interact. For example, a link may exist between CHD and prolonged hyperactivity of the SNS which accompanies the stress reaction. Hyperreactivity of the SNS seems to be related to atherosclerosis and increases in the low-density fraction of cholesterol. The TABP has been linked to hostility, hyperreactivity of the SNS, and CHD. Thus, there is a complex relationship between elevated cholesterol, hostility, underlying hyperreactivity of the SNS and elevated catecholamines, age, and CHD.

PTSD occurs in some individuals after exposure to extreme stress. The same physiological response occurs in PTSD as in GAS. The GAS activates the HPA, which produces glucocorticoids from the adrenals. Long-term discharge of these glucocorticoids can be toxic to the brain. In addition, there may be increases in the glucocorticoid receptors in the brain to compensate for the reduced cortisol secretion that occurs in individuals who continue to suffer from the effects of chronic stress in PTSD. It is not clear why the symptoms of PTSD do not then dissipate.

Food for Thought

1. Of what value are our stress reactions? Why can they be so toxic today?
2. What is the General Adaptation Syndrome? What are some of the problems associated with it?
3. Describe some of the psychological variables that modify the stress response.
4. What are the functions of the glucocorticoids and the gonadocorticoids? What happens to them during prolonged stress reactions?

GLOSSARY

adrenal medulla: inner layer of the adrenal glands; secretes adrenaline and noradrenaline which are involved in stress reactions.

adrenocorticotrophic hormone (ACTH): A hormone produced by the anterior portion of the pituitary gland, which stimulates the adrenal gland cortex and is involved in the stress response.

androgens: a class of gonadal hormones of which testosterone is the major hormone.

autonomic nervous system: part of the peripheral nervous system that is less under voluntary control and serves internal organs.

corticoids: a class of steroids released from the adrenal cortex.

cortisol: a glucocorticoid that controls inflammation from tissue injury and regulates carbohydrate metabolism.

estrogen: a major gonadal hormone.

fight-or-flight: mechanisms of survival in organisms when threatened.

General Adaptation Syndrome (GAS): Hans Selye's term for the body's generalized reaction against stress consisting of the stages of Alarm, Resistance, and Exhaustion.

gonadosteroids: the hormones secreted by the gonads.

homeostasis: state of balance in physiological systems.

hypothalamic-pituitary-gonadal axis (HPA): the reciprocal control exerted by the hypothalamus, pituitary, and gonadal glands on each other.

post-traumatic stress disorder: acute psychological reaction to intensely traumatic events such as wartime combat, rape, and natural disasters.

progesterone: hormone that prepares the uterus for the implantation of the uterus for a fertilized ovum.

strain: the organism's response to a stressor.

stressors: internal or external stimuli that the organism perceives as a threat.

sympathetic nervous system: network of nerves that innervate the internal organs and prepare the body for fight or flight and other vigorous activity.

testosterone: a prevalent type of androgen.

CHAPTER 6

Coping with Stress

In this chapter, we will consider the following subjects:

- Psychoanalytic theory and its emphasis on early experiences as a way to explain how people cope with stress
- Cognitive and behavioral methods to deal with stress
- Personality attributes such as hardiness, optimism, self-efficacy, and hopefulness which improve responses to stress

Many years ago, Dale Carnegie reported in his book, *How to Stop Worrying and Start Living* (1948 p. 17), that he had learned about a rapid-acting recipe for coping with stress ("handling worry") from Willis H. Carrier, the founder of the Carrier air-conditioning industry. Apparently, Mr. Carrier met with severe disappointment after trying to install a new method to clean gas so that it could be burned without damaging industrial engines. He was so upset by this failure that he developed symptoms that might be diagnosed today as an acute stress disorder. However, he is reported to have figured out a way to handle his problems "without worrying." It consisted of three steps. "1. Ask yourself, What is the worst that can happen? 2. Prepare to accept it if you have to. 3. Then calmly proceed to improve on the worst." Mr. Carrier went on to solve his problem and became successful in business by reportedly never forgetting these rules. According to Dale Carnegie, once we have accepted the worst that can happen to us, which upon close analysis is often not as bad as we think, then we have everything to gain by taking action. These "rules" are now part of what is now known as *cognitive restructuring*. In cognitive restructuring, negative thoughts are turned into more adaptive ones with direct positive effects on behavior. They are important aspects of Aaron Beck's Cognitive Behavioral Therapy and Albert Ellis's Rational Emotive Therapy, both of which are systems designed to cope with stress, anxiety, and depression. Dale Carnegie reported many other ideas in his book that were forerunners to the approaches used in modern cognitive and behavioral stress management.

In this chapter, we discuss several influential theories, including cognitive and behavioral ones, that explain how people cope with stressful experiences in their lives. An early theory that stems from the psychoanalytic tradition proposes that stable traits learned at an early age set the coping style of the individual throughout life. Another influential theory is a process approach that suggests coping strategy is much more dependent on the context in which it is found. Some of the theoretical concepts relating to coping strategies discussed in this chapter, such as *hardiness* and *explanatory style*, show the underlying tension between stable personality styles and more fluid contextual coping strategies. Regardless of underlying mechanisms, effective stress management procedures have been developed.

PSYCHOANALYTIC THEORY

Life has always been full of stressful experiences forcing individuals to cope with them in one form or another. Sigmund Freud's *psychoanalysis* was the earliest systematic attempt to develop an extensive theory on how the human mind copes with this pervasive problem. Anxiety, an unpleasant and stressful emotion that we consciously experience, is generated by ego conflict in three different ways in Freud's system. *Neurotic anxiety* is the result of the struggle between the need for immediate gratification of infantile impulses (the id) and the attempt of the ego as integrator of internal and external demands to modify and control these impulses. *Moral anxiety* is the struggle between internalized absolute values demanding us to do "the right thing" (superego) and the ego's attempts to modify these values to pacify the infantile demands of the id and perceived threats from the external world. *Reality anxiety* is generated by real or perceived threats from the external environment. Individuals develop certain unconscious styles and approaches to deal with the anxieties held over from childhood.

Sigmund Freud and his daughter, Anna Freud, developed various defense mechanisms to describe how we unconsciously deal with these anxieties. These defense mechanisms (Freud, 1965) increased the importance of the ego over other forces such as the id and the unconscious. The various defense mechanisms saved the individual from painful anxieties but at the cost of distorting of reality. For example, Sigmund

Freud's earliest and most important defense mechanism, repression, automatically places unwanted painful experiences in the unconscious where they are not consciously perceived. This, then, reduces the psychological pain of anxiety and stress. According to psychoanalysts, however, the repressed painful experiences have an unconscious effect on ongoing thoughts and behavior monitored by the ego. The operation of these psychodynamic processes is difficult to document experimentally.

Later work modifying the earlier psychoanalytic approach with its concentration on psychopathological defense mechanisms revealed that some defenses tended to be healthier and more adaptive to the individual than others (e.g., Haan, 1969). Individual responses to stressful experiences varied all the way from coping successfully to defending oneself by distortion of reality to severe distortions and breaking with reality and "ego-failure," which formed the basis of psychosis.

PROCESS THEORY

According to Lazarus (1993), a major development in coping research occurred in the late 1970s. At that time, the psychodynamic way of coping with its emphasis on an individual's permanent traits or style of coping with stressful experiences became superseded by coping as a process. In the process approach, individuals interact with environmental and social pressures that vary over time. It is dynamic and fluid rather than constant. The trait approach, which emphasizes more permanent responses to the environment and the acting out of unconscious forces, is downplayed in the process approach.

After many years of research in the area of stress and coping, Lazarus (1993) and his colleagues developed the following set of principles which they believe are representative of process approaches rather than as trait or personality approaches.

1. The effectiveness of coping processes depends on the particular person, the types of situations that person encounters over time, and the types of outcome that are of interest—for example, social functioning, physical health, and positive attitudes. According to Lazarus (1993), there may be no universal good or bad coping processes; rather some may be better more often than others. This stance coincides with Haan's in the psychoanalytic tradition, but it has more contextual flexibility. For example, the defense mechanism of denial may be good at some times (e.g., immediately after a particular traumatic event such as a heart attack or the death of a loved one) and bad at other times such as later on after the traumatic event when the individual must come to terms with the loss or trauma.

2. Coping varies with the particular problems that develop once an illness, such as a heart attack, progresses in time. It is necessary to determine the particular threats of immediate concern to the patient, and not prematurely generalize about the effects of the overall illness on the patient. An advanced cancer

victim may have different concerns, such as the possibility of imminent death, and so will require coping mechanisms different from those needed by individuals who are newly diagnosed and may be dealing with familial and financial concerns.

3. What individuals are thinking and doing while coping with stressful encounters should be measured. A professional observer should be able to make both cross-sectional and longitudinal measurements with the measurement instrument. This approach is necessary to determine the value of trait and process distinctions.

4. Coping efforts are independent of outcome. The term *coping* is used whether the process is adaptive or nonadaptive and whether it is fluid and changing or more permanent. Coping is defined as ongoing cognitive and behavioral efforts to manage specific external or internal demands that are assessed as taxing or exceeding the resources of the person (Lazarus, 1993). Note that there is no mention of adaptiveness or permanence in the definition.

5. Coping conceived of as a process emphasizes two major functions, *problem-focused* and *emotion-focused coping*. Problem-focused coping is to change the interaction between the environment and the person by acting on the environment or oneself in a direct manner. Emotion-focused coping is to change the way the relationship with the environment is attended, such as going from paying close attention (*hypervigilance*) to actively or passively avoiding what is happening. This coping strategy weakens the stress that is being perceived, even though the relationship between the individual and the stressors has not been changed.

   Although our society has a strong bias toward problem-focused coping, sometimes emotion-focused efforts are the best coping strategy. For example, in some chronic pain situations such as back pain or migraine headaches, as well as in terminal cancer cases, distraction and refocusing techniques weaken the perception of the chronic stress.

   According to Lazarus (1993), at least two problems are associated with the research on problem-focused and emotion-focused coping research: there is a need for prospective studies that will examine these coping strategies and how they affect individuals' ongoing adaptation to the environment; and there are some weaknesses in the self-report method on which a lot of coping research is based. That is, confounding variables of context and experience may be operating on the individual of which the individual is unaware. Individuals may be influenced by psychosocial factors operating between the interviewer and the interviewee, and reconstruction of memory of coping strategies may conform to a subject's preferred response style but may be inaccurate.

Lazarus (1993) states that we should also look at how the varieties of emotions that we experience relate to coping with stress. He believes that a description of the individual's emotional states can provide us with a much more multidimensional look at how an individual copes than the somewhat unidimensional concept of stress (e.g., see Lazarus, 1991). These emotions are likely connected to particular forms of coping in the individual. For example, anger would suggest coping strategies such as attack and defense, whereas anxiety would suggest other coping strategies such as compromise and conciliation. According to Lazarus, in the future, research should center on coping as a kind of a goal in which one must consider the specific emotions that the individual is experiencing, what the individual wants to accomplish, and what is allowable in the present situation in order to reach successful resolution of stressful encounters—that is, to cope successfully. This approach would give us a better understanding of how coping strategies are selected and used.

Regardless of which coping strategies are used, some individuals seem to be more consistently successful in coping with stressful experiences than others. They seem to possess a trait of resistance to the effects of stressful experiences which some researchers have labeled hardiness.

STAYING HEALTHY UNDER STRESS: HARDINESS

More than two decades ago, Kobasa and Maddi (1977) developed the concept of hardiness. Hardiness is a trait that refers to an individual's abilities to withstand stress consistently that others cannot. Such hardy individuals seem less likely to develop stress-related diseases and are less likely to break down under stressful conditions (Kobasa, 1979). Kobasa identified three different parts of hardiness: commitment, control, and challenge. Commitment is intense belief and involvement in what one is doing and the belief in the importance and value of one's work. People low on commitment are more likely to feel angry, frustrated, and separated from their work and social lives.

Control is the belief that the world is largely controllable, especially in the important dimensions of one's life. People high in control believe that they can influence events and master significant tasks in their lives most of the time. They think that much of what happens is within one's control and less likely to be the whims of "outrageous fortune." In contrast, those low in control tend to believe that fate and chance rule people's lives.

Challenge is the ability to see each new obstacle as an interesting problem to be overcome rather than as a threat to one's ego. Those who have a high sense of challenge see each task as something to accomplish and to overcome. Those who are low on this dimension tend to see many obstacles as threats and irritants to the ongoing progress of their lives. A prospective study carried out by Kobasa, Maddi, and Courington (1981) collected data on over 250 executives over several years and found that hardy individuals were less likely to become ill. However, Lazarus and Folkman (1984) question whether the personality measures used in the research that supports the trait accurately measures the trait. Smith

(1993) believes the research that supports the hardiness trait is weak, even though the trait is widely cited as a personality attribute that protects against stressful experiences. Underlying the debate on hardiness is the question of whether or not this enduring trait in individuals really exists (Funk & Houston, 1987).

LEARNED HELPLESSNESS AND EXPLANATORY STYLE

When we view events as uncontrollable and believe we can't do anything about them, we usually feel a great deal of stress. On the other hand, when we feel that we have some control over the stress, then we usually feel less stressed. In the late 1960s, Seligman and his colleagues (Overmeier & Seligman, 1967; Seligman & Maier, 1967) began research using dogs in shuttle boxes. Although the research was difficult for the experimental animals, the development of the concept of *learned helplessness* from this research has made a significant impact on the behavioral sciences' ability to explain mental and physical health. Seligman and his colleagues found that when dogs were exposed to severe inescapable shock, they became helpless and nonreactive both in the inescapable shock situation and in situations where the opportunity existed to escape the shock. Some of these animals could eventually learn to escape shock, but they took an incredibly long time to do so. In effect, animals had learned that they were helpless against environmental events. Even when placed in a situation where they could have escaped and avoided painful stimuli, they were helpless to do so without an incredible effort to teach them. There was a "cognitive lag" between what they had learned and their abilities to adjust to the present reality. Other animals that had not been exposed to the inescapable shock had no trouble learning to escape, being able to do so in one or two trials. Whereas they could help themselves out of a painful situation, the helpless animals exhibited apathy, lack of interest in their surroundings, and inability to learn new responses that would allow them to avoid their difficult predicament.

Seligman and his colleagues argued that this may be a model for reactive (situational) depression in humans. Many of the symptoms of reactive depression parallel the symptoms mentioned above for learned helplessness. Later, Abramson, Seligman, and Teasdale (1978) developed modifications of this learned helplessness idea with *attribution theory*. Attributions are what we believe are causes of events in the world. According to attribution theory, an individual understands and explains particular events in his or her environment and life as either internal or external, global or specific, and stable or temporary. How individuals explain events in their lives (their explanatory style) may have an effect on their experience of stress. When bad things happen, optimistic explanations attribute causes for the events to forces that are external to the individual, temporary in nature, and specific to the events. Pessimistic explanations attribute causes for events to forces that are internal, stable, and global (Peterson & Seligman, 1987; Peterson, Seligman, & Vaillant, 1988). The pessimistic individual assumes that stressful events occur because of an internal character flaw, that these flaws are a permanent part of the individual, and that these flaws will show up at every opportunity. These pessimistic explanations promote stress, depression, feelings of ill-health, facilitation of physical diseases, and death (Kamen-Siegel, Rodin, Seligman, & Dwyer, 1991; Peterson, Seligman, & Vaillant, 1988). This more permanent trait of explanatory style seems to be a valid predictor of future health.

SELF-EFFICACY AND HOPE

Albert Bandura (1977) developed the concept of *self-efficacy* as an enduring trait affecting an individual's ability to cope successfully with stressful experiences. He divided the trait into two parts. The first, self-efficacy expectancy, is the individual's intention to cope successfully and to believe that one can do it; the second, outcome expectancy, is the belief that certain behaviors will accomplish the task. Believing one can do it, having the intention to do it, and knowing certain behaviors to accomplish the task lead to high self-efficacy, and not being able to affirm any of these three conditions reduces self-efficacy.

Earlier, we discussed learned helplessness. Seligman and his colleagues found that learned helplessness implies that individuals learn there is no connection between their behaviors and desired outcomes. However, the helpless individual can still hope for a positive outcome. For example, being helpless in bed from a severe heart attack does not preclude hope that medication or surgery can make a person better. Beck, Weissman, Lester, and Trexler (1974) regard hopelessness as having negative expectations about the future. They developed a scale that measures hopelessness, but not necessarily hope. Thus, it has been difficult to define hope operationally so that research can proceed. Jacoby (1993) attempted to put hope into a developmental and existential perspective, but finally lamented that he could not. Nevertheless, research on the concept has begun (Snyder et al., 1991).

Whether the various traits that seem to reduce stress—notably hardiness, optimistic explanatory style, high self-efficacy, and hope—will continue to do so in further research remains to be seen. The seemingly more static nature of these concepts must be considered against the backdrop of the process approach (e.g., Lazarus, 1993), which asks us to consider the changing context in which coping strategies occur as well as the enduring characteristics of the coping individuals.

SOCIAL SUPPORT

Another form of stress reduction is derived not from internal charac-teristics, but from the social environment. We often talk of our social network and the social support that we receive from others. The social network is defined as the number of acquaintances with whom we have contact. Notice that this definition does not consider the quality of the contacts. In contrast, social support considers quality of relationships (Sarason, Sarason, & Pierce, 1990). Social support can take the form of buttressing self-esteem, giving advice, spending time in social activities, and providing services such as the use of a car and other material forms of support (Cohen & Wills, 1985). Just the fact of believing that someone is there to help you, whether or not they actually are, seems to reduce the perception of stress (Singer & Lord, 1984). Smith (1993) cites research showing that decreased social support is associated with increased mor-tality from all causes and increased ill-health and disease.

How does perceived social support reduce stress in the individual? One approach is that social support buffers the individual when stressful experiences occur. The other approach is that social support has direct effects on the individual whether or not stressful experiences occur. Both theories have received research support (Cohen & Wills, 1985).

Smith (1993) points out that the issues surrounding social support are complex. For example, it is hard to determine cause and effect. Do social support systems reduce stress directly, or are events stressful because they lead to loss of social support? Consider the often stressful event of divorce: supportive social relationships may decline because the rela-tionships that were formed during the marriage no longer seem appro-priate after the marriage is over.

Also, men and women seem to make different uses of social support systems (Ratliffe-Crain & Baum, 1990). Women seem to involve them-selves more deeply and extensively in social support networks than do men. Research is still unclear whether their more extensive involvement reduces women's stress (Smith, 1993), or alternatively, causes them to seek more support because of more perceived stress.

Human–Pet Companionship

The literature on the role of pets in reducing stress is new and as complicated as the research on human social support (Siegel, 1993). In Siegel's study, 938 subjects were enrolled through Medicare in a health maintenance organization. Subjects were interviewed by telephone at the outset of the study and then every two months for a year. Siegel assessed degree of responsibility for the pet, time with the pet, affective attach-ment to the pet, and perceived benefit-minus-cost difference. The data showed that dogs as pets reduced office visits to physicians among the elderly. More than other pets, dogs met their owners' needs for companionship and attachment. This area of research has exciting possibilities for reducing stress among individuals who otherwise have lost their social support systems.

STRESS MANAGEMENT

Psychologists and other behaviorally oriented health professionals employ a variety of techniques in order to get individuals to deal with and control stressful experiences in their lives. Some of these techniques change the way the body responds to the stressful experiences, some change the way a person thinks about and interprets these experiences, and some directly change the world's demands on a person. Further elaboration and expansion of stress management techniques can be reviewed in Smith (1993) and other books on coping with stress (e.g., Schafer, 1992).

Biofeedback

A stress management device that psychologists often use is *biofeedback*. Biofeedback is the use of an instrument that basically makes you aware of normal bodily processes of which you are not normally aware. It is based on behavioral principles pioneered in the late 1960s by Neal Miller (1969) which utilize environmental signals to amplify and feed back rates of bodily responses to a person to make them more amenable to control. Just as reinforcement controls rates of various forms of behavior, biofeedback signals can control rates of bodily responses. You might note that a mirror, which gives us a truer picture of ourselves than if we scanned ourselves, is a biofeedback device. So is a weight scale, which gives us a more precise estimate of our weight than our own or others' estimates. Both of these devices can affect rates of behavior related to how we look and what we eat.

Biofeedback instrumentation provides feedback of biological information in an amplified form to an individual. Various types of biofeedback instruments of the following variety are used: electromyographs (EMGs) that measure muscle tension; thermistors that measure body temperature, Galvanic Skin Response (GSR) instruments that measure changes in electrical conductance produced by the sweat glands; and electroencephalograms (EEGs) that measure brain wave patterns, most notably increases in alpha wave patterns associated with increases in relaxation.

Biofeedback seems to help some individuals reduce overall muscular tension and migraine and tension headaches. It is sometimes used to

---

Box 6.1
Simple Breathing Techniques That Can Be Used Quickly to Reduce Stress in the Immediate Situation

Six-Second Quieting Response

1. Draw a long, deep breath.
2. Hold for two or three seconds.
3. Exhale long, slowly, and completely.
4. As you exhale, let your jaw and shoulders drop.
5. Feel relaxation flow into your arms and hands.

This can be done with eyes open or closed, in the presence of others or alone.

Breathing Slowly for Calming Effect

This technique can be done before a speech, performance, interview, or a physical or athletic performance. Deliberately breathe calmly and slowly, thinking of this slow breathing as soothing and calming your entire body. Leaving your breath out longer than normal can increase the calming effect.

Source: Stress management for wellness, second edition by Walt Schafer. New York: Holt, Rinehart and Winston. Copyright © 1992 by Holt, Rinehart and Winston, reprinted by permission of the publisher.

---

train people whose limbs have been incapacitated by trauma or stroke. The biofeedback device provides cues such as lights and sounds, which indicate whether an individual's physiological processes are changing in the desired directions, and promotes better control over processes that are contributing to stress. After sufficient biofeedback training accompanied by other techniques such as visual imagery and role playing, individuals learn to generalize their biofeedback experiences to the real world. However, biofeedback does not seem to have notable benefits over other more cost-effective techniques such as progressive muscle relaxation techniques, autogenic (self-generated) imagery, breathing techniques, and hypnosis. See Box 6.1 for sure-fire methods to reduce stress quickly. (Parenthetically, many of the same techniques used in stress management are also used in coping with chronic pain partly by reducing the stress responses that accompany pain.) One of the earliest breathing techniques was developed by a physician, Dr. Herbert Benson (see Box 6.2) of the Harvard Medical School, who capitalized on the changes that he observed from individuals who practiced Transcendental Meditation (Benson, 1975, p. 114).

Progressive muscle relaxation therapy involves the progressive tensing and relaxing of the various major muscle groups of the body. The procedure was originally developed by E. Jacobson (1929), a physician, and

Box 6.2
The Benson Relaxation Response

1. Sit quietly in a comfortable position.

2. Close your eyes.

3. Deeply relax all your muscles, beginning at your feet and progressing up to your face. Keep them relaxed.

4. Breathe through your nose. Become aware of your breathing. As you breathe out, say the word "one" silently to yourself. For example, breathe in . . . out, "one,"; in . . . out, "one"; etc. Breathe easily and naturally.

5. Continue for 10 to 20 minutes. You may open your eyes to check the time, but do not use the alarm. When you finish, sit quietly for several minutes, at first with your eyes closed and later with your eyes opened. Do not stand up for a few minutes.

6. Do not worry about whether you are successful in achieving a deep level of relaxation. Maintain a passive attitude and permit relaxation to occur at its own pace. When distracting thoughts occur, try to ignore them by not dwelling on them and return to repeating "one." With practice, the response should come with little effort. Practice the technique once or twice daily, but not within two hours after any meal, since the digestive processes seem to interfere with the elicitation of the Relaxation response.

Source: Benson, H. (1975). *The relaxation response.* New York: William Morrow, pp. 114–115.

required extensive practice. The procedure has now been shortened and can be taught in one or two hourly sessions. This muscle relaxation is then generalized to the real world by the individual recalling how she relaxed in the training situation. Since it is impossible to be tense and relaxed at the same time, the client learns to be relaxed where she had heretofore been stressed.

The autogenic technique requires the individual to imagine various parts of the body being relaxed and free of stress. Based on procedures developed by a German neurologist, Dr. H. H. Schultz (Benson, 1975), it is designed to elicit a relaxation response through "passive concentration" rather than intense effort (Benson, 1975, p. 72).

Cognitive-Behavioral Stress Management

Cognitive approaches are used to change the way an individual thinks about a situation and to attempt to reinterpret the situation more in the individual's favor. Cognitive restructuring is a widely used technique for changing stress-inducing thought to promote health (Mahoney, 1977). Cognitive restructuring is a standard technique in the cognitive-behavioral approach to psychotherapy in which individuals under severe stress are taught to reinterpret their stressful experiences. Aaron Beck has developed a highly influential cognitive therapy for depression (Beck, 1976) which emphasizes negative perceptions of oneself, the future, and the environment as sources for stress that leads to depression. Albert Ellis (e.g., 1962), in the same vein, indicates that irrational beliefs, high expectations for oneself, and desire for positive approval from everyone lead to excessive stress and depression which affect behavior. His system, first known as Rational-Emotive Therapy (RET), is now called Rational-Emotive-Behavioral Therapy (REBT).

Ellis proposed a system called the ABCs of stress in his RET system. First, activating events (A) are followed by irrational beliefs regarding these events (B) and the stressful consequences (C) generated by these beliefs. The REBT system involves identifying these irrational beliefs, disputing and changing them, and then generalizing them to the external world in the form of behavioral change. In this way, more realistic approaches to life can be expected, with a reduction in experiencing stress.

Assertiveness Training

One way in which you can change the world's demands on you is through assertiveness training (see Box 6.3).

Being assertive involves stating your feelings about other people without diminishing their self-respect. This is not the same thing as aggressiveness. When people are aggressive, they do not consider others' feelings or try outrightly to damage them. Assertiveness falls in between aggressiveness and passivity. The passive person is often shy, withdrawing, reluctant to assert his or her rights and privileges, and socially inhibited (Girdano, Everly, & Dusek, 1990). According to these authors, passive people have learned that sometimes they can manipulate others through their style of behavior. They passively wish that someone will take care of their needs, or they arrange for subtle and nondirective ways to get what they want. Sometimes they play the martyr and make others feel guilty because they will not engage in activities that others know they enjoy.

Three types of assertive behavior can be distinguished (Christoff & Kelly, 1985): (1) refusing others' unreasonable requests (refusal assertiveness), (2) expressing positive feelings toward others (commendatory assertiveness), and (3) making requests from others (request assertiveness). All three types of assertiveness are not necessarily found together in the same individual.

Various authors (e.g., Girdano, Everly, & Dusek, 1990, p. 190; Jakubowski & Lange, 1978, pp. 80–81) have suggested that one should keep certain rights in mind as one learns to be more assertive. They are:

Box 6.3
Assertiveness Training

An acronym for being more assertive is LADDER.

L = Look at rights
A = Arrange a time
D = Define problems
D = Describe feelings
E = Express requests
R = Reinforce

Look at your rights, such as the right to have your own opinion and the right to protest unfair treatment or criticism. Arrange a time and place to discuss the problem with the other party. Define the problem as specifically as possible. Describe feelings using "I" messages, making sure not to blame others for your feelings, e.g., "I feel hurt," rather than "You hurt me." Express your request in simple, easy-to-understand sentences, remaining specific to the problem and firm. Reinforce your request by stating positive consequences for the other person if they agree and cooperate with you.

Source: Resnick, S. (November 1988). Stress management: A necessary and useful tool. *Carrier Foundation Letter*, No. 138, p. 3. Copyright by The Carrier Foundation. Reprinted by permission.

- Saying no and not feeling guilty
- Changing your mind
- Taking your time in planning your answer or action
- Asking for instructions or directions
- Demanding respect
- Doing less than you possibly can
- Asking for what you want
- Experiencing and expressing your feelings
- Feeling good about yourself, no matter what

These assertiveness rights are not justifications for running roughshod over other people. They are grounds for negotiations and compromises, and a delicate line exists between being aggressive, assertive, or passive. Of course, there are occasions when any one of the three approaches may be most appropriate.

SUMMARY

Human beings have had to cope with stress since time immemorial. The earliest theory developed to explain how the human mind copes with stressful experiences was the psychoanalytic, which was developed by Sigmund Freud and elaborated upon by his daughter, Anna. This approach emphasized a stable way of responding to the world based on early experiences. An alternative approach was developed in the 1970s based on cognitive and behavioral theories that emphasized changing and contextual determinants of coping strategies. Stress as a concept began to be considered as unidimensional and limiting as a way to describe how individuals coped with their environment.

Regardless of the stressful experiences, some individuals do a better job at coping than others. Research suggests that traits such as hardiness, an optimistic explanatory style, high self-efficacy, and hope determine better success at coping. However, much research is still needed in these areas before we can be confident of their validity.

Techniques have been developed to help individuals cope with stressful experiences in their lives. One technique is biofeedback, which generates awareness of physiological responses so that they can be changed to reduce stressful responses. Other techniques that produce much the same effects are progressive muscle relaxation, autogenic imagery, and hypnosis.

Cognitive strategies are used to change how individuals think and feel about the stressful events in their lives. Two of the most influential cognitive strategies are Aaron Beck's cognitive therapy, which has been very effective for depression but has been shown effective for stress reduction as well; and Albert Ellis's RET therapy which has proven effective in reducing the perception of stress by changing illogical beliefs.

Assertiveness training is used to confront directly the social environment in order to get needs met without damaging others' self-esteem. Aggressiveness and passivity are other approaches used to meet needs. Though often destructive to all parties involved in the transactions, these two approaches can be appropriate options in some circumstances.

Food for Thought

1. Discuss the different forms of anxiety postulated by psychoanalytic theory. How do we deal with these anxieties according to the theory? What is the main criticism of postulates in psychoanalytic theory?

2. What are the general differences between trait (e.g., psychoanalytic) theory and process theory? Describe the principles as developed by Lazarus and his colleagues.

3. Describe the personality attribute of hardiness. Are there any problems with it? What might they be?

4. Describe a couple of cognitive-behavioral methods you would train someone in who had trouble with anger and stress in the workplace. Are there any methods you would not use? Why?

GLOSSARY

attribution theory: a theory by which people attempt to explain why they or other people do what they do.

biofeedback: use of instrumentation to enhance bodily responses of which we are not normally aware.

cognitive restructuring: changing thought processes from self-destructive ones to more adaptive ones.

emotion-focused coping: approaches people use to change the way they feel about a stressful situation by passively or actively avoiding or escaping the situation.

explanatory style: how individuals explain events that happen to them.

hardiness: a collection of personality characteristics that certain individuals possess so that they can withstand stress with which others have great difficulty.

hypervigilance: paying excessively close attention to the environment for threats.

learned helplessness: a state of inactivity or passivity that individuals develop when they are exposed to chronic uncontrollable stress.

moral anxiety: anxiety in the Freudian system that stems from the superego and threatens to punish the individual for doing or thinking something that violates an accepted standard of behavior.

neurotic anxiety: a strong desire stemming from unconscious forces to engage in some thought or behavior that is destructive or socially harmful.

problem-focused coping: approaches people use to change the stress they feel by acting on the environment or themselves in a direct manner to reduce the stress.

psychoanalysis: a talking-based psychological therapy based on the principles of Freud's theory of personality which involves unconscious forces that determine behavior such as the id, the ego, and the superego.

reality anxiety: in the Freudian system, threats from the external world.

self-efficacy: beliefs that people have about their abilities to be successful.

PART IV

Chronic Diseases and Behavior

CHAPTER 7

Diabetes

In this chapter we will consider the following subjects:

- What diabetes is
- Different types of diabetes
- Bodily changes that occur from diabetes
- Lifestyle issues relating to diabetes
- How stress interacts with diabetes
- Stress management and diabetes
- Sense of self-efficacy and diabetes management

Kathryn was 28 years old when she was pregnant with her third child. At this time, the physician noticed high blood glucose levels and glucose spilling into the urine. These findings were symptoms of gestational diabetes that continued after the birth of her child. Kathryn was subsequently placed on insulin in order to regulate her blood glucose. During the initial stages of her disease, she experienced severe sweating, heart racing, dizziness, extreme nervousness, and feelings of losing consciousness. Following a period of adjustment of her insulin dosage, Kathryn no longer experienced these feelings of dizziness and changes in consciousness. However, she developed *agoraphobia* in which she had extreme panic reactions when she was out of the house and in public places. Her fear was that her blood glucose would drop and she would faint from abnormally low levels. It required several years of behavioral therapy in order for her to appear in public in a relatively comfortable state. From the time of her diagnosis of diabetes, Kathryn had trouble with weight control and with her desire for high caloric foods and sweets. Adherence to the diabetic regime was extremely difficult with its several daily insulin injections, blood testing for glucose, and adherence to a strict diet and exercise program. Kathryn developed loss of eyesight, heart disease, and circulatory problems because of her difficulty in adhering to the medical regime. Kathryn's particular form of adult onset diabetes, gestational diabetes, was initiated by changes in the body from pregnancy and from a genetic predisposition for diabetes in her family. Because she was unable to control her diabetes with diet and exercise, she was required to take insulin injections daily.

To begin this chapter, take the Diabetes Risk Test (Box 7.1) to see if you are prone to this disease.

ANATOMY AND PHYSIOLOGY

In order to discuss diabetes more thoroughly, an understanding of the anatomy and physiology related to the development of diabetes is necessary. The problems of diabetes originate in an organ located behind the stomach about the length of a human hand called the pancreas. The pancreas is necessary for both digesting food and regulating energy. It is the regulation of energy for the body that is important in the development of diabetes. The pancreas produces hormones that metabolize food. These hormones regulate the use of glucose, a simple sugar, which is used for most of the activities in our bodies. The pancreas regulates energy in a variety of behaviors in which humans engage such as exercise and movement, responding to trauma and stress, and infections.

The pancreas secretes three different types of hormones. *Insulin* is the first hormone that is produced when glucose rises in the blood. Insulin usually rises after eating a meal, and excess glucose that is not used is stimulated by insulin to be stored in muscles and fat cells so that energy can be used later. The liver also stores excess glucose in the form of a carbohydrate called glycogen. The second type of pancreatic hormone is *glucagon*. Glucagon breaks down glycogen stored in the liver so that it can be used as energy when blood glucose supplies are down. The third type of pancreatic hormone is called somatostatin, thought to be important in regulating both insulin and glucagon.

When diabetes develops, this balanced control system does not operate properly. The glucose in the bloodstream increases, and the cells are not able to utilize it. The individual develops *hyperglycemia* (excess glucose in the blood). This can be detected by measuring the glucose in the blood from a blood sample, or if the glucose is elevated enough, it can be detected in the urine as spillover. This sort of situation occurs when there is not enough insulin to permit the cells to utilize the glucose, or there

Box 7.1
Diabetes Risk Test

Could you have diabetes and not know it? Take the test. Know the score.

16 million Americans have diabetes—and millions of them don't even know it! Take this test to see if you are at risk for having diabetes. Diabetes is more common in African Americans, Hispanics/Latinos, and American Indians. If you are a member of one of these ethnic groups, you need to pay special attention to this test.

To find out if you are at risk, write in the points next to each statement that is *true* for you. If a statement is *not true*, put a zero. Add your total score.

1. My weight is equal to or above that listed in the chart.   Yes 5 _____

2. I am under 65 years of age *and* I get little or no exercise
     during a usual day.   Yes 5 _____

3. I am between 45 and 64 years of age.   Yes 5 _____

4. I am 65 years old or older.   Yes 9 _____

5. I am a woman who has had a baby weighing more
     than nine pounds at birth.   Yes 1 _____

6. I have a sister or brother with diabetes.   Yes 1 _____

7. I have a parent with diabetes.   Yes 1 _____

                                                                   TOTAL _____

Scoring 3–9 points: You are probably at low risk for having diabetes now. But don't just forget about it—especially if you are Hispanic, African American, American Indian, Asian American, or Pacific Islander. You may be at higher risk in the future. *New guidelines recommend that everyone age 45 and over should consider being tested for the disease every three years. However, people at high risk should consider being tested at a younger age.*

Scoring 10 or more points: You are at high risk for having diabetes. Only a doctor can determine if you have diabetes. See a doctor soon and find out for sure.

At-Risk Weight Chart

Height (feet/inches without shoes)	Weight (pounds without clothing)
4'10"	129
4'11"	133
5'0"	138

(continued)

Box 7.1 *(continued)*

5'1"	143
5'2"	147
5'3"	152
5'4"	157
5'5"	162
5'6"	167
5'7"	172
5'8"	177
5'9"	182
5'10"	188
5'11"	193
6'0"	199
6'1"	204
6'2"	210
6'3"	216
6'4"	221

If you weigh the same or more than the amount listed for your height, you may be at risk for diabetes. This chart is based on a measure called the Body Mass Index (BMI). The chart shows unhealthy weights for men and women age 35 or older at the listed heights. At-risk weights are lower for individuals under age 35.

Diabetes Facts You Should Know:

—Diabetes is a serious disease that can lead to blindness, heart attacks, strokes, kidney failure and amputations.

—It kills more than 187,000 people each year.

—Some people with diabetes have symptoms. If you have any of the following symptoms, contact your doctor:

• extreme thirst

• frequent urination

• unexplained weight loss

For more information on diabetes, call the American Diabetes Association at 1-800-DIABETES (1-800-342-2383).

Source: American Diabetes Association. (1998). Diabetes risk test. Available on Internet: http://www.diabetes.org/ada/risktest.html

is resistance most likely at the cellular level to the presence of insulin. Both cases produce diabetes.

Some of the symptoms of Diabetes Mellitus are (a) increased thirst, (b) increased urination, (c) weight loss even though the individual is eating more, (d) fatigue, nausea, and vomiting, (e) skin infections, vaginitis, blurred vision, bladder infections, and (f) impotence in men and cessation of menses in women (Larson, 1990, p. 707).

One severe symptom of diabetes is *diabetic ketoacidosis*. This symptom sometimes produces slightly sweet-smelling breath that is caused by acetone, a metabolic byproduct, when the body is forced to burn fatty acids rather than glucose. This process becomes more and more toxic to the body as it continues; the individual may develop diabetic coma and die. Ketoacidosis occurs when individuals are either not getting enough insulin or the insulin is not adequate to allow cells of the body to utilize the glucose.

Another severe symptom of unregulated diabetes is *hypoglycemic coma* (insulin shock). This condition is usually brought about by too much insulin. A hypoglycemic reaction causes trembling, weakness or drowsiness, and headache, dizziness, confusion, double vision, and difficulty in coordination. Eventually, convulsions or unconsciousness can follow (Larson, 1990, pp. 707–708).

The American Diabetes Association (1997) estimates that about 15.7 million Americans have diabetes (see Box 7.2), with most having *Type 2 diabetes* and the others having *Type 1*. About 10.3 million are aware of the disease, and 5.4 million are not. Half of the 16 million have the disease but are unaware of it, and people from minority groups are more likely to go undiagnosed. The disease itself may go undetected for years because the symptoms are sometimes so mild. Diabetes increases in frequency with aging so that about 18.4 percent of all Americans over 65 may have it (American Diabetes Association, 1997). For more information on diabetes, see Box 7.2.

The most severe type of diabetes is Type 1 or Insulin-Dependent Diabetes Mellitus (IDDM). Type 1 diabetes is also known as juvenile, or juvenile onset diabetes. Until the discovery of insulin in 1921, individuals with IDDM would almost inevitably die. Persons who usually develop IDDM are children and young adults. Apparently, for unclear reasons young males are at somewhat greater risk than young females (Larson, 1990, p. 708). Diabetics diagnosed before the age of 19 are classified as having IDDM. Those with IDDM need insulin for treatment because the pancreas usually produces little or no insulin. This type of diabetes develops rapidly, perhaps in a matter of months or even weeks. It is very likely caused by an autoimmune process in which the beta cells that produce insulin in the pancreas are destroyed by the body's own immune system (Palmer & McCulloch, 1991). Genetics seem to be important

---

Box 7.2
Diabetes Facts and Figures

- About 15.7 million people in the United States have diabetes, and 5.4 million do not know it!
- Diabetes is the seventh-leading cause of death by disease in the United States.
- Diabetes is a chronic disease that has no cure.
- Diabetes is the leading cause of blindness in people between the ages of 20 and 74.
- Approximately 27,900 people started treatment for end-stage renal disease because of diabetes.
- The risk of a leg amputation is 15 to 40 times greater for a person with diabetes.
- People with diabetes are two to four times more likely to have heart disease.
- People with diabetes are two to four times more likely to suffer a stroke.
- Health care and related costs for the treatment of diabetes are about $92 billion annually.

Source: American Diabetes Association. (1997). Facts and figures. Available on Internet: http://www.diabetes.org/ada/C20f.html

---

in that two out of every three diabetics are from families that have some history of the disease. However, only 50 percent of identical twins are concordant for the disease, so other factors such as the environment must play a role (Palmer & McCullogh, 1991). The genetics of diabetes is a topic of active research, with more research needed to describe how genetics affects the development and course of the disease. A large multi-center project called the GENNID study was launched in 1995 to attempt to identify genes responsible for Type 2 diabetes. The term GENNID comes from the genetics of noninsulin dependent diabetes (American Diabetes Association, 1995a).

The most common form of diabetes is Type 2 or Non-Insulin-Dependent Diabetes Mellitus (NIDDM), also known as adult onset diabetes. Usually, people who develop NIDDM are over 30 years of age. People with this disease usually do not have an absence of insulin. They may have a less than normal amount, but they are also equally likely to have a normal or even elevated amount of insulin in their blood. Much of their problem is the result of the body's resistance to insulin (Larson, 1990, p. 708). Apparently, the cells have developed a resistance possibly because of the high levels of fat and glucose that routinely circulate in the blood. Nine out of ten individuals with NIDDM are overweight or actually obese (American Diabetes Association, 1995b). Obesity exacerbates the effects of diabetes, and if individuals lose weight, many of the symptoms of diabetes dissipate. Weight-loss programs may reduce or eliminate the need for externally introduced insulin. Oral medication that increases the availability of insulin and reduces insulin resistance is also useful in treating NIDDM.

As we discussed in the opening section of this chapter, pregnant women sometimes develop gestational diabetes. This type of diabetes often takes the form of adult onset diabetes (NIDDM).

Some individuals with uncontrolled diabetes (adult onset is the most common) develop extremes of high and low concentration of sugar in the blood, which is sometimes termed brittle, unstable, or labile diabetes. These individuals may require hospitalization in order to become stabilized. Brittle diabetics may need three and four insulin injections a day and a very closely monitored lifestyle, with diet controls and activity levels carefully controlled.

Diabetes has two types of long-term effects. One type is associated with blood vessel involvement. Damage to the large vessels puts the diabetic at greater risk of stroke, heart attack, and gangrene of the feet. When small blood vessels are damaged, eyes, kidneys, and nerves become damaged. The other long-term effect is nerve damage usually in the feet, but also occasionally in the hands. This nerve damage is called *diabetic neuropathy*. This damage may cause a painful burning sensation with loss of sensation over time, making the body part more subject to injury and infection (Larson, 1990, p. 712). Foot ulcers and gangrene can develop, with further damage in the extremities. In men, diabetic neuropathy may cause erectile impotence.

HYPERTENSION, ATHEROSCLEROSIS, AND CORONARY ARTERY DISEASE

In an individual with high blood pressure (hypertension), the heart pumps blood through the body under abnormally high pressure. This condition may damage blood vessels, tissues, and organs through which blood passes. Atherosclerosis is produced by fatty deposits that thicken the lining of the arteries and eventually close off pathways for the blood. Atherosclerosis in the coronary arteries closes off oxygen and nutrients required by the heart. Hypertension, atherosclerosis, and coronary artery disease caused by atherosclerosis are more likely to occur in diabetics than in other people. Apparently, high levels of blood glucose damage blood vessel walls and promote the collection of solid material in the blood at the sites of injury.

Diabetics are prone to develop vision problems from changes in the small arteries that provide blood to the retina of the eye. One-half of all diabetics experience eye problems after having this disorder for ten years, and these problems are found in almost everyone who has diabetes for 30 or more years (Larson, 1990, p. 711). These small vessels in the back of the eye sometimes produce very small *aneurysms* which burst and cause blind spots. As they progress in their deterioration, more and more blind spots occur. The use of lasers for *diabetic retinopathy* sometimes retards the progression of this disease by improving blood circulation to critical parts of the retina, thereby sparing these areas.

There is also long-term deterioration in the blood vessels serving the kidney. Often no symptoms are apparent until kidney function has decreased to less than 25 percent of what is considered normal. Along with this blood vessel deterioration small amounts of protein escape into the urine. This escape of protein is further indication of renal deterioration. Progressive renal deterioration can lead to end-stage renal disease in which renal dialysis or a kidney transplant is necessary.

Medications are essential in treating people with IDDM and in many cases, people with NIDDM. Other important lifestyle components play a significant role in improving the prognosis of an individual with diabetes such as development of an appropriate diet and weight control plan, and participation of a moderate exercise program. Box 7.3 describes the differences between Type 1 and Type 2 diabetes.

STRESS AND DIABETES

As mentioned earlier in this chapter, Type 2 diabetes in its varied forms can usually be treated with a controlled diet, weight reduction, or oral medications that stimulate additional insulin secretion and reduce insulin resistance. Sometimes insulin therapy is necessary for these patients if other methods do not work. It has been difficult to find causes of Type 2 diabetes. Researchers have looked for defects in the beta cells of the pancreas and for mechanisms that produce insulin resistance in body cells. However, these defects have not as yet been found (Bell, 1991).

Stress and Glucose Metabolism

Surwit and Feinglos (1988) have suggested that the autonomic nervous system is involved in Type 2 diabetes. Epinephrine is produced by stimulation of the adrenal gland medulla by the sympathetic nervous system. Hyperglycemia has been found to occur with injections of epinephrine (Lori, Lori, & Buchwald, 1990), and stressful stimuli produce a prolonged sympathetic nervous system discharge that increases the production of epinephrine (Woods, Smith, & Porte, 1981).

Stress hormones seem to have a hyperglycemic effect at least at higher levels (Surwit & Schneider, 1993). At low levels, epinephrine seems to act as an insulin stimulant that reduces blood glucose levels, but at high

Box 7.3
Type 1 and Type 2 Diabetes

Type 1 diabetes results from the body's failure to produce insulin. Insulin allows glucose to enter cells to provide energy for metabolism and body functions. The failure most often comes from attacks by the body's immune system (T-cells) which destroy the insulin-producing cells (beta cells) of the pancreas. Glucose then builds up in the blood while the cells of the body starve. People with Type 1 diabetes must take daily injections of insulin and closely monitor their blood glucose. The American Diabetes Association estimates that there are about 700,000 people with Type 1 diabetes in the United States. The peak incidence for Type 1 diabetes is about age 10 to 12 in girls and 12 to 14 in boys. Type 1 diabetes tends to run in families, although environment must also be considered. The highest incidence of Type 1 diabetes is in whites with Scandinavian countries leading the world.

Type 2 diabetes results from the body not being able to make enough or to use insulin properly. In many cases it is possible to control diabetes by proper diet and exercise, but occasionally medication is required. Ninety-five percent of all cases of diabetes are of the Type 2 variety. People are most likely to develop Type 2 after age 30. Type 2 increases with age. By ages 65 to 74, about 17 percent of U.S. whites, 25 percent of African Americans, and 33 percent of Hispanics will have Type 2 diabetes.

Warning Signs of Diabetes:

Type 1 Diabetes:

1. Frequent urination
2. Unusual thirst
3. Extreme hunger
4. Unusual weight loss
5. Extreme fatigue
6. Irritability

Type 2 Diabetes:

Any of the above Type 1 symptoms and . . .

1. Frequent infections
2. Blurred vision
3. Cuts and bruises slow to heal
4. Tingling and numbness in hands and feet
5. Recurring skin, gum, or bladder infections

Source: American Diabetes Association. (1997). Facts and figures. Available on Internet: http://www.diabetes.org/ada/C20f.html

levels it seems to inhibit insulin secretion which increases blood glucose levels (Surwit & Schneider, 1993). A variety of other stress hormones, such as norepinephrine, cortisol, and pituitary growth hormone, seem to increase blood glucose as well (Surwit & Schneider, 1993). On the other hand, branches of the vagus nerve from the parasympathetic nervous system innervate the pancreatic beta cells and stimulate increased insulin secretion which acts to decrease blood glucose (Williams & Porte, 1974). Both the sympathetic and the parasympathetic innervation of the pancreas control the regulation of carbohydrate metabolism. In addition, cortisol, increased by chronic stress, causes increased glucose production by the liver and increased cellular resistance to insulin. Both effects promote higher blood glucose levels, which may lead to obesity and a predisposition to diabetes (Bjortorp, 1991).

A variety of studies have examined the relationship between stressful events and fluctuations in blood glucose in both NIDDM and IDDM subjects. For example, subjects have been exposed to stressful interviews (Hinkle & Wolf, 1952), video games (Carter, Gonder-Frederick, Cox, Clarke, & Scott, 1985; Stabler, Lane, Ross, Morris, Litton, & Surwit, 1988), viewing a gory film (Gonder-Frederick, Carter, Cox, & Clarke, 1990), and public speaking (Kemmer et al., 1984). The results of these studies conflict in terms of the direction and amount of blood glucose change. Lack of agreement in the studies could be from different stress stimuli used among the studies, from metabolic and psychological differences in the diabetic subjects used, and from the varying amount of experimental control that each study achieved.

Stress and Type 1 Diabetes

Surwit and Schneider (1993) argue that the weight of evidence from animal and human investigations argues for a role of stress in the course of Type 1 diabetes. However, the research contains many inconsistencies, which seem to be attributable to methodological problems. It is not clear, however, that stress effects can be modified with behavioral interventions. According to Surwit and Schneider (1993), most of the research on stress management interventions in Type 1 diabetes has had methodological problems: some researchers have not employed proper control procedures, and many studies have had small subject pools that prevent meaningful generalizations. The methodologically sound studies that have been done have failed to find significant effects. In addition, there may be a lot of individual differences among subjects. Thus, the role of stress management procedures in the treatment of Type 1 diabetes has not yet been made clear. Studies using larger groups of subjects matched for age of onset, personality characteristics, sex, and type of stress should help clarify this picture.

Stress and Type 2 Diabetes

According to Surwit and Schneider (1993), studies exploring the effects of stress and stress management procedures have been more consistent in finding positive results for Type 2 diabetes than for Type 1 diabetes research. These researchers point to studies showing how stress affects glucose levels in Type 2 diabetics both acutely and chronically. Evidence from both animals and humans (e.g., Lammers, Naliboff, & Straatmeyer, 1984; Rosenbaum, 1983) indicates that individuals with Type 2 diabetes have altered adrenergic sensitivity in the pancreas which may make them susceptible to stressful environmental conditions. If stress can increase blood glucose, then training in relaxation should lower glucose. This seems to be so (e.g., Miley, 1989, on unstable Type 2 patients), but subject pools have been small, with a great deal of subject variability.

Goetsch et al. (1993) investigated psychological stressors on blood glucose in adults with Type 2 diabetes. They attempted to control for methodological problems in earlier studies. Twenty-two adults with poorly controlled NIDDM and nine healthy nondiabetic adults were subjected to personally stressful imagery which subjects generated themselves, and a more standardized stressor which was the threat of the shock. During this time, measurements of blood glucose, cardiovascular, electrodermal, and subjective reports were obtained on a Likert Scale with 1 = completely relaxed and 10 = highly stressed. The diabetic group's blood glucose rose significantly after the threat of shock, but the nondiabetic group's blood glucose remained stable throughout the assessment. The cardiovascular, electrodermal, and subjective data measured on the Likert Scale all showed similar increases in both groups and did not differ statistically. The imagery condition was not standardized, and subjects may have used a variety of different images varying in emotional intensity and duration, which would reduce group differences. However, the hyperglycemic responses in the NIDDM group to the threat of shock showed an average increase of 13 percent with a range from 2 to 38 percent.

Threat of shock in the laboratory situation may be less powerful and briefer than naturally occurring stressors and could underestimate the magnitude of the blood glucose increase in natural situations. There were also several nonresponders in the diabetic group, which highlights the importance of individual differences in responses to disease processes such as diabetes. The authors point out that an understanding of individual differences in blood glucose responses may help to identify those with NIDDM who could benefit from stress management strategies and a corresponding improvement in health status. Further research would also necessitate investigating individuals in their natural social environment where other factors may be playing roles.

Surwit, McCaskill, Ross, and Feinglos (1991) investigated whether relaxation training could improve therapeutic results over an intensive medical therapy program involving 38 patients with Type 2 diabetes. Volunteers were assigned to relaxation training and diabetes education or a diabetes education-alone group. They were admitted to the hospital for metabolic assessment and then given outpatient relaxation training for eight weeks. Assessments were repeated at 24 and 48 weeks. The researchers found that individuals who showed high trait anxiety and neuroticism scores on paper-and-pencil personality tests and who showed large glycemic responses to epinephrine experienced greater improvements in glucose tolerance after relaxation training than patients who did not score high on anxiety and neuroticism.

In a recent study by McGrady, Graham, and Bailey (1996), the researchers looked at the effects of biofeedback-assisted relaxation training on 16 insulin-dependent diabetics (range of ages: 21–60). Nine of the subjects in the experimental (E) group received 30 minutes of biofeedback-assisted relaxation weekly for 12 weeks and biweekly meetings with a nurse to review their blood glucose levels and to receive diabetic supplies. Biofeedback consisted of electromyograph (EMG) readings from the forehead and thermal feedback from the index finger. The control (C) group received biweekly 30-minute meetings with the nurse only. Results showed that the E group reduced their blood glucose levels to normal target levels better than the C group. The study had several problems, however. The groups were small, making results difficult to generalize, the E group had less control over their glucose levels at the start of the experiment than the C group; adherence to diet and exercise regimes was not known; and long-term data on blood glucose control were missing. Regardless of limitations, studies such as this suggest a role for biofeedback and relaxation in controlling diabetic blood glucose levels.

According to Surwit and Schneider (1993), human stress studies and stress management procedures are difficult to do properly, and methodological differences between studies make them difficult to compare. Even though chronic sympathetic nervous system stimulation may play a role in Type 2 diabetes, deterioration of biological systems which develops from chronic hypergylcemia may make stress and neural factors less important in the later than the beginning stages of the disease. More well-controlled studies that evaluate stress-reducing behavioral and pharmacological interventions as adjunct treatments of diabetes are needed before the clinical importance of stress management in treating either Type 1 or Type 2 diabetes can be clarified. In addition, Surwit and Schneider point out that individuals vary in their responses to stress management interventions, just as they do in glycemic responses to stress. Research to date has largely neglected psychological characteristics of individuals who respond to stress management interventions. Paying attention to these characteristics will be important in the future if stress management techniques are to be of maximum effectiveness.

DIABETES MANAGEMENT

Psychological Factors

Diabetes is a good model for the study of chronic disorder management because there are ways to measure blood glucose over varying lengths of time. In the short term, one can measure daily blood glucose levels, glycosylated hemoglobin, which represents average blood glucose levels over six to eight weeks, and fructosamine, which measures blood glucose levels over shorter time periods. Short-term complications of diabetes occur such as diabetic ketoacidosis and hypoglycemic episodes. Diabetic ketoacidosis occurs, as we have seen, from the body's inability to utilize glucose. Thus, the body burns fatty acids which become toxic. Hypoglycemia occurs from too little glucose available often from faulty insulin regulation. The development of hypoglycemia can be an extremely aversive state, and some patients develop a fear of it. Diabetics may maintain elevated blood glucose levels just to reduce this hypoglycemic fear (Cox, Irvine, Gonder-Frederick, Nowacek, & Butterfield, 1987). In the long run, complications such as retinal destruction, kidney disease and failure, foot ulcers, gangrene, and male erectile impotence develop.

Psychological variables are important because the health beliefs, knowledge, and behavior of both people with diabetes and of health care professionals involved in dealing with these people affect how diabetics control their disease. According to Bradley (1994), patients and staff show enormous variation in their beliefs, knowledge, and behavior regarding diabetes. When diabetics tightly control their disease, they reduce long-term complications (DCCT Research Group, 1990; American Diabetes Association, 1995a). Since metabolic control of diabetes is an important determinant of whether or not an individual develops severe long-term complications, there is increased pressure for those involved in diabetic care to improve metabolic outcomes.

Because diabetes is so difficult to control effectively over the long run, it is important to pay attention to diabetic patients' psychological well being, as well as metabolic control. According to Bradley (1994), psychological outcomes that are measured by existing paper-and-pencil personality inventories may be inappropriate with people with diabetes. Personality measures of depression and anxiety include items that may be indicative of depression in the general population, but may reflect the symptoms of poor blood glucose control in diabetics. For example, fatigue, appetite disturbances, weight loss, anxiety, irritability, and loss of sexual interest may be symptoms of abnormal blood glucose levels rather than depression. Bradley (1994) and Bradley and Lewis (1990) have developed measures of psychological adjustment designed for diabetics and include measures to determine well being and energy as well as depression and anxiety. Ideal diabetic management occurs when the diabetic is satisfied with the treatment regime as well as maintaining effective blood glucose control. However, measurement of psychological processes may give us clues to what is going wrong with individuals who are maintaining poor diabetic control. It may also provide ideas on ways to approach patients based on their personality styles to improve control.

Optimizing blood glucose monitoring is one of the most important aspects of diabetic control. According to Gillespie (1991), some people are remarkably accurate in recognizing blood glucose levels. However, some think they can tell but are not very accurate; some have idiosyncratic but reliable physical symptoms and moods associated with high and low blood glucose levels; but most, if not all, can learn to recognize their blood glucose levels. Patients can increase their ability to recognize abnormal blood glucose levels through blood glucose awareness training. Subjects with IDDM have improved estimation accuracy of their blood glucose and have increased their long-term diabetic control as indicated by glycosylated hemoglobin compared to untrained control groups (Cox, Gonder-Frederick, Julian, Carter, & Clarke, 1989; Cox et al., 1991).

Weight

Some researchers (Wing, Epstein, Norwalk, Koeske, & Hagg, 1985) found that combinations of nutrition education, behavior modification techniques, very low calorie diets, and exercise produced dramatic weight losses in some patients with Type 2 diabetes. However, these individuals showed wide variation in weight-loss maintenance at followup. This variation indicates that individual tailoring of treatment regimes is necessary to match patients with their preferred treatments (Bradley, 1994). Nevertheless, most programs have resulted in impressive weight losses, but maintaining the weight loss has been the problem. This problem has affected not only diabetics, but also those treated for weight problems (see Chapter 3).

Psychologists can aid diabetics in other ways, including assisting in tailoring treatment regimens to patients' individual needs and social context, providing coping strategies for families with diabetics, and helping health care professionals improve their communication skills with their diabetic patients (Bradley, 1994). Diabetic adolescents are also prone to eating disorders. According to Bradley (1994), young, mostly female diabetics may binge and then omit insulin injections so that they do not gain weight from their binging. These all pose special challenges for the psychologist.

Adherence to Treatment

Management of chronic illnesses such as diabetes necessitates lifetime behavioral changes. In diabetes, patients are asked to measure their blood glucose, administer insulin, make significant and difficult dietary changes, and engage in a consistent exercise regimen. It is important to identify variables that affect a person's ability to maintain these treatment objectives after they have been educated in what to do. Over the past decade, self-efficacy has received increased attention as a predictor of treatment adherence (O'Leary, 1985). *Self-efficacy* judgments reflect individuals' beliefs about their ability to maintain their behavior changes successfully in the face of changes in situations (Bandura, 1982; O'Leary, 1985). A study by McCaul, Glasgow, and Schefer (1987) found that ratings of self-efficacy predicted general adherence when measured both cross-sectionally and prospectively. Their study did not differentiate between efficacy expectations and adherence to the different individual tasks with which a diabetic must deal. Their study was also restricted to IDDM subjects.

Recently, Kavanaugh, Gooley, and Wilson (1993) examined how effectively perceptions of self-efficacy predicted how both NIDDM and IDDM diabetics handled their separate tasks of glucose testing, diet, and exercise. During two client visits separated by two months, 63 adult outpatients completed information on diabetic history, current treatment, diabetic control, adherence, and self-efficacy about adherence to treatment. The results showed that self-efficacy was a significant predictor of adherence to the separate components of diabetes management over a subsequent eight-week period. The authors found that reports of adherence had a significant positive relationship with concurrent glycosylated hemogoblin even after severity of the disorder was controlled statistically. The authors noted some limitations in the generalizability of the results. Sixty-two percent of the subjects in the study were Type 2 diabetics, possibly resulting in weighting the results in their favor over Type 1 diabetics. The authors could not clearly separate out the relative effects of each type of diabetes on the results. Further research with larger samples of each type of diabetes would clarify the effects of self-efficacy on each type. The authors point out that self-efficacy for adherence and diabetes management regimens should be routinely monitored and used as predictors of the long-term consequences of diabetes. In addition, they suggest that interventions aimed at enhancing a person's self-efficacy may be important to overall management of diabetes.

SUMMARY

Diabetes involves the disregulation of carbohydrate metabolism by the pancreas and cellular processes in the body. In Type 1 diabetes, the pancreas makes little or no insulin; therefore, the body cannot metabolize glucose for its energy needs. It is thought that Type 1 diabetes is caused by an autoimmune process whereby the body's immune system destroys the beta cells of the pancreas that make insulin. In distinction to Type 1 diabetes, Type 2 diabetics have functioning beta cells that may be making too little insulin, appropriate amounts, or an excess. The problem can be that the cells which absorb glucose have developed a resistance to the effects of insulin owing in part to lifestyle factors such as a high-fat diet and a sedentary lifestyle. Both short-term and long-term complications develop from the disease. Deterioration of the circulatory and neural systems is likely. Treatment consists of medications and changes in lifestyle, including diet, weight control, and regular, moderate exercise. Because of the complex treatment required to combat the disease, adherence to treatment regimes is not high.

Stressors seem to affect the course of diabetes. Stress hormones such as epinephrine and cortisol have been linked to hyperglycemia with its concomitant long-term complications for the diabetic patient. Recent research suggests that stress management strategies may help diabetics control their hyperglycemia, but more research is needed to fine tune methodological problems and to identify the personality variables that respond favorably to stress management techniques.

Food for Thought

1. What is Diabetes Mellitus? What biological processes contribute to its effects? Describe the different types.
2. What are the factors within our control and the factors that are not within our control in the origin and progression of diabetes?
3. Why is adherence difficult in managing diabetes? How would you go about improving adherence?
4. Describe the effects of stress on diabetes. What psychological techniques might be useful in managing the disease? What factors might make them effective?

GLOSSARY

agoraphobia: fear of open spaces, often preventing individuals from leaving home.

aneurysm: swelling and weakening of a blood vessel wall, making it more susceptible to rupture.

diabetic ketoacidosis: a symptom produced by acetone produced by the metabolism of fatty acids rather than glucose.

diabetic neuropathy: diabetes-induced deterioration of the neurons in the peripheral areas of the body with consequent tingling, pain, and numbness.

diabetic retinopathy: diabetic-induced deterioration of the blood vessels supplying the optic retina.

glucagon: a pancreatic hormone that retrieves stored energy for use by the body.

hyperglycemia: excess glucose in the blood.

hypoglycemic coma: loss of consciousness from drastic reduction in the amount of glucose in the blood often brought on by too much available insulin.

insulin: a pancreatic hormone that provides energy to cells and stores excess energy as fat.

self-efficacy: individuals' perceptions of whether certain situations can be handled and whether they can do it.

Type 1 diabetes: diabetes that often begins early in life (childhood or adolescence) and originates from the failure of the pancreas to produce insulin.

Type 2 diabetes: diabetes that often begins later in life (40s or 50s) and is more likely brought on by a sedentary lifestyle, lack of exercise, a high-fat diet, and excess body fat.

CHAPTER 8

Coronary Heart Disease

In this chapter we will consider the following subjects:

- Anatomy and physiology of the heart
- Development of heart disease
- Psychological and biological risk factors
- Psychological and biological treatments
- Prevention of heart disease
- Personality styles and heart disease

John was a 48-year-old man who had been in good health until recently. He had not paid much attention to his diet and had eaten red meat at least once a day for most of his adult life. He had been smoking about a pack and a half of cigarettes a day since he was 18. He had not been getting any consistent exercise since high school. He had little control over his job as a bookkeeper at a plumbing and hardware supply store, but he liked his boss. Occasionally he would have to work long hours to get the books up to date during audits. He had many friends and a close-knit family. One day in the dead of winter, there was a heavy snow, and John had to shovel the snow from the front of the garage to get his car out. While shoveling, he got extremely short of breath, and came into the house and momentarily lost consciousness. His wife immediately summoned emergency rescue. They rushed him to the local hospital where he was diagnosed with an acute myocardial infarction (heart attack). It took John several weeks to be convinced that he had had a heart attack. From that time on, however, he stopped cigarette smoking and started a walking program consisting of two miles a day four times a week. His change in habits probably contributed to his good health for another 20 years.

As we will see in this chapter, many psychosocial and behavioral factors contribute to heart disease along with inherited propensities for the disease. In this chapter we will consider the anatomy and physiology of the heart, followed by a consideration of what can go wrong with this muscle. We will consider coronary artery disease, how it develops, the physiological and psychosocial risk factors associated with it, and medical and psychological treatments used in prevention of, and rehabilitation from, a cardiac event.

ANATOMY AND PHYSIOLOGY

The heart is a hollow cone-shaped muscular pump located in the chest and resting on the diaphragm. It is necessary to circulate blood for oxygen and nutrients and to eliminate waste substances. According to Hole (1993), the heart is about 14 centimeters long and 9 centimeters wide (5½ by 3½ inches) in an average adult. It is encased in a fibrous bag called the pericardium. The wall of the heart is composed of three layers, an outer epicardium, a middle myocardium, and an inner endocardium. The middle layer or myocardium is relatively thick and consists largely of cardiac muscle tissue, which pushes blood from the heart chamber. Internally, the heart is divided into four hollow chambers. The two upper chambers are called atriums, which receive blood from veins into the heart. The lower chambers, called ventricles, force blood out of the heart into arteries. (Veins carry blood toward the heart, and arteries carry blood away.) Blood low in oxygen and relatively high in carbon dioxide enters the right atrium. As the right artrial wall contracts, the blood passes into the right ventricle. The right ventricular wall contracts, and the blood goes out to the pulmonary arteries. From these vessels the blood enters into the capillary networks in the lungs where oxygen and carbon dioxide are exchanged. The blood, which is now freshly oxygenated and low in carbon dioxide, passes into the left atrium. The left atrial wall contracts, and blood is transferred to the left ventricle. When the left ventricle wall contracts, the blood passes into the large aorta, which branches to supply oxygen and nutrients to the body. (For a discussion on the anatomy of the heart, see Figure 8.1.)

The blood is supplied to the heart myocardium through the right and left coronary arteries. If a branch of a coronary artery becomes restricted or occluded by a thrombus (a blood clot formed at the site) or an embolus (a substance that is carried by the blood from another site and obstructs a blood vessel), the myocardial cells that are supplied by the blood may experience an oxygen deficiency, which is called ischemia. A person may

Figure 8.1
Anatomy of the Heart and the Coronary Arteries

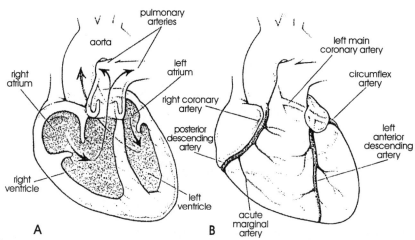

The heart is comprised almost entirely of muscle and contains four hollow chambers—the left atrium, the right atyrium, the left ventricle, and the right ventricle. Each heart beat is a muscular contraction that sends blood through the body's circulatory system (A). The left ventricle pumps oxygenated blood out of the heart via the aorta—the body's largest artery—which branches off into smaller arteries throughout the body. These arteries in turn divide into even smaller blood vessels, called arterioles, and eventually into capillaries, which are microscopic blood vessels that deliver oxygen and nutrients to the cells and pick up carbon dioxide and other waste products.

After the blood, now depleted of oxygen and nutrients, passes through the capillaries, it enters tiny veins called venules and then travels back to the heart through progressively larger veins. When the blood reaches the heart, it enters the right atrium and flows into the right ventricle, which pumps it through the pulmonary arteries into the lungs. In the lungs, carbon dioxide is exchanged for fresh oxygen through respiration. The reoxygenated blood then passes through the pulmonary veins into the left atrium, flows into the left ventricle, and the cycle begins again.

Like other tissues in the body, the heart muscle needs a steady supply of oxygen-rich blood in order to function. However, heart muscle cells do not extract oxygen and nutrients directly from the blood that continually fills the heart's chambers. Instead, the heart receives its blood supply via the coronary arteries, which emerge from the base of the aorta (B). The two primary coronary arteries— the left main coronary artery and the right coronary artery—lie on the surface of the heart and branch off into smaller arteries. The left main artery splits into the left anterior descending and the circumflex arteries, and the right coronary artery divides into the acute marginal and the posterior descending arteries. These branches, in turn, split into even smaller arteries (and eventually capillaries) that extend deep into the heart muscle, providing oxygen and nutrients to all portions of the heart and picking up waste products. The blood then passes through the coronary veins and drains directly into the right atrium. Coronary arteries are susceptible to developing atherosclerotic plaques. If the plaques grow large enough to narrow the space within the artery, the portion of the heart supplied by that artery will suffer from a lack of oxygen (ischemia) that may result in anginal pain. Blood clots can easily form in a narrowed coronary artery and cause a heart attack.

Source: Margolis, S., & Goldschmidt-Clermont, P. J. (1995). *Coronary heart disease*. The Johns Hopkins White Papers. Baltimore, MD: The Johns Hopkins Medical Institutions, p. 5. Text: Reprinted with permission from The Johns Hopkins White Papers, Coronary Heart Disease 1995 © Medletter Associates, 1995. The White Papers are updated and published annually. For further information, please call (800) 829-9170. Illustration: Robert Duckwall, Courtesy of The Johns Hopkins University Department of Art as Applied to Medicine © The Johns Hopkins University, 1995.

Figure 8.2
Electrical Activity in the Heart

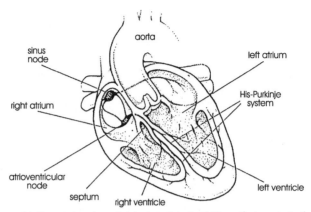

The heart's conduction system is an intricate network of fibers that controls the speed and timing of the heart's contractions. Each heart beat originates in the sinus node—a bundle of cells located in the upper part of the right atrium. The sinus node is known as the heart's natural pacemaker because it sets the rhythm for the heart's contractions by spontaneously generating an electrical impulse about 72 times per minute—the average resting heart rate. (This sinus rate can be adjusted according to your body's needs by messages from the autonomic nervous system; for example, the rate increases with exercise and decreases during sleep.) This electrical impulse travels through both atria, causing the muscle cells to contract. When the impulse reaches the atrioventricular, or AV, node—located in the septum (the wall between the two ventricles)—the current slows down for a moment to permit the atria to push blood into the ventricles an instant before the ventricles contract and pump blood to the lungs and the rest of the body. After this brief pause, the current continues through the ventricles via a specialized network of conduction tissue called the His-Purkinje system. It takes about one-quarter of a second for the electrical current initiated by the sinus node to reach the ventricles and complete each heart beat.

Source: Margolis, S., & Goldschmidt-Clermont, P. J. (1995). *Coronary heart disease*. The Johns Hopkins White Papers. Baltimore, MD: The Johns Hopkins Medical Institutions, p. 13. Text: Reprinted with permission from The Johns Hopkins White Papers, Coronary Heart Disease 1995 © Medletter Associates, 1995. The White Papers are updated and published annually. For further information, please call (800) 829-9170. Illustration: Robert Duckwall, Courtesy of The Johns Hopkins University Department of Art as Applied to Medicine © The Johns Hopkins University, 1995.

then experience a condition known as *angina pectoris*, a painful condition caused by a reduction of blood supply. Sometimes a part of the heart dies because of lack of blood supply. This condition is called a *myocardial infarction*, or a heart attack. A myocardial infarction is one of the leading causes of death in the United States.

In addition to angina pectoris and myocardial infarctions, there are some disorders of the heart called *cardiac arrhythmias*. See Figure 8.2 for a discussion of the electrical activity of the heart. One type of cardiac arrhythmia, tachycardia, is characterized by an abnormally fast heart-beat, usually over 100 beats per minute (Hole, 1993). It may be caused by heart disease, exercise, lack of physical conditioning, or various drugs or hormones. A second type of arrhythmia, bradycardia, means a slow heart rate, usually less than 60 beats per minute (Hole, 1993). It may be caused by decreased body temperature and lack of sleep. It also occurs in well-conditioned endurance athletes. Well-conditioned athletes show bradycardia because their hearts have developed the ability to pump a greater amount of blood with each beat. A third type of arrhythmia, called premature heartbeat, is characterized by a heartbeat that occurs before it is expected in the normal cardiac cycle. This disorder may stem from lack of blood to cardiac tissues or from muscle fibers that are irritated from disease or drugs (Hole, 1993). A fourth type of arrhythmia is called flutter. It occurs when the heart chamber is contracting regularly but at a very rapid rate such as 250 to 350 contractions per minute. This condition is likely to be due to damage to the myocardium (Hole, 1993). The last type of arrhythmia, fibrillation, is characterized by rapid heart actions, but the contractions are uncoordinated. The myocardium fails to contract as a whole, and the walls of the fibrillating chambers are ineffective in pumping blood. Ventricular fibrillation is very likely to cause death; it is the most common cause of sudden cardiac death in a seemingly healthy person (Hole, 1993). Sometimes defibrillation (stopping fibrillation) is accomplished by exposing the heart muscle to a strong electrical current for a short time. This stops the irregular contractions and initiates the normal rhythm of the heart. The normal pacemaker in the heart, which is controlled by innervation from the brain, sometimes malfunctions as well, necessitating that an artificial pacemaker be implanted. This device includes an electrical pulse generator and a lead wire that communicates with a portion of the myocardium. A microprocessor can sense the cardiac rhythm and increase or decrease its rate of contraction as needed. Its functions can be adjusted from the outside by an external programmer (Hole, 1993).

Blood Pressure

Arterial blood pressure rises and falls corresponding to the phases of the cardiac cycle. The ventricles of the heart contract and the walls squeeze the blood inside their chambers, forcing it into the pulmonary arteries and aorta. The maximum pressure during ventricular contractions is called systolic pressure. When the ventricles relax, arterial pressure drops, and the lowest pressure in the arteries before the next ventricular contraction is termed diastolic pressure. The alternate expanding and contracting of arterial walls can be felt as a pulse in any artery that runs close to the surface of the skin. Blood pressure varies with cardiac output. High blood pressure or hypertension is the result of elevated arterial pressure. When the reason for this elevated pressure is unknown, it is called essential hypertension. If it is related to some other problem like arteriosclerosis or kidney disease, then it is called secondary hypertension. Arteriosclerosis is the decreased elasticity of the arterial walls and is often accompanied by a narrowing of the passage-ways (lumens) between these walls from atherosclerosis. This narrowing and decreased elasticity cause an increase in blood pressure (Hole, 1993).

DEVELOPMENT OF DISEASE

About 20 million Americans suffer from *cardiovascular disease*, which affects the blood vessels of the heart, the brain, and extremities (Margolis & Achuff, 1998). *Coronary heart disease* (CHD) and cerebral vascular ac-cidents (CVAs) or strokes account for about half of all deaths in the United States. Cardiovascular disease occurs because of plaque buildup. Plaque is an accumulation of cholesterol in macrophages (lymphocytes that attack invading organisms) caught in injured arterial walls. This accumulation leads to the development of fatty streaks, which eventually clog the arteries if untreated. Partial blockage by plaque can limit the blood flow and thereby the oxygen reaching heart muscles supplied by an artery. If the plaque grows too large and blocks off a coronary artery, then the individual has a myocardial infarction. If it blocks blood going to the brain, it causes a stroke. Many people die of a heart attack before reaching the hospital (nearly 500,000 a year). If reached in time, blocked arteries can often be reopened with drugs, angioplasty (mechanical di-lation), stents (stainless steel mesh devices placed against the blood ves-sel plaque blockage), or bypassed with surgery. The strategic use of aspirin and lifestyle changes in diet and exercise patterns can also reduce the mortality rate from heart attacks.

The depositing of cholesterol in the arteries is now thought to be the first step in *atherosclerosis* (Margolis & Goldschmidt-Clermont, 1994). Cholesterol and the triglycerides are carried by lipoproteins. Triglycer-ides are carried by very low density lipoproteins (VLDLs), and choles-terol is carried by low density lipoproteins (LDLs). LDLs are the major contributors of atherosclerosis. High density lipoproteins (HDLs) protect against atherosclerosis by removing cholesterol from the arterial walls and returning it to the liver to eliminate. According to Margolis and Goldschmidt-Clermont (1994), HDLs may help prevent oxidation of LDLs. It seems that LDLs must be oxidized before they can be deposited on arterial walls.

Risk Factors

Some of the risk factors for heart disease (see Box 8.1) that cannot be changed are age—men over 45 and women over 55 have a higher risk

---

Box 8.1
Cardiovascular Disease: What Are Your Risk Factors?

1. Age	65 years and older
2. Gender	Male
3. Heredity	Close relatives who had heart attack before age 50
4. Race	African American
5. Cigarette Smoking	
6. Hypertension	B/P 140/90 and higher
7. Blood fats	Cholesterol 200 mg/dl +
8. Weight	Excess body fat
9. Diabetes Mellitus	Especially adult onset
10. Lack of exercise	Inactive lifestyle
11. Stress	Type A personality, job stress, life stress

Source: Knight, S., Vail-Smith, K., Jenkins, L., Phillips, J., Evans, L., & Brown, K. (1994). Instructor's manual for Williams, B. K., & Knight, S. M. (1994). *Healthy for life: Wellness and the art of living*. Pacific Grove, CA: Brooks/Cole Publishing Company. Copyright © 1994 Brooks/Cole Publishing Company, Pacific Grove, CA 93950, a division of International Thomson Publishing Inc. By permission of the publisher.

---

of CHD; gender—CHD is more common in men than in women; and heredity—the risk of CHD is higher if a first-degree relative such as a parent or sibling had a heart attack before age 50 in men or 60 in women. CHD is the major cause of death among women after menopause because the low levels of estrogen produced after menopause lead to an increase in LDL cholesterol and a drop in HDL cholesterol.

Some of the risk factors for CHD that can be changed are cigarette smoking, which apparently is the most dangerous risk for CHD; and high blood pressure, which increases chances of stroke, kidney disease, and heart attack. High levels of cholesterol and its major carrier LDLs are atherogenic. There are no definitive studies as yet that indicate triglycerides by themselves are a risk factor in healthy men (Margolis & Goldschmidt-Clermont, 1994). However, a high level of triglycerides may be a risk factor in women, diabetics, and people over 65 (LaRosa, 1997).

Apparently, diabetes carries with it as yet unidentified risk factors for CHD. Often, diabetics have abnormal blood lipids, high blood pressure, and obesity, risk factors that are independent of diabetes.

Weight that is above 20 percent of ideal body weight is considered a risk factor. An abundance of fat within the abdomen which produces an apple-type body shape, as opposed to excessive fat in the hips and thighs producing a pear-like shape, is also related to a higher incidence of CHD.

Lack of physical activity appears to be a major risk factor for CHD. However, most of the studies have been observational in nature and show only a correlation between exercise and reduced heart disease. Other factors involved in the differences between exercisers and sedentary individuals, such as personality variables, and strategies to cope with stress, may produce the differences in CHD. However, a best guess is that sedentary activity is causally related to a higher incidence of CHD.

Finally, an increase in forming clots has been considered a cause of increased risk of heart attack. One factor that lends support to this hypothesis is the fact that aspirin is an anti-platelet (platelets are clotting cells in the blood) medication and is a good agent for reducing heart attacks in patients with CHD.

BIOLOGICAL TREATMENTS

Treatment for a heart attack usually begins when the stricken individual is transported to the hospital by the rescue squad, which is usually capable of providing oxygen, *cardiopulmonary resuscitation* (CPR), and nitrates which dilate the coronary arteries to relieve angina. The heart attack victim is usually transported to the coronary care unit at the hospital and administered oxygen. Morphine is often given to relieve pain and to reduce anxiety in the patient. Heart monitoring is done to determine that the individual had a heart attack and to monitor for cardiac rhythm disturbances. There are a variety of drugs that can open up a closed coronary artery by dissolving the blood clot blocking the flow of blood through the heart. Some of those drugs include Streptokinase, Urokinase, and tissue Plasminogen Activator (Margolis & Goldschmidt-Clermont, 1994). Patients are given aspirin or Coumadin after the initial drug therapy to reduce the possibility of further clot formation.

If the patient remains stable, he or she is discharged in about one week. The individual resumes a full schedule in about two months after leaving the hospital. Ideally, following the heart attack lifestyle factors should be assessed and changed if necessary. Aspirin and specialized drugs such as beta blockers and Angiotension-Converting Enzyme (ACE) inhibitors reduce the possibility of a second heart attack.

Surgery

Sometimes drug therapy is not enough and surgical treatment is necessary. One technique that has been used extensively in recent years is Percutaneous Transluminal Coronary Angioplasty (PTCA). According to Margolis and Goldschmidt-Clermont (1994), PTCA was performed 367,000 times in the United States in 1992. This procedure is much less invasive than the coronary artery bypass surgery that has traditionally been used to correct cardiac problems. PTCA is done by inserting a needle into the femoral artery in the groin and then placing a plastic straw or sheath into the groin artery. A hollow catheter is inserted through the sheath into the femoral artery. The catheter is guided with fluoroscopic visualization to the heart and to the blocked coronary artery. The catheter has a balloon at its tip, and it is forced past the plaque blocking the coronary artery. Using a guide wire, the catheter is placed so that the plaque straddles the uninflated balloon. The balloon is then inflated several times. The procedure widens the channel for blood flow by squeezing the plaque against the wall of the artery. According to Margolis and Goldschmidt-Clermont (1994), about 90 percent of patients notice immediate improvement from PTCA and the artery becomes at least 50 percent open.

Another recently developed procedure is the use of a stent. It is a mechanical wire-meshed device inserted into a coronary artery to keep it propped open. It may be an improvement over PTCA because it may decrease the rate at which the artery closes (restenosis). However, the long-term effects of this procedure are still under investigation (Margolis & Achuff, 1998).

The alternative procedure is coronary artery bypass surgery. In 1994, approximately 318,000 patients were subjected to 501,000 coronary artery bypass graft surgeries (Margolis & Achuff, 1998). In this procedure, a portion of a blood vessel from the patient's leg or chest is used to shunt blood around the occluded segment of the coronary artery. This procedure requires general anesthesia and about seven to ten days of hospitalization. During this time, the heart is stopped and the blood is circulated by a heart/lung machine. According to Margolis and Goldschmidt-Clermont (1994), if necessary, as many as five grafts can be constructed during a single operation. The choice between PTCA and bypass surgery depends on a thorough individual analysis. The best candidates for PTCA are those with blockage in a coronary artery close to where it enters the heart. Bypass surgery is often preferred when there is more than one coronary artery occluded or narrowed, or a PTCA complication such as artery closure may occur. There is also higher mortality in women than men during and immediately after PTCA.

The death rates for PTCA and bypass surgery are each about 2 percent. The short-term risk of bypass surgery is greater than that of PTCA if the patients are low risk and in good health. However, within six months about a third of angioplasty patients show reappearance of angina from narrowing of the previously dilated vessel, thereby necessitating another PTCA or bypass surgery. Bypass surgery usually provides good relief of angina for five years or more. According to Margolis and Goldschmidt-Clermont (1994), bypass surgery does not increase life expectancy any more than medication or PTCA except in certain cases because of the underlying continuing development of atherosclerosis.

Of course, when worse comes to worse, heart transplants can be considered. According to Margolis et al. (1994), about 85 percent of transplant patients are alive after one year and 65 percent survive for at least five years. Many of these patients do develop heart disease, but the disease may be controlled by the same lifestyle changes and medications used to control CHD in nontransplant patients.

TRADITIONAL RISK FACTORS

Some of the traditional risk factors, briefly discussed earlier in the chapter, include high blood cholesterol, high blood pressure, cigarette smoking, obesity, sedentary lifestyle, and Diabetes Mellitus. In addition to traditional risk factors, there are psychosocial factors, including stressful life events, stress on the job, and lack of social support.

Cholesterol

Considering the traditional risk factors first, elevated cholesterol levels and blood pressure seem to be major risk factors for CHD. The risk of CHD rises directly with increasing total blood cholesterol above 180 milligrams per deciliter. The higher the total blood cholesterol, the greater the risk of CHD (Stamler, Wentworth, & Neaton, 1986). The average blood cholesterol of middle-aged men in the United States is approximately 210 to 220 milligrams per deciliter, whereas it is recommended that cholesterol be reduced to below 200 milligrams per deciliter (mg/dl) (The Expert Panel, 1988). The ratio of HDLs to total cholesterol is also a very important factor. If total cholesterol is over 200, it is important to determine how much HDLs are contributing to the elevation. The higher the HDLs (over 35 mg/dl), the better. There is even a cholesterol factor, LP(a), which is not measured in normal cholesterol screenings. Elevations of LP(a), which seem to run in families, are also detrimental (Abel, 1995). According to Blackburn (1987), there is overwhelming evidence that a causal connection exists between cholesterol levels, severity of atherosclerosis, and risk of CHD.

Cholesterol is a waxy substance found in cell walls in humans and other animals. Although it is necessary for the manufacture of hormones and steroids, too much cholesterol in the human body becomes a risk factor for cardiovascular disease (CVD). A variety of experiments involving diet and comparisons of populations with different eating habits have strongly suggested that blood cholesterol levels are affected by the amount of saturated animal fat and associated cholesterol in the diet (Blackburn, 1987; Keys, 1970; Keys, Anderson, & Grande, 1965).

Although evidence is overwhelming regarding the effects of high cholesterol, there is more and more evidence that low cholesterol is also associated with health risks. Muldoon and Manuck (1992) have identified several detrimental conditions associated with low blood cholesterol: higher levels of cancer, higher levels of hemorrhagic stroke, and increases in automobile accidents, violence, and suicides. With regard to cancer, it is difficult to determine which comes first, the chicken or the egg. That is, did the cancer precede the low cholesterol, or did low cholesterol precede the cancer? For example, early subclinical symptoms of cancer may have produced the low levels of cholesterol often found in cancer patients. There is evidence that stroke levels are high in Japan, for example, and as Japanese move to an American-style diet and their cholesterol levels go up, they tend to have fewer strokes. Could fewer strokes result from a reduction in the amount of salt intake as fat intake increases in their diet, or could saturated fat protect against strokes (Gillman, Cupples, Millen, Ellison, & Wolf, 1997)?

Some studies (e.g., Cummings & Psaty, 1994; Hillbrand, Spitz, & Foster, 1995; Morgan, Palinkas, Barrett-Connor, & Wingard, 1993) have suggested that people with behavioral disorders such as violent criminals, those who attempt suicide and commit alcohol-related violence, depressed people, and those with mania often have low blood cholesterol levels. Precisely which factors interact to produce the relationship between behavioral disorders and low cholesterol is not known at this time. For example, could diet play a role? Some studies have shown that when cholesterol levels are lowered, those in the lowered groups have a higher risk for violent death than those who receive placebos. Reduced fat diets may affect neural transmitters in the brain. Monkeys fed a low-fat diet become more aggressive than those on a high-fat diet. There is some indication that serotonin, which is a neural transmitter, may be reduced in low-fat diets and is also lower in criminals. Low serotonin levels may be linked to increases in violence and antisocial behavior. The point is that if your cholesterol level is below 200 milligrams per deciliter (mg/dl), you should not take medications in order to reduce this cholesterol level even further because of possible risk factors associated with lower levels. Further research may clarify optimum levels of blood cholesterol, but levels associated with least risk at this time seem to be between 160 and 200 (mg/dl).

Hypertension

Elevated levels of systolic pressure (which is the upper reading of a blood pressure measurement) or diastolic pressure (which is the lower reading of a blood pressure measurement) increase the risk of CHD. Hypertension (high blood pressure) studies have shown that even slightly elevated readings of systolic and diastolic blood pressures increase the risk of heart attacks and strokes (Blackburn, 1987; Kannel, 1986; Leon, 1987). Apparently, increased blood pressure damages the lining of the coronary arteries by the extra pressure against the arterial walls (Smith & Leon, 1992). Hypertension seems to contribute to the depositing of cholesterol at sites on the artery walls which have been damaged by the high blood pressure. According to Smith and Leon (1992), hypertension increases the heart muscle's need for oxygen by requiring stronger contractions to pump blood against increased resistance in the arteries. Over time this also causes an enlargement of the left ventricle of the heart, further increasing oxygen demands of the heart muscle. According to Smith and Leon (1992), these mechanisms increase the chances of ischemia (reduction in blood supply) and increase the chance of CHD. According to most sources, the cutoff numbers for hypertension are 140 millimeters of mercury systolic over 90 millimeters of mercury diastolic. That is, if you consistently have a blood pressure reading of 140/90 or above you have hypertension. Smith and Leon (1992) indicate that about 60 million Americans have systolic and diastolic blood levels high enough to require treatment. They caution, however, that aggressive pharmacological intervention should only be started after repeated measurements of high blood pressure have been made.

Cigarette Smoking

Cigarette smoking, along with high blood cholesterol and high blood pressure, are the three most important risk factors for CHD. The incidence of heart attacks and sudden cardiac death is directly related to the number of cigarettes routinely smoked. According to Kannel (1986), the extensively cited Framingham Heart Study indicates that if one stops smoking, the risk for CHD declines eventually to the level of individuals who have never smoked. However, the British Regional Heart Study (Cook, Shaper, Pocock, & Kussick, 1986) reported that even after 20 years of not smoking, some increased risk was still evident in men. Smith and Leon (1992) suggested that it is the number of years that a person has been smoking which appears to be the strongest measure of risk for CHD. Therefore, individuals should be caught when they are young, before they develop a long history of smoking to have a significant impact on the risk of CHD.

Leon (1987) reported that smoking can cause an increase in atherosclerosis directly correlated with the number of cigarettes smoked. Nicotine and carbon monoxide from cigarettes smoked promote arterial damage and increase cholesterol absorption into arterial walls. Smoking also reduces HDL cholesterol. Nicotine can increase the work of the heart by raising the heart rate and blood pressure. Platelet aggregation and clot formation are promoted by smoking, which increases the possibility of a coronary thrombosis. Carbon monoxide is increased in smokers. This means that the red blood cells (hemoglobin) do not carry as much oxygen when they are carrying more carbon monoxide. If there is weight gain in smokers, it is more likely to occur in the abdominal region, which also increases risk for CHD. Of course, tobacco smoke also does lung damage.

According to Perkins (1985), an elevation of two or more of the risk factors mentioned above combine in a synergistic rather than an additive fashion. That is, their combination is more than the sum of each of the risk factors combined. According to Smith and Leon (1992), about 25 percent or more of men in their 30s and 40s in this country show simultaneous elevations of any two or all three of the major risk factors. Individuals who smoke and have high blood cholesterol and blood pressure are as much as 16 times more likely to develop CHD. In summary, smoking, high blood pressure, and high cholesterol are the most potent risk factors now identified for CHD.

Other factors include obesity, physical inactivity, and elevated blood glucose (Diabetes Mellitus). A lot of conflicting evidence has been published regarding obesity and CHD. It may be that only certain subgroups of individuals who are obese are at increased risk for CHD. For example, if individuals have the male-type or apple-shaped abdominal obesity rather than the female-type or pear-shaped obesity in the hips, buttocks, and thighs, they are at much higher risk of CHD. It may be that male-type obesity is the only obesity risk factor for CHD (Bjorntorp, 1985; Despres, Moorjani, Lupien, Tremblay, & Modeau, 1990).

Physical Activity

Regular moderate physical activity (aerobic activity three or four times a week for 20 minutes or more) appears to offer some independent protection against CHD, even if the other major CHD risk factors are present. According to the Multiple Risk Factor Intervention Trial, participants who exercised 30 to 70 minutes per day doing light to moderate physical activity continuing over a seven-year period showed one-third fewer fatalities from CHD than those who exercised less than 30 minutes per day (Leon, Connett, Jacobs, & Rauramaa, 1987). According to Leon and Connett (1991), this relationship was still present after an eleven-year followup. Apparently, between 150 and 300 calories a day of physical activity appears to reduce the risk of CHD (Paffenbarger, 1986; Paffenbarger & Hyde, 1984). Regular exercise may also increase the size of the coronary arteries and reduce the severity of atherosclerosis produced by a high-fat diet (Kramsch, Aspen, Abramowitz, & Hood, 1981). Also, collateral coronary arteries may develop, which increases the chance of blood being supplied to the heart (Leon, 1972).

Diabetes

Persons with Type 1 (early onset) and Type 2 (adult onset) diabetes commonly have a more rapid development of atherosclerosis and CHD, stroke, and other cardiovascular diseases. Cardiovascular disease is three times higher among diabetic women, than among nondiabetic women (Smith & Leon, 1992). Approximately two-thirds of all diabetic deaths in Western societies are related to cardiovascular disease (West, 1978).

PSYCHOSOCIAL RISK FACTORS

Two parallel but growing bodies of research are beginning to link psychological and social factors to the development of cardiovascular disease (Smith & Christensen, 1992). Epidemiological studies have identified social support, isolation, and hostility (e.g., Krantz, Contrada, Hill, & Friedler, 1988; Syme, 1987). These studies suggest that psychological and social stressors influence the development of CHD by impacting on cardiovascular and neuroendocrine factors. For example, psychosocial stressors may be associated with prolonged and extreme increases in blood pressure, heart rate, and circulating levels of catecholamines and adrenocortical hormones. These hormones may increase blood pressure and speed up the development of coronary artery disease. However, according to Smith and Christensen (1992), there is need for further research. Research in psychophysiological factors mostly pertains to responses such as increases of blood pressure of single individuals to nonsocial stressful stimuli, including mental arithmetic during cognitive tasks. These psychophysiological responses may not correlate directly with the more complex interpersonal situations that are identified in epidemiological research (Smith & Christensen, 1992).

Social Support

Individuals who are socially isolated are at greater risk for CHD (Bland, Krogh, Winkelstein, & Trevisan, 1991). Changes in residence, occupation, and social class also seem to be associated with increased risk of CHD (Syme, 1987). Individuals who perceive low levels of control over job demands are at risk for increased levels of CHD (Karasek, Theorell, Schwartz, Pieper, & Alfredsson, 1982). Following a cardiac event, negative social interactions predict worse psychological adjustment to the event. For example, in the UCLA-Social Support Inventory (UCLA-SSI), the question assessing this area is, "Sometimes when we most want or need people we care about to be there to help us, they let us down, even if they don't mean to" (Helgeson, 1993, pp. 830–831). An index of negative social interactions was created from questions such as this in the UCLA-SSI, which was given while the patients were in the hospital recovering from the cardiac event (mainly MIs). This index predicted worse psychosocial adjustment to the illness three months later. In this study Helgeson also found that perceived social support had greater impact on psychosocial adjustment than received support and that receiving support does not always mean that the patients psychological needs are being met. Perceptions of social support may reduce the threat of a situation, but receiving too much support, such as in the form of excess information, may be unhelpful and distressing to the patient. The most effective social support seems to match the specific form of social support needed (e.g., emotional, informational, physical aid, and assistance).

Type A Behavior Pattern and Hostility

Another factor involved in CHD is the *Type A Behavior Pattern* (TABP). (See Box 8.2 for an exploration of the characteristics of Type A behavior.) Research in this area abounds with inconsistencies. Hostility seems to have become the best predictor of subsequent CHD (Dembroski, MacDougall, Costa, & Grandits, 1989). Williams, Barefoot, and Shekelle (1985) posit that hostile persons may experience more intense and frequent episodes of anger and thus monitor their environment more intensely. The physiological arousal associated with this anger and vigilance may contribute to the development of CHD. Interestingly, according to Gorkin, who reported these results at the Society of Behavioral Medicine's annual meeting (1994), the *Type B Behavior Pattern* is a better predictor of mortality than TABP among patients showing cardiac symptoms. He observed that these symptoms may serve as a wakeup call to the TABPs to be more vigilant about their health, whereas Type Bs may become more socially isolated and depressed over time because of their less vigilant approach to life.

Cardiovascular reactivity (CVR) may be the mechanism underlying the arousal and anger episodes in hostile individuals. For others, trust and agreeableness have a beneficial effect on CVR and health by reducing conflict and creating social networks that buffer against stress and limit struggles for dominance and control in social situations. Smith and Christensen (1992) state that modifying the social environment and attempting to enhance social competence and reduce thoughts about mistrust of others should reduce excessive CVR and stop the associated unhealthy interpersonal interactions.

REHABILITATION

Coronary heart disease is a lifestyle problem, and the sooner intervention occurs in an individual's life, the better off the individual will be in terms of preventing the development of CHD. However, if the individual does have a myocardial infarction (MI) followed by coronary artery bypass surgery or other invasive procedures, rehabilitation must be planned so that the individual can minimize damage. Increasing physical activity, going on a low-fat and low-cholesterol diet, losing weight,

Box 8.2
What Are Your Usual Reactions?

____ 1. When I stop at a red light while driving, I find it difficult to patiently wait for the light to turn green.

____ 2. When I talk to other people, I find myself finishing their sentences for them.

____ 3. I often find myself trying to do several things at once (like reading while I eat).

____ 4. I have difficulty relaxing.

____ 5. I cannot sit still long enough to watch one program on television.

____ 6. I'm often involved in too many projects at once.

____ 7. I tend to overextend myself.

____ 8. People tell me that I am a fast talker, eater, and walker.

____ 9. I cannot stand waiting in lines.

____ 10. I am very competitive.

____ 11. I am frequently angry and frustrated.

____ 12. When I am driving, I usually race through yellow lights and often speed.

____ 13. In order to enjoy sports or playing games I need to win.

____ 14. I never seem to have enough time.

____ 15. I often eat "on the run."

____ 16. I am not a patient person.

____ 17. I get upset with people who drive, move, talk, or think slowly.

____ 18. People tell me that if I don't slow down, I'm going to get an ulcer or high blood pressure or have a heart attack.

____ 19. I probably have Type A behavior.

The above statements invite you to explore the characteristics of Type A behavior, a behavioral pattern characterized by time urgency, competitiveness, and being hurried and driven by deadlines. This questionnaire is not a diagnostic of that problem but if you answered "yes" to several items, you may want to consider the possibility of Type a behavior as a potential pattern for you that may present health problems, especially if you answered yes to #19 and also have strong, recurrent feelings of hostility and anger.

Source: Knight, S., Vail-Smith, K., Jenkins, L., Phillips, J., Evans, L., & Brown, K. (1994). Instructor's manual for Williams, B. K., & Knight, S. M. (1994). *Healthy for life: Wellness and the art of living*. Pacific Grove, CA: Brooks/Cole Publishing Company. Copyright © 1994 Brooks/Cole Publishing Company, Pacific Grove, CA 93950, a division of International Thomson Publishing Inc. By permission of the publisher.

stopping smoking, and managing stress are important aspects of a rehabilitation program.

Muscle strengthening and regular aerobic exercise are important in reducing the chances of further MIs. According to Smith and Leon (1992), exercise programs have had inconclusive results because of high rates of nonadherence, small numbers reported (thus low statistical power), and treatment programs that do not last long enough to show a benefit. However, a statistical technique called meta-analysis (pooling data from a large number of studies) produced results showing a reduction of 25 percent in subsequent mortality from exercise programs (May, Eberlein, & Furberg, 1982; O'Connor et al., 1989). According to Smith and Leon (1992), exercise has physiological benefits, including reduction of heart rate and blood pressure and the ability to work harder without producing myocardial ischemia. Exercise also has a beneficial effect on the emotional functioning of CHD patients, at least in the short run (Mayou, 1981; Prosser et al., 1981). However, many patients do not adhere to the exercise regimen. Most patients drop out after three months (Carmody, Senner, Malinow, & Matarazzo, 1980). Some of the reasons for dropout include smoking, having a nonprofessional occupational status, a history of leisure pursuits involving low levels of physical activity, depression and anxiety, hypochondriasis, and chest pain (Blumenthal, Williams, Wallace, Williams, & Needels, 1982). Increasing a sense of control, group and family support, and written contracts are social and behavioral methods that may help individuals stick to their exercise regimen (Duppert, Rappaport, & Martin, 1987; Oldridge, 1986).

Diet

Studies involving relatively small numbers of subjects indicate that a low-fat diet (less than 10 percent dietary fat) accompanied by aerobic exercise and stress management may reduce symptoms of ischemia in CHD patients (e.g., Ornish et al., 1983). In a controlled clinical trial, Ornish et al. (1990) indicated that individuals participating in an intensive cholesterol-lowering diet with very low-fat, moderate exercise, and stress management techniques such as meditation show reductions in the severity of angiographically documented coronary artery disease. One of their control groups which followed the American Heart Association's recommendation of 30 percent dietary fat showed a progressive increase in their CHD.

Smoking Cessation

Smoking relapse is as significant a problem for recovering MI patients as it is for others who smoke. Smoking cessation techniques that are described in Chapter 4 are appropriate here for CHD patients. Patients may begin smoking soon after they had their MI and may be aided by friends and family who bring them cigarettes when they come to visit. Specific attention and planning for relapse prevention (Marlatt, 1985) are vital to the smoker who has had an MI because of the significant danger that he or she will resume smoking once the initial crisis has passed.

Reduction of Type A Behavior Pattern

Results of the Recurrent Coronary Prevention Project (Friedman et al., 1984, 1986) show that changes in Type A behavior can reduce cardiac risk in CHD patients. Treatment procedures were instituted to help Type A patients develop alternative responses to their aggressiveness. According to results of this study, the Type A treatment group had about a 50 percent reduction in recurrent MIs. Intervention techniques reduced both Type A behavior and risk of subsequent CHD.

Patel, Marmot, and Terry (1985) found that relaxation therapies helped reduce the risk of MI. Combining stress management and a reduced fat and cholesterol diet improved heart performance, produced less chest pain, and caused less severe CHD as assessed by angiography (Ornish et al., 1983, 1990). The bulk of available evidence strongly suggests that stress management is useful in improving the prognosis of CHD patients (Smith & Leon, 1992).

DEPRESSION AFTER A HEART ATTACK

One of the common occurrences after an MI is depression. Prolonged and severe depression occurs in a significant number of post–MI patients (Carney, Rich, & Tevelde, 1987; Croog & Levine, 1982). However, Smith and Leon (1992) point out that it is not easy to identify a mood disorder because of the side effects of medications and heart damage caused by the heart disease. Self-report questionnaires may be inadequate to separate out the effects of the physical problems, the side effects of medication, and clinical depression.

In a groundbreaking study of depression following myocardial infarction, Frasure-Smith, Lesperance, and Talajic (1993) found that major depression as assessed by the Diagnostic and Statistical Manual of Mental Disorders, Third Edition, Revised (1987) (the standard diagnostic source for mental health professionals now in its fourth edition) was an independent risk factor for mortality at six months for a mixed-gender population of patients, 78 percent of whom were male. The impact of depression was at least as important as a history of previous MI and left ventricular dysfunction. Frasure-Smith reported at the Society of Behavioral Medicine's annual meeting (1994) that the Beck Depression Inventory, which measures levels of depression, was the best predictor of cardiac mortality over eighteen months. The evidence is now convincing that depression leads to increased rates of fatal and nonfatal heart disease. However, the mechanism(s) underlying this connection remain speculative (Glassmon & Shapiro, 1998).

A study by Folks, Blake, Freeman, Sokol, and Baker (1988) showed a negative correlation between sexual adjustment and postoperative depressive symptoms. Decreases in sexual adjustment were related to increases in depression. Patients were assessed preoperatively with the Psychosocial Adjustment to Illness Scale (PAIS) and other depression rating scales. Assessments were made three, six, and twelve months postoperatively as well. In five of the six subscales, items addressing sexual dysfunction were significantly correlated with persistent depressive symptoms. Sexual dysfunction was highly related to depression both pre- and postoperatively. Preoperative sexual adjustment disturbances predicted depression postoperatively at three, six, and twelve months. The authors suggest that clinically predisposed depressed patients are more likely to report sexual adjustment disturbances prior to surgery. Temporary reduced sexual activity after an acute MI is normal. Continued impairment in sexual activity may be associated with marital distress (Smith & Leon, 1992). Behavioral interventions during the acute coronary crisis and treatment of depression during rehabilitation may improve sexual adjustment, quality of life, risk of further coronary episodes, and mortality rates.

Finally, a study by Follick et al. (1988) randomly assigned post–MI patients to a standard care control group or a telephone intervention group. The telephone group was given a hot line number to call if any member of the group felt they were experiencing symptoms of an MI. Each patient was equipped with an instrument to transmit an electrocardiograph signal over the phone, and this transmission was evaluated by medical staff. If the client was experiencing a cardiac episode, the patient was instructed to administer medication and an ambulance was called. The telephone patients experienced a significant reduction in depression and returned to work more rapidly following discharge from the hospital. The results of this study suggest that increasing a patient's sense of control may improve psychological function during the rehabilitation phase.

SUMMARY

The heart is a muscular pump that circulates blood, oxygen, and nutrients, and eliminates waste products from the body. Heart disease accounts for half of all deaths in the United States. It develops with the depositing of cholesterol on blood vessel walls. Various biological and psychosocial risk factors increase the incidence of the disease. Treatments consist of both biological and psychological approaches. Much of prevention and treatment of heart disease consists of changing unhealthy behaviors to healthier ones. Studies are now showing that personality styles that emphasize negative emotional states such as excessive anger, hyperreactivity to stimuli, and depression are predictive of cardiac events and mortality. Research is now looking into psychotherapeutic and pharmacologic approaches to cardiac treatment.

Food for Thought

1. What do the four chambers of the heart do? What is the sequence of circulatory events?
2. How does heart disease develop? Discuss the biological and psychosocial risk factors for the disease.
3. How would you advise someone to prevent heart disease? What behaviors do you consider most important? Least important?
4. Describe personality characteristics that increase the chances of heart disease. Do you think anything can be done to change these characteristics? If so, what? How?

GLOSSARY

angina pectoris: chest pain from depriving the heart muscle of oxygen caused by a restriction or closure of one or more of the coronary arteries of the heart.

atherosclerosis: a buildup of plaque and loss of elasticity of the blood vessels of the body.

cardiac arrhythmias: atypical heart rhythms that could signal heart disease.

cardiopulmonary resuscitation: a method to revive a person after that person's heart or lungs have failed from trauma or disease.

cardiovascular disease: malfunction of the blood vessels of the body from buildup of atherosclerotic plaque.

cardiovascular reactivity: strong and immediate reactions by the heart and blood vessels to perceived environmental stressors and a slower than normal return to cardiovascular baseline.

coronary heart disease: malfunction of the vessels of the heart caused by narrowing or closure of the coronary vessels.

myocardial infarction: heart failure from the blockage of the coronary vessel(s) by a clot or atherosclerotic plaque.

Type A Behavior Pattern: behavior that is motivated by underlying hostility, which produces time-driven behavior and minimal tolerance for others' mistakes.

Type B Behavior Pattern: behavior that is less time-driven and motivated by cooperation and a pleasant personality style.

CHAPTER 9

AIDS

In this chapter we will consider the following subjects:

- Incidence and prevalence of worldwide cases of AIDS
- Biology of the immune system and HIV infection
- Controversy in research on AIDS
- Origin and development of the new field of psychoneuroimmunology
- Behavioral approaches that may bolster the immune system
- Lack of research on women and minorities

By now, virtually everyone has heard about AIDS (Acquired Immunodeficiency Syndrome). One of the general assumptions regarding AIDS is that it has sprung full blown as a new disease and was caused by a new virus that emerged in Europe and in North America during the last half of the 1970s and early 1980s. It is generally accepted that AIDS first came to the attention of the medical community in 1981 when small groups of healthy young men in San Francisco suddenly became infected with a rare malignancy known as Kaposi's sarcoma and a rare form of pneumonia known as Pneumocystis carinii, which is normally dormant in most people. These diseases are known as opportunistic diseases, occurring in individuals who are weakened by other diseases. These young men in San Francisco progressed in a fairly regular fashion from infection with these rare diseases to death. They showed symptoms such as anorexia (inability to eat), chronically swollen lymph nodes in their necks, groins, and armpits, and chronic coughs. They picked up many unusual pathogens (disease-producing organisms) that infected their intestines and other body parts. Few of these men lived more than a year beyond their diagnosis of AIDS, or Gay-Related Immune Deficiency (GRID), the term used for the disease at that time. It was noted that every AIDS patient was identified as homosexual. These individuals were found to be drug abusing and promiscuous in their sexual relationships.

In a literature review of the field, Root-Bernstein (1993) indicated that several cases reported before 1981 had all of the opportunistic symptoms and disease patterns of AIDS. Based on this review, prior to this time he argued that hundreds of AIDS-like cases were documented in medical journals for decades before the recognition of AIDS. Recently, it has come to light that the AIDS virus that infects many in North America may have developed shortly before 1959. Researchers have located the earliest present strain of virus in a man in Africa at about this time (Zhu et al., 1998).

The problem with the AIDS/HIV (Human Immunodeficiency Virus, or first stage of the disease) infection is that we have developed no cure or preventative vaccine for it. It is as true now as it was in 1981 that behavior changes are the only means to prevent the spread of AIDS. The HIV epidemic poses incredible challenges to behavioral science to come up with strategies for primary prevention and behavior change (Kelly, Murphy, Sikkema, & Kabikman, 1993).

STATISTICS ON AIDS

In 1982, only 250 AIDS cases had been diagnosed; by 1993 the number had jumped to nearly 300,000 cases (Centers for Disease Control and Public Health Service, 1993). According to Kelly et al. (1993), it took eight years for the first 100,000 AIDS cases in this country to be diagnosed, and in just two years the second 100,000 cases had been identified. AIDS is now the leading cause of death in men and women between the ages of 25 and 44 (Tillman & Pequegnat, 1996). In some geographical areas such as New York City, it is the leading cause of death in women 18 to 30 years of age (Chin, 1990). The incidence (new cases) of HIV disease is escalating faster than that of other prevalent diseases in this country such as cancer and cardiovascular disorders. As of 1996, however, the incidence and mortality of AIDS has slowed down. These results likely reflect better treatment strategies (Centers for Disease Control and Prevention, 1998).

AIDS is communicable, and an individual can pick the HIV virus up with relatively few exposures; however, most exposed people must be exposed to a fairly large amount of virus in bodily fluids (e.g., blood and semen, which are the best vehicles for transmission). According to Kelly et al. (1993), this is the only high-incidence disease that requires individuals to make and maintain highly consistent behavioral changes, allowing few, if any, occasions for relapse. This is particularly difficult in emotionally charged areas such as sexuality.

HIV is unlike other types of chronic illnesses in terms of exposure. For example, lung cancer, which is strongly related to cigarette smoking, and cardiovascular disease, which is strongly related to a high-fat diet, require exposure to smoke and diet for years before a pathological process becomes evident. Because of the long latency of this particular disease, which averages about ten years (Baccatti & Moss, 1989), the prevalence (existing cases) of AIDS and related illnesses reflects exposure approximately ten years before.

Studies confirm that as many as 50 percent of gay men and intravenous drug users already have HIV infection, depending on the study and area in which the study was done (Curran et al., 1988; Kelly et al., 1992). Rates seem to be increasing in areas where there are drug abuse and high rates of sexually transmitted diseases such as in American inner cities (McCray & Onorato, 1992; Quinn, Groseclose, Spense, Provost, & Hook, 1992). These statistics are ominous and are portents for disaster if nothing significant is done. In 1992, the World Health Organization estimated that about 10 to 12 million individuals were infected with HIV worldwide and may exceed 20 percent of the rural population and 30 percent of the adult urban population in regions of Sub-Saharan Africa (Allen et al., 1992; Chin, 1990; Preble, 1990). By the year 2000, it is estimated that there will be 110 million HIV infections among the heterosexual populations of Africa, India, and Asia (Mann, 1992).

These heterosexual epidemics seem to be stimulated by traditional sexually transmitted diseases such as syphilis and herpes simplex II which weaken immune systems. In addition, cultural values may not favor monogamy or condom use. Malnutrition, poor public and personal health, warfare, "ethnic cleansing," and an abundance of other social problems can take a significant toll on the immune systems of individuals exposed to the HIV virus (Kelly, Murphy, Sikkema, & Kalichman, 1993; Ulin, 1992).

According to the World Health Organization (1997), there are about 16,000 new HIV infections in the world each day. More than 90 percent of the new infections are in developing countries. About 1,600 are in children under age 15, and 14,000 are in adults.

IMMUNITY

To understand more about how AIDS affects the human body, it is necessary to understand more about the *human immunity system*. This system is incredibly complex, and more is being discovered regarding its operations every day. The immune system prevents us from getting sick from the huge numbers of bacteria, toxins, viruses, fungi, and other possible sources of human destruction that are in the air, water, and everywhere we are. Our immune system has evolved over millions of years in order to protect us and to keep us alive so that we can survive like other animals and pass on our genetic material to future generations. The immune system's first line of defense consists of several layers: the skin, the mucous membranes, the gastrointestional tract, and the respiratory tract, all of which defend us from foreign material such as *antigens* (foreign substances) which can get into our bodies and infect us. Any foreign material that does get in and elicits an immune response is called an antigen. We are born with some of this immunity, which is called natural immunity, from our mothers and their immune systems, and we acquire immunity (not surprisingly called acquired immunity) through experience with these disease-producing organisms in the environment. After childhood diseases such as measles, chicken pox, and even colds, we develop an immunity to the antigens from these diseases. We can even be injected with vaccinations that carry a weakened or dead form of the antigen. The vaccinations elicit immune responses from our body so that we will be able to defend ourselves against the antigen when it comes at us full strength.

If the antigen succeeds in penetrating the first line of defense consisting of the skin and the mucous membranes, scavenger cells called *macrophages* (big eaters) may engulf the antigen and eat it through a process called *phagocytosis*. A *cell-mediated immunity* may then be induced in which *T-lymphocytes* (T is for thymus-activated or coming from the thymus) may directly attack the antigen. Finally, *B cells* (B from bursa because they were isolated from a particular bursa or sac associated with joints in chickens) are activated in our bone marrow to produce *antibodies*. These antibodies are specialized proteins that are secreted into our body fluids; they include blood and lymph to attack the antigens. Once the antibody hooks on to the antigens, a chemical reaction occurs which destroys the antigen.

AIDS involves primarily the destruction of macrophages and a special type of T cell called a Helper T cell (CD4 cell). The AIDS virus attaches itself to particular molecules of T cells called the CD4 molecule. It then enters the cell and changes the DNA of the cell in such a way as to render it ineffective. Since it works from RNA outside the nucleus of the cell to the DNA in the nucleus instead of the other way around, it is called a *retrovirus*.

Another system, called the Suppressor T lymphocytes, is also involved in regulating the immune response. These Suppressor T cells decrease the reaction of the immune system in attacking the antigen. Suppressor T cells suppress the activities of Helper T cells and are thought to protect us from accidentally attacking our own bodies. It is thought that over-stimulation of the Suppressor T cells occurs when the AIDS virus infects its victims. After a particular infection has subsided, normally there are a few clone cells from the immune system that remember the invader and remain on duty; if that particular antigen returns, there will be a swift and massive immune response. The normal healthy human being has about twice as many Helper T cells to Suppressor T cells so that a typical Helper T/Suppressor T ratio is about 2:1 (Root-Bernstein, 1993). In contrast, AIDS patients often have ratios that are less than 1. That is, they have many fewer Helper T cells than a normal, healthy human being.

This marked reduction in Helper T to Suppressor T cells has tremendous ramifications throughout the entire immunological system. All of the other immune responses are deleteriously affected in some way. In AIDS, diseases that a healthy immune system with a proper Helper T/Suppressor T ratio can easily handle (opportunistic diseases) establish themselves and reproduce to the detriment of physical health. Thus, the body loses its ability to distinguish between what is the "self" and natural and what is "nonself" and not natural.

General Immunity

Researchers in the field of Psychoneuroimmunology (PNI) recognize various types of immunity. *Nonspecific immunity* is the most general type and provides a broad defense against many different types of antigens. Specialized lymphocytes called phagocytes, as previously mentioned, seek out antigens and digest them. Other lymphocytes, called *monocytes* circulate in the blood and consume antigens that may be circulating. Still another group of defense cells are called *natural killer (NK) cells*. These cells attack and destroy body cells that are infected or cancerous. They attack viruses and other antigens once they enter body cells where phagocytes cannot go. They are nondescriminating and respond to any antigen-like substance.

Specific Immunity

The *specific immunity* component of the immune system responds in a more exact way to specific invaders. This type of immunity occurs through experience with specific types of antigens that have invaded the body. Once they are consumed by phagocytes, the phagocytes show the genetic material to lymphocytes, which can either continue with the defense or build new lymphocytes that will respond to the new antigen. These new lymphocytes destroy either the antigens in body fluids or infected cells. The process by which lymphocytes attack antigens in body fluids is known as antibody-mediated immunity. As mentioned earlier, antibodies are proteins that develop from plasma cells which produce special types of lymphocytes called B cells. These antibodies can slow the antigen down so that they can be caught and consumed by phagocytes, blow the antigens up, or neutralize the toxins produced by the antigens.

These antibodies are divided into five types of immunoglobulins: IgG, IgM, IgA, IgD, and IgE. Some of the immunoglobulins defend the surface of the body, some of them are found in lungs and skin and mucous membranes, and some of them defend against pollens or molds in the air. In addition, some of them are specialized to remember antigens that they have encountered previously.

Cell-Mediated Immunity

Cell-mediated immunity is the action of the T cells that detect and destroy body cells that have become infected or abnormal and pose a risk to the organism. There are several different types of T cells. One type of T cell is called a Memory T cell, and it carries information regarding previously encountered antigens so that if they are encountered again, there is a rapid previously learned response to destroy the antigen rather than a slower response brought about by the necessity of learning about the new antigen.

Another type of T cell, called a Killer T cell, is specialized to attack and kill antigens directly. When Killer T cells detect an antigen, they will attack it by dissolving the antigen's outer membrane. These Killer T cells also respond to a variety of other foreign tissues, and sometimes they cause problems when individuals receive transplanted tissues and organs from outside donors. These Killer T cells attack the transplanted material, causing its rejection.

Two other types of T cells are affected by the AIDS virus. The Helper T cells, mentioned previously, are important in stimulating the body's immune response to the antigens invading the system. These cells stimulate other cells to reproduce and attack the invading organisms.

After the proper adjustments have been made and the invading antigens have been destroyed, the Suppressor T cells, mentioned earlier, turn the system off. The balance between the Helper and the Suppressor T cells is basically the way in which the immune system maintains a proper balance; too much of an attack and resources are exhausted, too little of an attack and the antigens take over the organism. In the case of the AIDS virus, the ratio between the Helper and Suppressor T cells is unbalanced so that more Suppressor cells and fewer Helper cells are available.

In summary, the body has an initial line of defense consisting of the skin and mucous membranes of the body with their antibodies protecting against antigens. However, when the skin or mucous membranes are penetrated, further specific and nonspecific immune responses occur. The phagocytes with nonspecific immune responses consume antigens and present their remnants to B and Helper T cells. Helper T cells then stimulate the immune response, along with the B cells that stimulate antibodies, to destroy the antigen. If the antigen invades the cells, then Helper T cells signal the Killer T cells that there is antigen in the cell tissue. The Killer T cells then multiply and attack the cell destroying the antigen and their infected hosts.

Controversy: Does HIV Cause AIDS?

A relatively small group of "maverick" researchers believe that present research does not justify the statement that "HIV causes AIDS." Root-Bernstein (1993), for one, has argued that there are too many anomalies or scientific problems to warrant this conclusion. For example, certain symptoms are as highly correlated with AIDS as is HIV; diseases such as Kaposi's sarcoma and Pneumocystic carinii pneumonia are also universal symptoms characteristic of AIDS. Root-Bernstein does not believe the scientific case has been made that HIV is necessary or sufficient to cause AIDS. For example, he reports cases in the literature of HIV seronegative AIDS patients, and other diseases such as the Herpes Simplex viruses and Mycoplasma (an extremely small form of bacteria), that seem to be present as often as the HIV viruses in AIDS cases. Essentially, Root-Bernstein's critical question is this: Is it not true that a certain number of other-than-HIV immunosuppressive processes must be present in order for a full-blown case of AIDS to occur? He believes the data suggest that HIV spreads only to individuals with at least some additional risk factors other than the HIV virus.

For example, Root-Bernstein reports a comprehensive study of HIV transmission from prostitutes to their clients in New York City. Of the 340 male subjects in the study who regularly had sex with prostitutes, and who denied ever having had sex with a man or using intravenous drugs, only three out of the 340 had evidence of HIV infection. Furthermore, there are no data on whether these three men who showed evidence of the HIV infection had other immunosuppressive risks such as intravenous drug use, chemotherapy, surgical procedures, and nutritional deficiencies. Root-Bernstein believes that when such factors are taken into account, prostitutes represent virtually no risk for spreading HIV to heterosexuals with none of the other immunosuppressive risks. However, this result may also be partly explained by lower exposure to HIV because it is less concentrated in vaginal mucosa and saliva.

Root-Bernstein (1993) made the provocative suggestion that many of these studies imply that nondrug abusing heterosexual males and females have little or no risk of HIV or AIDS. Only when other predisposing factors, called co-factors, are present does the incidence of HIV infection markedly increase. Apparently, there are cases of patients known to be infected with HIV who have successfully controlled, and seemingly eliminated, the virus from their bodies without medical intervention. There are also several cases in which individuals have acquired a HIV virus and then lost the virus at subsequent testing (Root-Bernstein, 1993). These results occurred prior to the advent of protease inhibitor drugs which have also led to some individuals converting from HIV seropositive status to seronegative status. For example, Magic Johnson (the former professional basketball player), once diagnosed HIV positive, is now seronegative (as of 1998). He apparently has no other risk factors, he is taking protease inhibitors and exercising regularly, and he appears to have an extremely positive mental outlook.

Regardless of Root-Bernstein's opinion, the great majority of investigators believe that HIV is the primary cause of AIDS and that HIV infection alone will cause severe immune dysfunction over time, often leading to death (Greene, 1993). The majority of researchers acknowledge that the presence of opportunistic diseases during end-stage disease complicates the cause-effect relationship, but they believe HIV must be understood in order to understand AIDS.

PSYCHONEUROIMMUNOLOGY

Psychoneuroimmunology is the study of how people's attitudes, emotional states, and behavior interact with the nervous and immune systems. Robert Ader and others in his lab initiated germinal research in this area in the early 1970s. Ader and Cohen (1975) attempted to produce conditioned taste aversion to a saccharin solution in rats by injecting them with the drug cyclophosphamide (CY) just after they had drunk some of the saccharin solution. The CY rapidly produces sickness and nausea, and rats have a strong aversive reaction to saccharin thereafter. After Ader had conditioned this taste aversion, he stopped the administration of the CY to see how long the conditioned aversion would last in terms of conditioning. The animals returned to drinking the saccharin as the conditioning extinquished, but surprisingly began to die from infections and cancer. CY is a known immunosuppressant, and although one dose of this drug by itself would not cause immune system impairment which would bring on cancer, infections, and death, the pairing of this chemical with the conditioned stimulus, saccharin, was enough to produce conditioned suppression of the immune system when the animals were exposed to the saccharin again. Subsequent studies confirmed that the drug CY was not the only drug that would cause conditioned suppression of the immune system. Other chemicals that were known immunosuppressants can also cause conditioned immunnosuppression

(Rogers, Reich, Strom, & Carpenter, 1976). Since then the immunosuppressive effects of CY have been verified under a variety of experimental conditions (Ader & Cohen, 1993).

Drugs are not the only factors that cause changes in the immune system. For example, Sato, Flood and Makinodan (1984) found that recovery was delayed when mice that were previously radiated were re-exposed to conditioned stimuli (CS) that had been previously paired with electrical shock. This electrical shock stimulation presumably is an analog to stress reactions and causes immunosuppressive effects in rats and mice. Thus, it seems that, through conditioning, cues associated with the immunosuppressive effects of stress can assume immunosuppressive properties themselves (Ader & Cohen, 1992).

Some studies show not only immunosuppression from conditioned stimuli, but also immunoenhancement. For example, Gorczynski, Macrai, and Kennedy (1982) used a procedure in which mice were repeatedly grafted with skin from other mice. This caused an increase in the number of T cells responding to the skin grafts. The experimental group of mice was repeatedly grafted over a period of days. On the test trial, both control and experimental animals were sham grafted. That is, they were exposed to all procedures leading up to the grafting procedure, but they did not receive the grafts. Only the mice that had been repeatedly grafted showed an increase in the T lymphocytes associated with the sham grafting on the test trial. This result shows that conditioning can produce an increase in T lymphocyte production.

Russell et al. (1984) found enhanced biological production of histamine, which is part of the allergic immune system response, in Guinea pigs by a conditioned stimulus (an odor) paired with a stimulus that elicited increased histamine. Unreinforced presentations (elimination of the stimulus that elicited the increased histamine) of the conditioned stimulus (the odor) produced extinction of the enhanced histamine response (Dark, Peeke, Ellman, & Salfi, 1987).

Rat mast cells, which are involved in immune reactions and found in the mucosal tissues of the intestine and lung, produce increased mast cell enzyme (Protease II) when injected subcutaneously with egg albumen. Protease II is a chemical that increases during immune reactions. Animals were exposed to audiovisual cues (CS) followed by the egg albumin (US). Animals were then reexposed to the CS and were found to have an enhanced production of Protease ll (MacQueen, Marshall, Perdue, Siegel, & Bienenstock, 1989). These data indicate that conditioning can produce an increase in a mediator chemical involved in immune reactions.

Ader and Cohen (1982, 1991) also report suppression of the effects of an overactive immune system in autoimmune diseases such as Systemic Lupus Erythematosus (SLE). In SLE, the immune system attacks its own cells and causes severe inflammation of the kidney, skin, nervous system, blood vessels, and so on. Ader and Cohen (1991) have shown that conditioning procedures can suppress some of this overactive immune response. The ability to condition the immune system has exceptional import for humans who have immunosuppressive or immunoenhancement deficiencies. Much less of a drug (and presumably fewer side effects) which promotes either effect can be used if a conditioned stimulus can enhance return to more normal responses. As Ader and Cohen (1991) have indicated, more research is required on these complex interactions between the nervous system, the immune system, and learned behavior.

PSYCHOSOCIAL INTERVENTIONS AND IMMUNE FUNCTION

Receiving a diagnosis of a life-threatening or terminal disease causes psychological as well as physical changes. Individuals often exhibit hopelessness, a sense of despair, and loss of control over their own destiny. Sometimes they even abandon and isolate themselves from family members and friends. If the diagnosis is AIDS or cancer, it is sometimes accompanied by social rejection. Interpersonal relationships seem to be capable of providing protection against the stresses of serious physical illnesses and other life events (Cohen & McKay, 1984; Kiecolt-Glaser & Greenberg, 1984).

Other factors are also important (Gruber, Hall, Hersh, & DuBois, 1988) such as the subject's belief that the psychosocial intervention will be successful. A sense of hope that individuals can do something about their health also seems to have a significant impact on their prognosis.

Some of the psychosocial interventions that some psychologists believe have health-promoting effects include guided imagery, biofeedback, and other forms of relaxation.

In an experiment by Gruber et al. (1988), there were ten adult subjects ranging in age from 34 to 69. All had a metastatic disease such as breast cancer, lung cancer, lymphoma, melanoma, and endometrial, bladder, or cervical cancer. Subjects were in treatment with their oncologists (cancer specialists). Relaxation was based on progressive muscle relaxation, and imagery training consisted of subjects formulating their own idiosyncratic images on how they could imagine destroying cancer cells. Active participation in developing one's own image patterns seems to be conducive to inducing a state of well being (Langer & Roden, 1976). The subjects practiced twice a day. They were evaluated weekly, and they also participated in group sessions for relaxation and imagery training once a month. Blood samples were drawn at the monthly intervals, and lymphocytes were examined. The subjects were given no information until six months into the study. A variety of psychological tests were given to the subjects, including the Minnesota Multiphasic Personality Inventory (MMPI), the Rotter Internal-External Locus of Control Scale, and the Sarason Social Support Scale. Briefly, these inventories determine personality style, a sense of personal control, and sense of social support, respectively. Over the course of the twelve-month study, insignificant increases in immunoglobulins were found as well as mixed-lymphocyte responsiveness and the ability of NK cells to kill a target population of tumor cells. There was also an increase in the production of Interleukin-2, which is produced mainly by Helper T cells.

Results of the psychometric testing indicated that individuals tended to increase their feelings of internal control from the psychosocial interventions, although this was not statistically significant. The MMPI indicated that the subjects had adequate coping skills and did not show undue stress and anxiety. All of the subjects perceived adequate social support throughout this study. The authors noted that the subjects in their study were volunteers and were self-selected; therefore, generalization of this study to other cancer victims is limited.

Electromyograph (EMG) biofeedback was incorporated into the Gruber et al. (1988) study when it was felt that some participants were not as relaxed as their self-reporting indicated. The authors observed that some of the most significant increases in immune systems measures were observed in those subjects who had the largest reduction in their EMG measures (suggesting reduction in stress).

The possibility that relaxation may work by enhancing the immune system was suggested by a study by Peavey, Lawlis, and Goven (1985). The study used 21 female and 20 healthy male volunteers whose ages ranged from 21 to 47. A number of psychological instruments were used, including the Social Readjustment Rating Scale, the Profiles of Mood States (POMS), a Stress Coping Rating Scale, and a symptom checklist. Physiologically, a white blood count and differential blood count were done, and a biochemical method was used for measuring phagocyte cells. Relaxation was measured by both an electromyograph and a thermal unit to determine level of relaxation. Training sessions lasted one hour and were carried out twice a week. Subjects were also given an audiotape which they took home to practice on how to relax. Subjects were then divided into high-and low-stress groups based on their responses to stress scales. Those individuals who had high-stress scores were found to have low-phagocyte activity, while those who had low stress had higher phagocyte activity. The high-stress group was assigned to either a biofeedback-assisted relaxation group or a control group. Those who were assigned to the biofeedback training had increased phagocyte measures in comparison to the control group. They also had diminished anxiety and improved overall coping ability (Peavy, Lawlis, & Goven, 1985). According to Peavy et al. (1985), this study shows a relationship between high-stress and low-phagocyte activity, and low-phagocyte activity can be enhanced with biofeedback-assisted relaxation training.

In another study, Jasnoski and Kugler (1987) showed that higher levels of IGA immunoglobulin could be produced by procedures that used relaxation. The researchers used a mild arousal or alertness control group to control for the possibility of change of alertness in any direction which could be a factor in increasing immunoglobulin levels. The arousal manipulation was done by having the control subjects discriminate between different tones.

Other studies have shown that adverse immunological responses to psychological distress can be lessened with positive interpersonal relationships (Kennedy, Kiecolt-Glaser, & Glaser, 1988). For example, less lonely medical students have enhanced immune capability in comparison to more lonely medical students (Kiecolt-Glaser et al., 1984). In addition, women with better-quality marriages tend to have better lymphocyte responsiveness as well as less depression than those with poor marriages (Kiecolt-Glaser et al., 1987).

WOMEN AND AIDS

In the United States, women represent 10 percent of all AIDS cases; disease transmission for more than half of these women is associated with injection drug use (Ickovics & Rodin, 1992). The majority of women with AIDS (72 percent) are black or Hispanic (Centers for Disease Control, 1991). Many of these women are poor, socially disadvantaged, and abuse drugs by injection. Many of them are sex partners of injection drug users.

According to Ickovics and Rodin (1992), differences in genetic and endocrine factors as well as social roles, social conditions, and socioeconomic factors likely influence exposure to the AIDS virus and the disease process. Ickovics and Rodin also point out that women are more likely than men to be poor, of minority status, and less connected to community organizations. In contrast, men in major studies such as the Multicenter AIDS Cohort Study (MACS) are described as relatively advantaged and with high levels of education, professional jobs, and sufficient income (Kaslow et al., 1987). According to the Centers for Disease Control (1991), the number of AIDS cases of women in the United States increased by more than 1000 percent between January 1987 and November 1991. In New York City alone, AIDS is the leading cause of death among women ages 20 to 40 (Chin, 1990). The primary route of HIV transmission is the practice of needle sharing and injection drug use (Ickovics & Rodin, 1992). The Centers for Disease Control (1991) reported that 51 percent of all women with AIDS have used injection drugs. In contrast, only 26 percent of AIDS cases among men were associated with injection drug use.

Using drugs seems to precipitate risky behavior. In several studies, over two-thirds of the injection drug users reported never using condoms (Centers for Disease Control, 1990; Lewis & Watters, 1991).

The second most common transmission category for women with AIDS is heterosexual contact with HIV-infected persons. Thirty-two percent of women and only 2 percent of men contracted HIV through heterosexual contact (Ickovics & Rodin, 1992). There appears to be at least two reasons for this effect. First, there are more infected men than women: this statistic simply means that women are more likely to encounter an infected partner in heterosexual contact by chance alone. Second, male to female transmission is apparently more effective than female to male transmission. Reasons for this lack of symmetry of transmission between the sexes include the following: semen has a greater concentration of HIV than vaginal mucosa; and the delicate membranes of the vaginal walls are more likely to be lacerated than the skin surrounding the penis during intercourse, allowing a gateway for the HIV infection to enter.

There is a third way to be infected with HIV. Infants may acquire the infection from their mothers either in the uterus as they are developing or during birth (Goedert, Duliege, Amos, Felton, & Bigger, 1991). The CDC (1992) reports a rising incidence of HIV-infected infants who have acquired the infection from their mothers. Apparently, there is a 30 percent chance of HIV transmission by this route if the mother is infected.

A woman's prerogative to use condoms may be reduced by her partner's resistance and threats of rejection or physical abuse in the sexual relationship. In studies of prostitutes, only 4 percent of women had sex partners who consistently used condoms (Centers for Disease Control, 1987). This was also true of women attending intercity sexually transmitted disease clinics (Quinn et al., 1988).

Minority women are disproportionately represented among women with AIDS. Among women with AIDS, 27 percent are white, 20 percent are Hispanic, and 52 percent are black (Ickovics & Rodin, 1992). Minority women are primarily at risk because of their drug use and their partner's drug use. Ickovics and Rodin argue that education alone will not be sufficient to encourage the reduction of high-risk sex behavior such as unprotected sex among minority women (Jaffe, Seehaus, Wagner, & Leadbeater 1988; Weissman et al., 1989).

One encouraging study by Kalichman, Kelly, Hunter, Murphy, and Tyler (1993) indicated that if care is given to use culturally sensitive AIDS prevention messages that are targeted at specific populations such as African-American urban women, changes in behavior can occur. In this study, African-American women were more likely to be tested for HIV antibodies and to request condoms following AIDS information presented around three themes that were deemed relevant to African-American women: cultural pride, community concern, and family responsibility.

According to Ickovics and Rodin, distinctions can even be made between ethnic subgroups. For example, there is a sevenfold higher rate of AIDS among Hispanics born in Puerto Rico compared to Hispanics born in Mexico.

Research is sparse regarding African-American adolescents. John Jemmott and Loretta Sweet Jemmott have been doing some of the critically needed research in this area (e.g., Jemmott & Jemmott, 1990; Jemmott, Jemmott, & Fong, 1992). According to these researchers, blacks are disproportionately represented in AIDS statistics. Since many cases show up when individuals reach their 20s, it is likely that they were infected in their adolescent years. But behavior change is possible. For example, Jemmott, Jemmott, and Fong (1992) found that AIDS risk intervention aimed at increasing AIDS-related knowledge and reducing risky activities and behaviors such as intravenous drug use and sex without a condom reduced later reports of risky sexual activity in a group of 157 black adolescent males.

Clinical Course for Women with AIDS

Fungal infections caused by Candida albicans were the most frequent defining characteristic in a group of 24 women being treated for AIDS in Rhode Island (Carpenter, Mayer, Fisher, Desai, & Durand, 1989). In contrast, Pneumocystis carinii pneumonia (PCP) and Kaposi sarcoma (KS) seem to occur less frequently in women in the United States with AIDS than in men. Infected women seem to show vaginal candidiasis as a clinical sign of HIV (Imam et al., 1990; Rhoads, Wright, Redfield, & Burke, 1987). Sex differences in clinical manifestations of AIDS could result from women not being diagnosed or misdiagnosed, and not being treated correctly once the diagnosis is made, by health care professionals.

Effective treatment for women may be substantially different from that for men (Carpenter et al., 1989). Women have been excluded from experimental studies and clinical trials of new AIDS medications (Rodin & Ickovics, 1990). They have been markedly underrepresented in clinical trials and have limited access to these treatments (Hamburg & Fauci, 1990). The original studies for Azidothymidine (AZT) involving 282 patients included only 13 women (Fischl, Richman, Grieco, Gottleib, & Volberding, 1987). Also, women seem to die significantly sooner after an AIDS diagnosis than men (Friedland et al., 1991). The poor prognosis of women AIDS victims may be due to diagnosis and treatment occurring later in the disease process. Physicians may be more confused about the course of HIV infection in women than they are in men to make an earlier diagnosis.

Clearly, there is a critical need for more research on women and minorities because of the rapidly expanding presence of HIV and AIDS in these populations.

SUMMARY

AIDS came to the attention of the medical community in 1981 when small groups of otherwise healthy men developed unusual symptoms and soon thereafter died of opportunistic diseases such as Kaposi's sarcoma and Pneumocystis carinii pneumonia. Since then, AIDS has developed into the leading cause of death in men and women between the ages of 25 and 44. As many as 50 percent of gay men and intravenous drug users may already have the HIV infection. There may be 110 million HIV-infected individuals in heterosexual populations by the end of the decade in Africa, India, and Asia.

The human body has several systems devoted to defense against pathogens that invade the body. These defenses consist of the skin and mucous membranes, cells such as macrophages which eat foreign antigens, B cells which produce antibodies to destroy antigens, and Helper T and Suppressor T cells which control the body's reaction to antigens. One effect of AIDS is to hinder the production of Helper T cells and thereby reduce the body's ability to respond to antigens.

The field of psychoneuroimmunology developed around 1974 when Robert Ader found that animals can learn to suppress their immune system. This led to the exciting idea that environmental variables directly affect the immune system. Not only immunosuppression can be learned, but immunoenhancement may also be possible.

A variety of techniques developed by behavioral scientists such as biofeedback, relaxation techniques, and guided imagery may bolster the immune system. Also, positive interpersonal relationships may attenuate the adverse effects of stress on the immune system.

There is a scarcity of AIDS research on women and minority groups. Differences in biological sex, social roles, social conditions, and socioeconomic factors no doubt play significant roles in the incidence and prevalence of the HIV infection. For example, the primary routes for HIV infection are more likely to be the use of intravenous drugs and heterosexual contact for women than for men. The clinical course of progression may also differ between women and men.

Food for Thought

1. What is AIDS? How is it acquired? What are the medical criteria for the diagnosis of AIDS? What are some of the symptoms? What are the best methods of prevention?
2. Describe the functions of the immune system. How is it affected by the AIDS virus? Specifically, where does the virus attack?
3. How was the field of psychoneuroimmunology started? Describe the experimental work. What is so important about this work?
4. Describe some of the psychological approaches to AIDS management. What might be the effects of these approaches? Does research demonstrate how these approaches work? Explain.

GLOSSARY

antibodies: proteins produced by B cells which act to destroy specific antigens.

antigens: any substance that is identified as foreign to the body and produces a reaction from the immune system to destroy it.

B cells: bone marrow cells that produce antibodies.

biofeedback: techniques developed by psychologists which provide information to individuals on physiological changes to stimuli in order to modify these changes and reduce stress.

cell-mediated immunity: immunity at the cellular level which uses T cells to eliminate alien cells.

human immunity system: the system that defends against invasion by disease and has both inherited and acquired components.

macrophages: large cells that are part of the nonspecific immunity system, and surround and destroy antigens.

monocytes: large cells that are part of the nonspecific immune response.

natural killer (NK) cells: cells that participate in the nonspecific response by killing cancer cells and viral-infected cells.

nonspecific immunity: immune responses to any antigen regardless of the type of antigen.

phagocytosis: ingestion and destruction of cells identified as alien to the body.

psychoneuroimmunology: the study of psychosocial factors such as stressors which impact on internal systems, including the nervous, immune, and endocrine systems.

retrovirus: a type of virus that carries instructions in RNA and transcribes into the DNA of a host cell.

specific immunity: the immune system's response to specific types of antigens.

T-lymphocytes: a type of cell that attacks antigens and controls other immune functions.

CHAPTER 10

Cancer

In this chapter we will consider the following subjects:

• Types of Cancer
• Factors that increase cancer risk
• Factors that decrease cancer risk
• Psychosocial interventions that affect life expectancy

When Bill was growing up, he lived in a small rural Pennsylvania town that was very cold in the winter and had few days of sunshine in the summer. As a matter of course, he ran around without a shirt and in shorts most of the time when the weather allowed it. It was a big thing at that time (the 1950s) as it is today to obtain a nice tan as a healthy look. Bill is light skinned and had a great deal of difficulty obtaining a deep tan of any sort. Often, at the very beginning of the summer, he would severely burn from the sun, and shortly thereafter, his skin would peel. While playing sports, he often ran around with his friends working out in the yard and running with a football to get in shape for the fall football season. He also had jobs where he worked outside renting boats on a lake during his high school summers. Then, in his 40s he noticed some red blotchy marks on his back that later became open sores. He thought it was from sweating under his T-shirts which he wore when he went running. Visiting a dermatologist for an opinion, he found out that he had *basal cell carcinoma*. Now in his 50s, he has basal cell carcinomas removed about every six months. Because basal cell carcinoma almost always remains localized, it can be removed by a relatively benign surgical procedure. Because of his bouts with basal cell carcinoma, Bill now wears a shirt and hat all the time and applies at least #15 sunscreen at all times (even in the winter). He avoids prolonged exposure to sunlight. Luckily for Bill, this relatively benign type of carcinoma was not the virulent *melanoma* which is more severe and more likely to spread to other parts of the body. Skin cancers of various forms seem to develop at least partially from ultraviolet radiation from the sun. If Bill knew when he was growing up what he knows now, he certainly would have reduced his exposure to the sun.

DESCRIPTION OF CANCER

The American Cancer Society (1997) defines cancer as a group of diseases characterized by uncontrolled growth and spread of abnormal cells. If the spread of these abnormal cells is not controlled, it can result in death. Causes of cancer include external chemicals, radiation from the environment, and viruses, and internal factors such as hormones, changes in immunity, and inherited mutations. Causal factors can operate together or in some sequence to start the process of cancer (American Cancer Society, 1996). Cancer does not immediately start when the causative agent is present. The American Cancer Society (1996) indicates that ten or more years may pass before the particular causative agent affects the individual and a detectable cancer occurs (such as Bill's skin cancer).

All cancers start as single cells in the body. A cancer begins when an original cell loses its ability to pass on normal characteristics because the DNA which is necessary for replication is damaged or functions improperly. The abnormal cells that come from this damaged replication process give rise to more and more deviant cells. These cells tend to reproduce more rapidly than normal ones (Greenwald, 1992). If the cell mass continues to grow, it may start invading other tissues and organs, impairing their ability to function properly. If some of the cells break off and circulate in the body to other sites, then this process is called *metastasis*. Other areas of the body may then develop tumors. These deviant cells hurt the individual because they do not function properly and they interfere with the normal activities of healthy organs and tissues. Cancers may also reduce the body's ability to fight infections such as pneumonia (Greenwald, 1992). If cancer therapies are instituted, individuals have more difficulty in eating and drinking, which increases the chance of dying from malnourishment or dehydration.

Cancer is diagnosed according to the stage of involvement. For example, one of the common stage schemes for prostate cancer is as follows: in Stage 1 the cancer cannot be felt (palpitated) and causes no symptoms; in Stage 2 blood studies for cancer may be positive, and the tumor may be palpitated, but the cancer remains in the *prostate gland*; in Stage 3 the cancer cells have spread outside the confines of the prostate gland to tissues around the prostate; and in Stage 4 cancer cells have spread to lymph nodes and organs and tissues far away from the prostate gland such as the brain, liver, or lungs. Cancer specialists agree that whether or not a cancer is curable depends on where the cancer originates, at what stage it is diagnosed, and of what specific cells the cancer is composed. The American Cancer Society (1996) estimates that the leading *sites* of cancer in women are the breast followed by lung, colon, and rectum, and then uterus and ovaries. In men, prostate cancer is first, followed by lung, and then colon and rectal cancer. The leading cancer *deaths by site* in women are lung, followed by breast, and then colon and rectal cancer. In men, it is lung cancer, prostate, and then colon and rectal cancer. Note that in both men and women lung cancer is the leading killer, and smoking is responsible for 87 percent of these deaths (American Cancer Society, 1996). The five-year survival rates for various cancers (the five-year survival rate is the standard for cure in the medical community) is highest for early diagnosed melanoma (skin cancer), followed by uterine, breast, and bladder cancer. The most lethal cancer site is the pancreas with only a 3 percent survival rate no matter when it is detected. Apparently, pancreatic cancer is very difficult to detect initially, and when it is detected it is too far advanced to control it effectively. According to the American Cancer Society (1998a), the observed survival rate for all forms of cancer in 1998 is estimated to be about 40 percent. That is, 4 in 10 persons who get cancer this year will be alive five years after diagnosis. When the statistics are adjusted for dying first of heart disease, accidents, and diseases of old age, a "relative" five-year survival rate is 58 percent for all cancers (American Cancer Society, 1998a).

Many cancers have major behavioral components that are modifiable. According to the American Cancer Society (1998a), many of the one million cases of basal cell, squamous cell, and melanoma skin cancers that are expected to be diagnosed in 1998 can be prevented by ultraviolet radiation protection from the sun. Other cancers caused by cigarette smoking and heavy use of alcohol can also be prevented. Cancer can also be prevented with regular screening and self-exams to detect cancers of the breast, tongue, mouth, colon, rectum, cervix, prostate, testis, and skin.

The American Cancer Society (1998a) maintains that many cancer fatalities could be prevented with proper behavior modification in the areas of smoking, diet, exercise, use of alcohol, and early detection. "The National Cancer Institute estimates overall annual costs for cancer at $107 billion; $37 billion for direct medical costs, $11 billion for morbidity costs (cost of lost productivity), and $59 billion for mortality costs" (American Cancer Society, 1998b). About one in every four deaths in this country is due to cancer. About 1,228,600 new cancer cases are expected to be diagnosed (American Cancer Society, 1998a). The incidence rate has been increasing steadily in men and women for several decades, mostly the result of lung cancer. Recently, however, the incidence rate of lung cancer in men has declined and has also started to slow in women. Death rates from other forms of cancer have been declining or leveling off (American Cancer Society, 1998a). Since 1987, more women have died of lung cancer than breast cancer, a major cause of death in women. The five-year relative survival rate for lung cancer is 13 percent when all stages of lung cancer are combined. If the disease is localized, the rate is 47 percent, but only 15 percent of all lung cancers are discovered that early (American Cancer Society, 1996). Cigarette smoking is responsible for 90 percent of the lung cancer cases in men and about 79 percent in women, and smoking accounts for 30 percent of all cancer deaths. Those who smoke two or more packs of cigarettes a day have a lung cancer death rate that is 12 to 25 times greater than that of nonsmokers (American Cancer Society, 1996). There has been a steady rise of cancer mortality in the last half century. The major cause of this increase has been lung cancer.

There are many different types of cancer. All cancers are characterized by the presence of *neoplastic cells*. Neoplastic cells, which can be either benign or malignant, develop new and nearly unlimited growth, which robs growth potential from neighboring cells. Benign cells are not likely to metastasize; malignant cells or cancer cells, on the other hand, are likely to metastasize. Masses of neoplastic tissue that grow together are called tumors. Benign tumors are much less likely to metastasize than malignant ones. In any case, if the tumor continues to grow, it becomes a threat to other tissue in the area by weakening their ability to reproduce themselves.

Malignant tumors can be divided into four main groups: carcinomas, sarcomas, leukemias, and lymphomas. Carcinomas are cancers of epithelial tissue, cells that line the surfaces of the body such as the skin, stomach, and mucous membranes. Sarcomas originate in bone, cartilage, muscles, and lymph. Leukemias are cancers of the blood, and lymphomas are cancers of the lymph system. These four types comprise the majority of the cancers found in humans, but there are a large variety of other cancers which are less prevalent. Incidence of cancer rises with age, with most cases affecting adults in midlife or older.

FACTORS SUSPECTED OF INCREASING RISKS OF CANCER

Diet

Fat in the American diet as a factor in increasing cancer rates has received a lot of attention. For example, a diet high in fat may be a factor in the development of cancer of the colon, rectum, prostate, and endo-metrium. The association between high-fat diets and breast cancer is much weaker (American Cancer Society, 1998a). It may be that fatty sub-stances in the diet give rise to high levels of hormones that promote the development of tumors (Greenwald, 1992). Enzyme and human fat tissue may enable the body to produce a potent hormone that stimulates neo-plastic tissue to multiply (MacDonald, Edman, Hemsell, Porter, & Siiteri, 1978). A study by the American Cancer Society in the 1970s followed 750,000 people for 13 years. Results indicated that overweight people were much more likely to die from cancer than people of normal weight. Women whose weight was 40 percent over the normal range had five times the death rate from *endometrial cancer* and twice the death rate from cervical cancer compared to those of normal weight (Lew & Garfinkle, 1979). Men whose weight was 40 percent above normal had a 70 percent greater chance of dying from colon cancer and a 30 percent higher chance of dying from prostate cancer. It has been difficult to determine why individuals with a low-fat diet are less likely to develop cancer (Green-wald, 1992). Meat eating does not seem to be related to malignancies. Serum cholesterol has not been isolated as a cause of cancer. However, there is some suspicion that individuals who have sufficient resources to consume processed food, meats, and other high fat-containing items rather than grains, fruits, and vegetables are more likely to develop colon and breast cancer. Comparisons of Japanese Americans living in Hawaii in the 1970s with both Hawaiian Caucasians and Japanese living in Japan seem to suggest this result. Among the Japanese Americans living in Hawaii, rates of colon and breast cancer approximated those of the Cau-casian population rather than those in Japan (Waterhouse, Muir, Correa, & Powell, 1976). The Japanese Americans in Hawaii may have adopted food habits such as increased fat content from their Caucasian neighbors and therefore developed similar cancer propensities.

Tobacco Use

According to the American Cancer Society (1997), smoking is the most preventable cause of death in our society.

As noted in Figures 10.1 and 10.2, the incidence rates of new cases of lung cancer has been rising for years. It began to decline in men from 1984 to 1992, but the incidence rate in women continues to rise. Lung cancer is responsible for more than one in six deaths in the United States. It is related to more than 400,000 U.S. deaths each year. A major source of lung cancer is smoking. According to the World Health Organization (1997), lung cancer is not only the biggest killer and the most common cancer in the world, causing almost a million deaths a year and over 1.3 million cases, but it is also preventable. Globally, 85 percent of the cancer cases in men and 46 percent of the cases in women are due to smoking.

Figure 10.1
Age-Adjusted Cancer Death Rates,* Males by Site, United States, 1930–1993

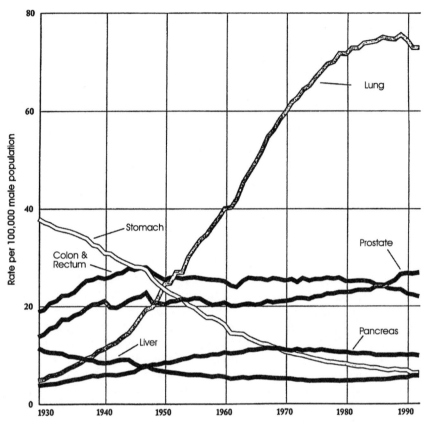

*Rates are per 100,000 and are age-adjusted to the 1970 U.S. standard population.

Note: Due to changes in ICD coding, numerator information has changed over time. Rates
for cancers of the liver, lung, and colon and rectum are affected by these coding
changes. Denominator information for the years 1930–1959 and 1991–1993 is based on
intercensal population estimates, while denominator information for the years 1960–
1989 is based on postcensal recalculation of estimates. Rate estimates for 1968–1989
are most likely of a better quality.

Source: American Cancer Society. (1997). *Cancer facts and figures—1997*. Atlanta, GA: Author.
Reprinted by the permission of the American Cancer Society, Inc.

Rates for men are increasing in most countries, and rates for women are
rising rapidly in countries where female smoking is long established.
Since tobacco consumption is increasing in many developing countries,
the lung cancer epidemic seems certain to continue and grow. Tobacco
is also associated with cancers of the mouth, pharynx, larynx, esophagus,
pancreas, uterine/cervix, kidney, and bladder, and is a major cause of

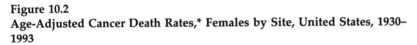

Figure 10.2
Age-Adjusted Cancer Death Rates,* Females by Site, United States, 1930–
1993

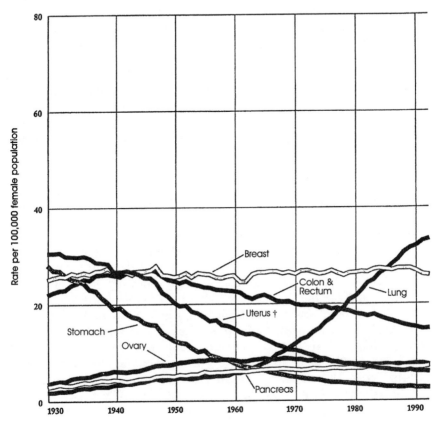

*Rates are per 100,000 and are age-adjusted to the 1970 U.S. standard population.
†Uterine cancer death rates are for cervix and corpus combined.

Note: Due to changes in ICD coding, numerator information has changed over time. Rates
for cancers of the uterus, ovary, lung, colon, and rectum are affected by these coding
changes. Denominator information for the years 1930–1959 and 1991–1993 is based on
intercensal population estimates, while denominator information for the years 1960–
1989 is based on postcensal recalculation of estimates. Rate estimates for 1968–1989
are most likely of a better quality.

Source: American Cancer Society. (1997). *Cancer facts and figures — 1997*. Atlanta, GA: Author.
Reprinted by the permission of the American Cancer Society, Inc.

heart disease. Tobacco use has been associated with conditions such as
colds, gastric ulcers, chronic bronchitis, emphysema, and cerebrovascular
disease. In 1990, the surgeon general indicated several benefits of smoking cessation: people who quit smoking live longer, people who quit

before age 50 have half the risk of dying in the next fifteen years compared to those who continue to smoke, cancer risks significantly decrease, and coronary heart disease and cardiovascular disease significantly decrease. According to the American Cancer Society (1996), cigarette consumption dropped about 35 percent from 1973 to 1991. By 1990 more than 44 million people in the United States had stopped smoking; this is nearly half of all the adults who ever smoked. In 1991, cigarette smoking levels had returned to the much lower 1942 levels. However, recently there has been a disturbing rise in teenage smoking, especially among young women, running counter to the national trend.

Along with the general decline in the United States, there has been a significant increase in cigarette exports to the rest of the world. These exports have increased about 200 percent since 1985. Some countries, such as Japan, have experienced an increase in cigarette imports of about 942 percent. The United States has tripled its tobacco exports to the countries of the former Soviet Union since 1985 (American Cancer Society, 1998a). China seems to be the next market being exploited, with an alarming increase in smoking-related deaths.

People who do not smoke but are exposed to the smoke of others have also increased risks. Although there are potential flaws in the research, environmental tobacco smoke may cause an estimated 35,000 to 40,000 deaths annually in the United States, about two-thirds of the deaths from heart disease, and about 3,000 from lung cancer (American Cancer Society, 1998a). Environmental tobacco smoke can aggravate asthmatic conditions and impair blood circulation, and has significantly higher concentrations of toxic and carcinogenic compounds than does mainstream smoke. Why is this? Environmental smoke is unfiltered by smokers' lungs, and nonsmokers are not adapted to the effects of smoke as smokers are. Thus, nonsmokers' lungs may react more strongly to the smoke.

The Environmental Protection Agency (1993) has classified environmental smoke as a known human carcinogen. Children exposed to second-hand smoke have increased respiratory infections and illnesses, as well as middle-ear infections. If mothers smoke while pregnant, the infants are more likely to die from Sudden Infant Death Syndrome.

Even smokeless tobacco (snuff and chewing tobacco) has its risks. A 1986 report of the Advisory Committee to the Surgeon General (American Cancer Society, 1996) indicated that snuff causes cancer of the oral cavity, and cheek and gum. About 20 percent of male high school students have reported using smokeless tobacco (American Cancer Society, 1998a).

FACTORS SUSPECTED OF DECREASING RISKS OF CANCER

Beta-Carotene

Vitamin A and substances such as beta-carotene have generated quite a bit of research in the last few years. Beta-carotene is found in green and yellow vegetables such as carrots, beans, and sweet potatoes, fruits, and other foods coming from plants. Beta-carotene is converted to vitamin A in the intestines. Beta-carotene apparently has antioxidant effects in preventing cancer. Some studies have shown that a diet rich in vitamin A substances reduce the chances of lung cancer even among cigarette smokers (see Greenwald, 1992, p. 78). The results, however, have not been consistent. Some studies, after examining all forms of cancer, found no evidence of beta-carotene or vitamin A protecting against malignancies (Paganini-Hill, Chao, Ross, & Henderson, 1987; Willett et al., 1984). A study published in *The New England Journal of Medicine* by the Alpha-Tocopherol, Beta-carotene Cancer Prevention Study Group (1994) found an unexpectedly higher incidence of lung cancer among men who received beta-carotene compared to those who did not. The study was done with over 29,000 male smokers 50–69 years of age from southwestern Finland. The study, a randomized double-masked placebo-controlled primary prevention trial, had subjects who continued in the study from five to eight years. The authors suggested that this clinical trial raises the possibility that beta-carotene may have harmful as well as beneficial effects in some clinical populations. However, another study by Mayne et al. (1994) suggests that dietary beta-carotene reduces lung cancer risk in nonsmokers in the United States. In addition, there may be cultural, genetic, and other demographic differences between smoking Finns and Americans. Also, the effects of smoking may react synergistically with other factors, confounding comparisons between smokers and nonsmokers. It is still difficult, however, to determine whether it is vitamin A, beta-carotene, or some other substance in fruits and vegetables, related or unrelated, which has possible preventative effects against cancer.

Commenting on the Alpha-Tocopherol Study Group in the same issue (1994), the editors of *The New England Journal of Medicine* suggested that the Finnish results may simply have been due to extreme random variation. They suggested this because the results are so much at variance with other evidence indicating a benefit of beta-carotene. The editors also suggested that the clinical trial may not have been long enough to show the beneficial effects of beta-carotene (about six years). Further research is needed to clarify the effects of beta-carotene on other nonsmoking human populations.

Fiber

During the 1980s, people were told to increase fiber in their diets for health. Definitions of fiber included indigestible fiber, partially digestible proteins, sugars, and starches; cellulose, gums, mucilages; shell material from shrimp and other crustaceans; waxes; and silicon (Trowell et al., 1976). Some of these substances dissolve in water, and others do not. Some are entirely digested, whereas others pass through the intestines largely unaffected. Even though somewhat inconsistent, studies in the 1980s have shown a relationship between high dietary fiber and low rates of colon cancer (Greenwald, 1992). However, studies attempting to relate fiber intake to cancers other than colon have been few (Greenwald, 1992).

Exercise

There is some evidence that people who exercise regularly are less likely to get colon and breast cancer (Greenwald, 1992). One possible explanation for the reduction in colon cancer from exercise is that exercise seems to stimulate peristalsis; this reduces contact time for *carcinogens* on the tissues that line the intestines (Greenwald, 1992, p. 83). The relationship of exercise to breast cancer is currently under investigation (American Cancer Society, 1998a).

Of course as we age, cancer rates go markedly up. In fact, aging may be the single greatest cancer risk factor. Internal events such as elevated estrogen in women and elevated testosterone in men may also be risk factors (Ghanadian, Puah, & O'Donoghue, 1979; Henderson, Ross, & Bernstein, 1988). Hereditary factors may also be involved in cancer—for example, for colon, breast, and ovarian cancers (Greenwald, 1992, p. 86). Greenwald (1992) contends that death rates from cancer may ultimately prove more resistant to individual preventative efforts than heart disease. He reports that the Multiple Risk Factor Intervention Trial (MRFIT), which followed 12,866 men for over ten years to assess the effects of habits and lifestyle on longevity, found an immediate drop in the risk of dying of a heart attack if smokers quit smoking. However, the ex-smokers continued to face the same risk of death from lung cancer as those who persisted in smoking. Greenwald contends that increased efforts to reduce cancer mortality should be aimed at treatment and not primarily at prevention.

Unfortunately, even the best informed and most careful individual still faces a significant risk of cancer. Most causes of cancer do not seem to be easily removed from humans or their environments.

PSYCHOLOGICAL INTERVENTIONS WITH CANCER PATIENTS

Considering psychological intervention with cancer patients involves a variety of problems. Much has to do with the type of therapy used, the psychotherapist's skills and personality, the receptiveness and personality of the patient, and how long the therapy continues. In addition, cancer is not just one disease but a variety of different diseases. Some cancer patients have much higher five-year survival rates than others. Physical impairment and the invasiveness of the disease are the best predictors of magnitude of mood disturbance (Cella et al., 1987). Cancer patients such as those diagnosed with melanoma, breast, and lung cancer have a low, moderate, and high risk, respectively. Mood disturbance is more likely the higher the risk level (Gordon et al., 1980). Anderson (1992) has indicated that psychological interventions seem to be important for reducing emotional stress, enhancing coping, and improving adjustment.

Controversy: Do Mood States Affect Cancer Outcomes?

Work in the 1970s relying on anecdotal evidence by the Simontons and others (Cousins, 1979; LeShan, 1977; Simonton, Matthews-Simonton, & Creighton, 1978) suggested that positive emotions and mental imagery techniques improve chances for recovery by increasing immune activity and decreasing abnormal cell counts. In the mid-1980s, Cassileth, Lisk, Miller, Brown, and Miller (1985) published a study on 204 patients with advanced cancer and tried to connect psychosocial factors and longevity. The study found no relationship between emotional well being and survival. Another study done in the 1980s, called the Seattle Longitudinal Assessment of Cancer Survival (SLACS) (Greenwald, 1992, Appendix), assessed psychological factors on survival over a five-year period using the Profile of Mood States (POMS). This study found no effects of negative emotional states, such as tension, depression, anger, confusion, fatigue, and vigor, on survival rates. Neither the Cassileth study nor the SLACS study indicated that patients' emotional states affected their chances for survival. These negative results did not ring true for many psychologists and physicians who often saw negative emotional states affecting disease outcomes.

In a landmark study by David Spiegel and his colleagues (Spiegel, Bloom, Kraemer, & Gottheil, 1989), the authors studied 86 patients with metastatic breast cancer prospectively. They intervened with a one-year intervention consisting of weekly supportive group therapy and self-hypnosis for pain. At the ten-year followup analysis, only three of the patients were alive. However, the mean survival rate for the group that had social support and self-hypnosis was 36.6 months compared to 18.9 months in the control group. This was a significant increase in survival rate for the intervention group. The study was undertaken with no assurance that participation would prolong their lives in any way. The work was basically done to replicate earlier studies with cancer patients showing improvement in mood, adjustment, and pain with social support (e.g., Goldman & Kennedy, 1979; Spiegel & Bloom, 1983). Nonetheless, psychosocial intervention increased average survival rates.

Temoshok and Dreher (1992) have suggested a particular cancer-related behavior pattern that she has named *Type C*. She believes that the Type C behavior pattern is excessive use of coping methods that others only sometimes use, such as appeasing others, denying our true feelings, and conforming to social standards. She studied a group of melanoma cancer patients for a period of ten years to determine the link between this Type C behavioral pattern and cancer development. On the average, her melanoma patients coped with their disease by keeping their feelings hidden from others, not expressing anger, and not acknowledging fear and sadness. They maintained a pleasant appearance even under the most difficult circumstances. They attempted to please others as much as they could.

In one study (Temoshok, 1985), subjects were videotaped in an interview on a seven-point scale on the following dimensions of emotional expression: (1) verbal articulateness in describing emotion, (2) consistent nonverbal expressiveness such as looking or sounding angry when describing an anger episode, and (3) differentiated affective expressiveness such as when relating a sad event. For example, does the subject describe or show sadness or mixed emotions? Temoshok broke general emotional responses into bodily sensations, thoughts, and actions. She found that less expressive patients had thicker tumors and more rapidly dividing cancer cells. They also had relatively fewer lymphocytes invading the base of the tumor. Their cancer defense systems seemed to be operating less effectively. Temoshok concluded that inhibiting emotions was associated with weaker defenses against cancer.

In their book, Temoshok and Dreher (1992) reported that the Cassileth et al. (1985) study in *The New England Journal of Medicine* caused a storm of controversy regarding the mind–body problem. For example, in referring to the Cassileth study, the deputy editor of *The New England Journal of Medicine* reported that the belief that disease is a direct reflection of mental states is largely a myth. She wrote that when people get sick or die, an unfortunate belief is prevalent that it is a personal failure. This belief is an unfortunate case of "blaming the victim." Temoshok argues that this opinion is not the true reflection of the mind–body approach used by responsible scientists. Most responsible scientists realize that mental state is only one factor in a complicated array of other factors.

We do not control our biological reality, but our mind may influence it in some way. The main idea is to try to understand what patterns of living are healthy, what risk factors are controllable, and in what areas we can engage in behaviors that enhance health. We are certainly not to blame for our disease, but we are not hopeless in its presence either.

In 1991, Levy, Herberman, Lippman, D'Angelo, and Lee suggested a weak, but direct, link with disease outcome through natural killer cell suppression in those who had recurrent disease and expressed more distress at baseline assessment. In their study of breast cancer victims, patients were immunologically and psychosocially assessed five days, three months, and fifteen months after surgery. All were followed for a minimum of five years, and 60 percent of the patients were followed for seven years or longer. Twenty-nine women reported disease reoccurrences during the entire followup period. Those who had higher natural killer cell activity at followup were more likely to be disease-free. Using the Profile of Mood States (POMS) as the assessment instrument for negative mood states, Levy et al. (1991) found that psychosocial factors such as negative mood states were predictive of recurrent disease and rate of disease progression. The authors suggested that in patients whose cancer does reoccur, the quality of psychosocial support as well as the extent of negative mood states may have the potential to predict progression of disease. House, Landis, and Umberson (1988) also reported evidence that social support has survival value.

Psychological distress and stressors from negative life events, both acute and chronic, are reliably associated with suppression of immune function (e.g., Herbert & Cohen, 1993). Herbert and Cohen (1993) did a meta-analytic review of studies of stress and immunity in humans. The meta-analysis showed consistent evidence for a relation between stress and decreases in immune measures such as mitogens (substances that increase the proliferation of lymphocytes) and natural killer cell activity. They also found changes in the number of circulating white blood cells, immunoglobulin levels, and antibodies. Variations in these variables depended on the type of stressful events that occurred, the duration of the stressful events, and whether the stressful events were interpersonal or nonsocial. However, they could compare only a few of these studies that had these variables. The authors point out that little knowledge is available as to what these changes in immune function mean and what effects different types of stressors have on the immune system and health and disease outcomes. They indicate that it is difficult to determine whether stressor-induced immune alterations have substantial implications for health outcomes.

Andersen, Kiecolt-Glaser, and Glaser (1994) have presented a biobehavioral model of adjustment to the stresses of cancer. They propose mechanisms on how behavioral and psychological responses can influence elements of the immune system and have possibly adverse effects on health. Women who were diagnosed with gynecological cancer showed more negative emotional states than control groups. The long-term presence of cancer, together with all of the problems and disruptions that cancer treatments cause, can produce chronic stress (Andersen, Kiecolt-Glaser, & Glaser, 1994). The Andersen et al. model considered the qualities of stressors that produce stress, lower the quality of life, and are likely to produce negative biological effects as well. Long-term naturalistic stressors such as bereavement and other interpersonal stressors are related to greater immune alteration than are nonsocial stressors (Herbert & Cohen, 1993).

Andersen, Kiecolt-Glaser, and Glaser (1994) indicated that lowered natural killer cell activity may represent one of the more reliable markers of suppressed immune function from these stressors. They suggest that stressed individuals often have appetite disturbances that cause them to eat less or to eat foods with lower nutritional value, to self-medicate with inappropriate drugs, and to have sleep disturbances such as insomnia. Stressed individuals also smoke more cigarettes and drink more coffee (Dews, 1984). On the other hand, cancer stressors can also decrease the frequency of positive health behaviors. For example, exercise seems to help mental health and mood, and cancer patients seem to do less of it (Andersen, Kiecolt-Glaser, & Glaser, 1994).

Substance abuse may affect immunity directly (Jaffe, 1980) and alter nutritional intake. If an individual is not eating properly, a variety of immunological impairments may result (Chandra & Newberne, 1977). Stressors affect the immune system by activating the sympathetic nervous system and by releasing hormones. A variety of hormones are released under stress, such as catecholomines and cortisol, growth hormone, prolactin, and opioid peptides. Andersen, Kiecolt-Glaser, and Glaser (1994) reported data from HIV-infected and cancer subjects which suggested that stressors are correlated with aspects of immune suppression. Of course, an argument can be made that the disease process itself may cause this immune suppression. Countering this argument, Andersen, Kiecolt-Glaser, and Glaser (1994) suggested that the effects of the cancer disease process are not unidirectional. Some immune processes rise and some decrease from cancer, indicating variability in immune responses to the disease process rather than unidirectional ones. There is no doubt, however, that further studies are necessary to confirm the stress–immunity–cancer link.

Kiecolt-Glaser and Glaser (1992) have reviewed psychological interventions that affect the immune system in noncancer populations. They have reviewed diverse strategies such as relaxation, hypnosis, exercise, self-disclosure, and cognitive behavioral strategies, and these interventions have produced generally positive responses. For example, Kiecolt-Glaser et al. (1985) have shown that relaxation training intervention produces increases in natural killer cell activity. However, these authors indicate several reasons why the effects of psychosocial interventions are not consistent and powerful. The reasons are as follows: (1) different types of cancers may respond differently to psychological interventions, (2) different types of biological treatments may produce different responses to psychological interventions, and (3) people of different ages and genders may produce different responses to these interventions. On the other hand, there is enough evidence regarding the positive effects of psychosocial interventions to pursue promising research leads. Studies have indicated that reducing emotional stress, increasing social adjustment, relieving symptoms such as pain, and improving coping skills does affect quality of life.

The effectiveness of psychological interventions may vary depending on the extent of the disease (Anderson, 1992). Morbidity and mortality risk from cancer can vary from low to moderate to high. For example, if the cancer is localized, the prognosis is usually favorable (low); if it is regional but has not spread to distant sites, it is guarded (moderate); and if it has spread to distant sites, then it has a high morbidity and mortality risk. Rapidly progressive diseases such as lung and pancreatic cancer also have high mortality and morbidity risks. For example, only 3 percent of pancreatic patients survive after detection (American Cancer Society, 1998a). In a study reported by Gordon and his colleagues (1980), cancer patients with melanoma (low mortality risk), breast cancer (more moderate mortality risk), and lung cancer (high mortality risk) were repeatedly assessed over a period of two years for the effects of psychosocial intervention. The intervention had three components: (1) education, with education regarding the medical system, disease and treatment side effects, and relaxation training; (2) counseling, including support and problem solving; and (3) environmental change, which included referral to additional services required by the patients. Compared to control groups, the greatest improvement in emotional distress occurred for the lung cancer patients. There was moderate improvement for the breast cancer patients, and the intervention and control melanoma groups showed no difference in emotional stress. However, the lung patients showed the highest levels of continuing stress, followed by moderate levels in the breast cancer patients and a decline in stress in the melanoma patients. The intervention groups as a whole resumed daily activities significantly sooner than the control groups, and the activities were more likely to be away from home. The intervention subjects tended to return to work more quickly than the controls. One of the main findings of this study was the interaction of cancer site (and mortality risk) by the effects of psychosocial intervention. The study helps us to unravel some of the complexities of psychosocial interventions on individuals with cancer (Anderson, 1992).

One of the best studies involving low mortality cancer patients was the Fawzy et al. (1990) study. This study was a six-week structured group intervention that consisted of health education, improvement of problem-solving skills and stress management techniques such as relaxation, and psychological support. The patients in this study had Stage 1 or 2 malignant melanoma and were under no treatment following surgical removal of the melanoma. Fawzy et al. found decreased psychological distress and significant positive immunological changes in the intervention group patients compared to the control group. The intervention group showed increases in lymphocyte production and activity. These increases were found not at a six-week followup but six months later.

As mentioned earlier, Spiegel, Bloom, Kraemer, and Gottlieb (1989) completed a landmark study on the effects of social support on morbidity rates of women with advanced, metastatic breast cancer. The members of the intervention groups survived an average of a year and a half longer than the controls over the ten-year course of the study. The improved survival rates in the intervention groups could have been from positive immunological changes (which were not examined in this original study). However, the social support groups' improved survival rates could also have been due to differences in other health factors such as compliance, exercise, diet, stress management, and other lifestyle variables.

According to Kiecolt-Glaser and Glaser (1992), much more is known about the effects of various negative stressors on the immune system than about the effects of positive behavioral and psychosocial interventions. These authors report that researchers have also not as yet collected much immunological data on various health behaviors such as sleep, smoking, physical activity, and alcohol and drug use, and these health behaviors may have immunological consequences. Poor personal relationships suppress the immune system (see Kiecolt-Glaser & Glaser, 1992). Kiecolt-Glaser and Glaser state that psychological or behavioral therapy outcomes combined with immunological measures are important areas for future research. Future research will be necessary to determine how positive immunological changes in individuals with suppressed immune systems translate into improvements in health.

SUMMARY

Cancer is defined as a group of diseases characterized by uncontrolled growth and spread of abnormal cells. This uncontrolled growth can result in death. The growth of the cancer cells is diagnosed by stages. Usually, larger stage numbers mean more involvement. Type of cell involved also affects the probability of recovery. The increased fat content of food has been implicated in promoting cancer growth. Some controversy has arisen regarding the effectiveness of beta-carotene in preventing cancer. Some studies have suggested that high-fiber diets aid in preventing cancer. Exercise has been implicated in reducing the chances of cancer.

Tobacco is the single most preventable cause of death and a leading cause of cancer. Lung cancer has been rising in direct relation to the amount of cigarettes consumed. Increased cigarette smoking among teen populations is a major source of concern.

Mood disturbances are common among cancer victims, and the more severe the cancer, the more severe the mood disturbance. Mood disturbances and stressors seem to have a suppressing effect on immune function. Recent studies have shown that social support and psychological interventions increase survivor rates in cancer patients. The exact mechanisms by which psychological mechanisms work awaits further research.

Food for Thought

1. List some of the causes of cancer. Speculate on how many of these causes are due to behavior. Discuss the leading kinds of cancer in women and men. Why do you think a discrepancy exists between the leading sites for cancer and the leading deaths by site from cancer?

2. Why do you think fat increases cancer rates? Speculate on how obesity may increase the chances of cancer. Explain why tobacco is so dangerous. Speculate on the reasons why exercise decreases the chances of cancer.

3. What are the best predictors of mood disturbance in cancer victims? What psychological interventions seem to help cancer victims? What might these interventions do? Describe the controversy surrounding the effects of psychosocial variables on cancer patients.

4. Describe the studies done by Spiegel and his colleagues showing the effects of psychosocial variables on cancer survival rates. Describe the work done by Temoshok and her colleagues on the Type C behavior pattern. Describe the studies done by Fawzy and his colleagues on low-morbidity cancer patients.

GLOSSARY

basal cell carcinoma: a malignant form of skin cancer that does not spread easily and that usually occurs on sun-exposed surfaces. Local surgery almost always provides a cure.

carcinogens: agents producing or inciting cancerous growth.

endometrial cancer: malignant neoplastic cells that develop on the inside of the upper portion of the uterus. The endometrium is the site where the egg implants and the baby attaches to the mother.

melanoma: a malignant form of skin cancer that must be caught early to prevent its spread to other sites in the body.

metastasis: spreading of carcinoma from the primary site to other sites in the body.

neoplastic cells: cells that grow without order or regulation, potentially resulting in the formation of either benign or malignant tumors.

prostate gland: the gland surrounding the urethra (urinary tract) and immediately below the bladder in males. The gland provides a liquid medium for sperm during ejaculation in males.

Type C: passive, nonassertive, and stoic personalities discovered by Temoshok in melanoma patients.

PART V

The Future

CHAPTER 11

The Future of
Health and Well Being

Matarazzo (1980, p. 815) has defined the field of health psychology, which is intimately related to the development and maintenance of well being, as the "educational, scientific, and professional contributions of the discipline of psychology to the promotion and maintenance of health, the prevention and treatment of illness, the identification of etiologic and diagnostic correlates of health, illness, and related dysfunction, and the improvement of the health care system and health policy formation." According to Glass (1989), the field of health psychology can be divided into three general categories. The first category is how physical diseases develop and how biobehavioral mechanisms impact on them. The second category deals with treatment of, and rehabilitation from, these diseases using nondrug methods such as biofeedback and coping skills training. The third category deals with promotion of healthy behaviors and prevention of chronic diseases with behavioral and lifestyle changes. This latter category is the focus of a psychology of well being. It is the focus that Matarazzo (1984) has suggested under the rubric of behavioral health.

No other area is as important for the development and maintenance of well being as how we deal with stress in our lives. As I mentioned in Chapter 5, Lazarus and Folkman (1984) defined coping with stress as a process of managing internal or external demands that are perceived as taxing or exceeding a person's resources. Lazarus and Folkman conceptualized coping as initiated by appraising the threat and assessing circumstances as harmful, threatening, or challenging. People judge their available resources such as time and personal characteristics, and then assess their coping skills and abilities to determine whether they will be sufficient to meet the threat or challenge imposed by the stressful event. Lazarus and Folkman (1984) suggested two general coping strategies: problem-solving strategies and strategies aimed at regulating emotions. Problem-solving efforts are especially useful for managing controllable stressors, and emotion-based efforts are more suited to managing uncontrollable stressors. However, individuals tend to use both types of strategies and to use them at different times depending on circumstances and the status of the stressor. For example, avoiding responses may be more effective for managing short-term threats, but vigilant coping may be more effective for long-term threats (Suls & Fletcher, 1985). Multiple coping styles may be necessary in managing some complex stressful events (Collins, Taylor, & Skokan, 1990).

People who feel they can exert some control over a stressful event, whether cognitively or behaviorally, seem to adjust better than those who have no such feelings of control (Taylor, 1990). However, as Taylor pointed out, there may be psychological costs to feelings of control. For example, individuals may feel they are to blame if they fail in their control efforts. Coping strategies for noxious medical procedures may be avoidant in nature such as cognitive distraction or active in nature such as inducing a person to reinterpret a stressful experience as a positive one. Relaxation techniques have had wide applicability in coping with the stress of obesity and smoking. Relaxation techniques are incorporated into stress management procedures, pain management procedures, and the treatment of chronic disease (Taylor, 1990).

Taylor (1990) has also suggested that self-help aids are other low-cost and effective intervention techniques that psychologists can use. Self-help manuals issued by various organizations such as the American Cancer Society and other reputable organizations are cost effective in helping people modify their habits (Cummings, Emont, Jaen, & Sciandra, 1988).

CARDIOVASCULAR DISORDERS

Cardiovascular disorders have been studied extensively by researchers interested in the interaction of behavior and disease. A great deal of attention has been devoted to personality–disease relationships. The most significant among these is the Type A Behavioral Pattern. As we have already discussed, this pattern is characterized by competitive drive, impatience, hostility, rapid motor and speech patterns, and the development of coronary artery disease (CAD). Researchers now believe that expressed hostility is a significant factor in the Type A Behavioral Pattern (TABP). Those who are more easily provoked to anger may be more likely to develop heart disease. This continued and easily activated response sets off a cascade of hormonal and physiological effects that damage the cardiovascular system. Other components of the TABP, such as competitiveness and time urgency, do not seem to be as detrimental as hostility. However, relationships between TABP and CAD tend to depend on the type of assessment done. For example, research suggests a stronger correlation between TABP and CAD when researchers use structured interview assessments rather than standardized paper-and-pencil personality tests (Friedman & Booth-Kewley, 1988).

ADHERENCE MODELS

Psychologists have found that failure to adhere to treatment recommendations increases with the complexity of treatment. Between 30 and 60 percent of all patients fail to take medications that have been prescribed (Kaplan & Simon, 1990). The more medications that patients have prescribed, the more nonadherence occurs (Cockburn, Gibberd, Reid, & Sanson-Fisher, 1987). When significant changes in lifestyle are called for (Brownell, Marlatt, Lichtenstein, & Wilson, 1986), research has indicated that positive expectancies of success, support from peers and the social environment, and a record of adherence in the past increase adherence rates in individuals. Physicians who present clear explanations for treatment, express positive verbal communication such as reassurance, support, and encouragement, and refrain from negative verbal communications such as anger and negative emotions produce more adherence (see Dimatteo et al., 1993).

Dimatteo and her colleagues (1993) studied the role of the physician's personal characteristics in patient adherence. They studied 186 physicians longitudinally and found that physicians' global job satisfaction has a positive effect on patients' general adherence. Physicians who were happier in their work showed improved patient adherence. The mechanism by which this happens is not clear, although we can speculate that they conveyed their positive feelings to their patients. This study is one of the few demonstrating that how health professionals feel about their work can influence patient adherence.

HEALTHY LIVING AND HEALTH DELIVERY

Recently, a report published by the Human Capital Initiative Coordinating Committee (HCICC) (American Psychological Society, April 1996) called for behavioral research to improve the health of all members of our population. With more than 40 million people not insured in this country, there is a need to make health care more affordable and accessible. More specifically, there is a need to concentrate on research that helps us in understanding and maintaining health and preventing disease across age, gender, and socioeconomic segments of our nation. We have spent a great deal of time and money on high-tech treatment of diseases. With decreases in the amount of money available for these expensive treatments, it is becoming increasingly clear that individuals must be health providers for themselves. That is, they must be well-informed consumers of health information and be willing to put what they have learned into practice. It is becoming more important to provide opportunities and training so that individuals can take care of their own health care; this is especially true in the areas of disease prevention and maintenance of health. This is a golden opportunity for a psychology of well being to have a significant impact in reducing health care costs and increasing quality of life in the United States.

The HCICC (1996) indicated that seven of the ten leading causes of death have significant aspects of modifiable behavior related to them. Some of these modifiable behaviors are stress, smoking, high-fat and nutritionally poor diets, obesity, and a sedentary lifestyle, which can increase the incidence of heart disease, cerebral vascular accidents, and cancer. HIV often occurs because of behavioral choices regarding sexual behavior or drug use. These behavioral choices should be changed as early as possible before they become well-ingrained patterns of behavior in adulthood. Research in health psychology may help improve these choices so that quality of life throughout the life span is enhanced and health care costs are less expensive. As the HCICC indicates, healthy behavior choices may seem less rewarding in the short run. Therefore, research should help individuals learn to span the gap between a healthy behavioral choice and its positive consequences later on.

Dean Ornish (1996), in his work with patients with coronary heart disease, takes an intriguing approach to the delayed positive reinforcement consequences of healthy behavioral choices. He has argued that making drastic behavioral changes (rather than using the more standard approach of making slow, gradual changes) is much more effective in establishing healthy lifestyles in the long run. He believes that these behavioral changes should begin all at once. Patients in his program are placed on vegetarian diets with less than 10 percent fat. They are encouraged to engage in an hour of meditation a day and in moderate physical activity. Ornish indicates that patients see improvements in their overall physical functioning rapidly enough to provide significant and relatively quick reinforcement. Thus, behavioral changes are more easily maintained. The success of his program in reversing heart disease by nonsurgical methods has caught the attention of other health professionals and the general public. More research such as Ornish's is necessary to increase our understanding of how to help individuals with other chronic diseases to make positive behavioral changes and maintain them.

Major tasks in the next few years are to make the prevention of disease and the promotion of health as important in the nation's agenda as treatment and cure of disease. In the early part of this century, infectious diseases were the major causes of death and disability. Vaccines and antibiotics have reduced these threats. In fact, the small-pox virus kept under the auspices of the World Health Organization will be destroyed in 1999 because it is no longer a threat to the human population. We must be wary, however, because new antibiotic-resistant strains of viruses and bacteria are constantly appearing as a result of the overuse and misuse of available antibiotics. In any event, chronic diseases such as heart disease, cancer, diabetes, and HIV infection are some of our present major worries. Behavioral choices affecting their incidence and prevalence are associated with all of these diseases. According to the HCICC (1996), the United States spent 12 percent of its gross national product in 1990 on health care, and it is estimated that over 13 percent would be expanded in 1998. With the increased incidence of chronic diseases, these health care costs will continue to escalate. It behooves us to spend time and money on behavioral research to change this picture.

ETHNIC, CULTURAL, AND GENDER ISSUES

Sensitivity to ethnic and cultural factors is fundamental to making major changes in health care. Behavioral research is needed to determine what works in the large number of minority populations in this country. Associated with this, individuals with fewer financial resources should have as much access to quality care as the more well-off members of our society do.

More attention will need to be paid to gender issues in disease. In a report issued by the National Center on Addiction and Substance Abuse at Columbia University (June 1996) on substance abuse in women, Joseph Califano (president of the Center) noted that women, and especially adolescent women, are closing the gender gap in drinking and using drugs. He also reported that research indicates women need different treatment than men. For example, 69 percent of women being treated for alcoholism were sexually abused as children, whereas only 12 percent of men were abused. Depression is common among women who use drugs, including tobacco. The report indicated that women are more likely than men to feel powerless and helpless before they become alcoholics, whereas men are more likely to become depressed after becoming alcoholics. In addition, most of the oldest people surviving in this country are women. Clearly, more research is needed on gender, aging, and disease progression.

CAREGIVER STRESS

We also need to pay attention to the stress that chronic illnesses cause caregivers and family members associated with the afflicted person

(American Psychological Society, April 1996). The effects of chronic disease on the caregiver can produce depression and other psychological disorders, reductions in the effectiveness of their immune systems, and possibly a reduction in life expectancy. There is a dire need for behavioral research to determine ways to improve these caregivers' and family members' quality of life during their activities with the afflicted family member, and a need for behavioral research on how to improve coping after the family member's death.

SELF-HELP

Finally, we need to pay attention to self-help in health care. Acknowledging this trend, the Center for the Advancement of Health (1996) has published *An Indexed Bibliography on Self-Management for People with Chronic Disease*. The bibliography was created to help health care professionals encourage patients to take more responsibility in managing their chronic illnesses.

We should pay particular attention to Herbert Benson's advice in his Master Lecture entitled *Balancing the Three Legged Stool*, at the Society of Behavioral Medicine Meeting in 1994. He indicated that the first two legs of the health care stool, drugs and surgery, have become inordinately important for health care in this country. The third leg of the stool, self-help, has collapsed so that only the first two legs hold the stool up. With the advent of managed care, drugs and surgery are becoming more expensive. Self-help is likely to be more cost-effective than the other two legs of the stool. Benson pointed out five categories of self-help involving the development of well being buttressing this third leg of the health care stool. These five categories are relaxation techniques which elicit the "Benson" relaxation response, exercise, group support, sound nutrition, and cognitive restructuring techniques. Paying more attention to these five categories of self-help in health care will improve our abilities to manage our own health and well being, decrease the costs of health care in this country, and improve our quality of life. Looks like a winner to me!

References

Abel, P. M. (1995). Your total cholesterol doesn't mean much. Available on Internet: http://www.icorp.net/cardio/articles/hdl.htm

Abramson, L. Y., Seligman, M. E. P., & Teasdale, J. D. (1978). Learned helplessness in humans: Critique and reformulation. *Journal of Abnormal Psychology, 87,* 49–74.

Ader, R., & Cohen, N. (1975). Behaviorally conditioned immunosuppression. *Psychosomatic Medicine, 37,* 333–340.

Ader, R., & Cohen, N. (1982). Behavioral conditioned immunosuppression and murine systemic lupus erythematosis. *Science, 215,* 1534–1536.

Ader, R., & Cohen, N. (1991). Conditioning of the immune response. *Netherlands Journal of Medicine, 39,* 263–273.

Ader, R., & Cohen, N. (1992). Conditioned immunopharmacologic effects on cell-mediated immunity. *International Journal of Immunopharmacology, 14,* 323–327.

Ader, R., & Cohen, N. (1993). Psychoneuroimmunology: Conditioning and stress. *Annual Review of Psychology, 44,* 53–85.

Agras, W. S., Schneider, J. A., Arnow, B., Raeburn, S. D., & Telch, C. F. (1989). Cognitive-behavioral and response prevention treatments for bulimia nervosa. *Journal of Consulting and Clinical Psychology, 57,* 215–221.

Agras, W. S., & Werne, J. (1977). Behavior modification in anorexia nervosa: Research foundations. In R. A. Vigorski (Ed.), *Anorexia nervosa* (pp. 291–303). New York: Raven Press.

Allen, S., Serufilia, P., Boggerts, J., Van de Perre, P., Nsengumuremyi, F., Lindan, C., Carael, M., Wolf, W., Coates, T., & Hulley, S. (1992). Confidential HIV testing and condom promotion in Africa: Impact on HIV and gonorrhea rates. *Journal of the American Medical Association, 268,* 3338–3343.

Alpha-Tocopherol, Beta-Carotene Cancer Prevention Study Group. (1994). The effect of vitamin E and beta-carotene on the incidence of lung cancer and other cancers in male smokers. *New England Journal of Medicine, 330,* 1029–1035.

American Cancer Society. (1996). *Cancer facts and figures—1996.* Atlanta, GA: Author.

American Cancer Society. (1997). *Cancer facts and figures—1997.* Atlanta, GA: Author.

American Cancer Society. (1998a). Cancer facts and figures—1998. Available on Internet: http://www.cancer.org/statmenu.html

American Cancer Society. (1998b). Cancer facts and figures—1998. Available on Internet: http://www.cancer.org/cancerinfo/acs_frame.asp? frame=statmenu.html

American College of Sports Medicine. (1991). *Guidelines for exercise testing and prescription* (4th ed.). Philadelphia: Lea & Fabiger.

American Diabetes Association (1995a). Research report, changing the future. Available on Internet: http://www.diabetes.org/C80.html.

American Diabetes Association (1995b). Weight loss. Available on Internet: http://www.diabetes.org/C40G.html.

American Diabetes Association. (1997). Diabetes facts and figures. Available on Internet: http://www.diabetes.org/ada/C20f.html

American Diabetes Association. (1998). Diabetes risk test. Available on Internet: http://www.diabetes.org/ada/risktest.html

American Psychiatric Association. (1994). *Diagnostic and statistical manual of mental disorders* (4th ed.). Washington, DC: Author.

American Psychological Society. (April 1996). Human capital initiative: Doing the right thing. *Observer, Report 4.*

Andersen, B. L., Andersen, B., & deProsse, C. (1989). Controlled prospective longitudinal study of women and cancer: I. Sexual functioning outcomes. *Journal of Consulting and Clinical Psychology, 57,* 683–691.

Andersen, B. L., Kiecolt-Glaser, J. K., & Glaser, R. (1994). A biobehavioral model of cancer stress and disease course. *American Psychologist, 49,* 389–404.

Anderson, A. E. (1992). Eating disorders in males: A special case? In K. D. Brownell, J. Rodin, & J. H. Wilmore (Eds.), *Eating, body weight, and performance in athletes: Disorders of modern society.* Philadelphia: Lea & Fabiger.

Anderson, B. L. (1992). Psychological interventions for cancer patients to enhance the quality of life. *Journal of Consulting and Clinical Psychology, 60,* 552–568.

Anderson, R. E., Barlett, S. J., Morgan, G. D., & Brownell, K. D. (1995). Weight loss, psychological, and nutritional patterns in competitive male body builders. *International Journal of Eating Disorders, 18,* 49–57.

Andrew, G. M., Oldridge, N. B., Parker, J. O., Cunningham, D. A., Rechnitzer, N. L., Jones, N. L., Buck, C., Kavanagh, T., & Shephard, R. J. (1981). Reasons for dropout from exercise programs in post-coronary patients. *Medicine and Science in Sports and Exercise, 13,* 164–168.

Appley, M. H., & Trumbull, R. T. (1967). On the concept of psychological stress. In M. H. Appley and R. T. Trumball (Eds.), *Psychological stress* (pp. 1–13). New York: Meredith Publishing Co.

Asterita, M. F. (1985). *The physiology of stress: With special reference to the neuroendocrine system.* New York: Human Sciences Press.

Baccatti, P., & Moss, A. R. (1989). Incubation period of AIDS in San Francisco. *Nature, 338,* 252–253.

Bahrke, M. S. (1993). Psychological effects of endogeneous testosterone and anabolic-androgenic steroids. In C. E. Yesalis (Ed.), *Anabolic steroids in sport and exercise* (pp. 161–192). Champaign, IL: Human Kinetics Publishers.

Baillie, A. J., Mattick, R. P., Hall, W., & Webster, P. (1994). Meta-analytic review of the efficacy of smoking cessation interventions. *Drug and Alcohol Review, 13*, 157–170.

Bandura, A. (1977). Self-efficacy toward a unifying theory of behavioral change. *Psychological Review, 84*, 191–215.

Bandura, A. (1982). Self-efficacy mechanism in human agency. *American Psychologist, 37*, 122–147.

Bassler, T. J. (1972a). [Letter to the editor]. *New England Journal of Medicine, 302*, 57–58.

Bassler, T. J. (1972b). Jogging deaths. *New England Journal of Medicine, 287*, 1100.

Bassler, T. J., & Cordello, F. P. (1976). Fiber-feeding and arteriosclerosis. *Journal of the American Medical Association, 235*, 1841–1842.

Bassler, T. J., & Scaff, J. (1976). Letter: Impending heart attacks. *Lancet, 1*, 544–545.

Beck, A. T. (1976). *Cognitive therapy and the emotional disorders.* New York: International University Press.

Beck, A. T., Weissman, A., Lester, D., & Trexler, L. (1974). The measurement of pessimism: The hopelessness scale. *Journal of Consulting and Clinical Psychology, 42*, 861–865.

Begleiter, H., Porgesz, B., Bihari, B., & Kissin, B. (1984). Event-related brain potentials in boys at risk for alcoholism. *Science, 225*, 1493–1495.

Beglin, J., & Fairburn, C. G. (1992). Evaluations of a new instrument for the detection of eating disorders in community samples. *Psychiatry Research, 44*, 191–201.

Bell, G. I. (1991). Molecular defects in Diabetes Mellitus. *Diabetes, 40*, 413–422.

Bennett, W. J., & Gurin, J. (1982). *The dieter's dilemma: Eating less and weighing more.* New York: Basic Books.

Benson, H. (1975). *The relaxation response.* New York: William Morrow and Co.

Benson, H. (March 1994). *Master lecture: Balancing the three-legged stool.* Fifteenth Annual Meeting of the Society of Behavioral Medicine, San Francisco.

Bernard, C. (1957). *An introduction to the study of experimental medicine.* New York: Dover Publications.

Bertalanffy, L. von. (1968). *General systems theory.* New York: Braziller.

Bjorntorp, P. (1985). Regional patterns of fat distribution. *Annals of Internal Medicine, 103* (Suppl. 5, Part 2), 994–995.

Bjorntorp, P. (1991). Metabolic implications of body fat distribution. *Diabetes Care, 14*, 1132–1143.

Blackburn, H. (1987). Epidemiologic evidence for the causes and prevention of atherosclerosis. In D. Steinberg & J. M. Olesfsky (Eds.), *Hypercholesterolemia and atherosclerosis* (pp. 53–98). New York: Churchill Livingstone.

Blair, S. N., Kohl, H. W., Gordon, N. F., & Paffenbarger, R. S., Jr. (1992). How much physical activity is good for health? *Annual Review of Public Health, 13*, 99–126.

Bland, S. H., Krogh, V., Winkelstein, W. S., & Trevisan, M. (1991). Social network and blood pressure: A population study. *Psychosomatic Medicine, 53*, 598–607.

Blum, K., & Payne, J. E. (1991). *Alcohol and the addictive brain: New hope for alcoholics from biogenetic research.* New York: Free Press.

Blumenthal, J. A., Williams, R. S., Wallace, A. G., Williams, R. B., Jr., & Needels, T. L. (1982). Physiological and psychological variables predict compliance to prescribed exercise therapy in patients recovering from myocardial infarction. *Psychosomatic Medicine, 44,* 519–527.

Bohman, M., Sigvardsson, S., & Cloninger, C. R. (1981). Maternal inheritance of alcohol abuse. *Archives of General Psychiatry, 38,* 965–969.

Boring, E. G. (1950). *A history of experimental psychology.* New York: Appleton-Century-Crofts.

Bouchard, C., Shepherd, R. J., Stephens, T., Sutton, J., & McPherson, B. (Eds.) (1990). *Exercise, fitness and health. A consensus of current knowledge.* Champaign, IL: Human Kinetics Publishers.

Bouchard, C. L., Perusse, C., Tremblay, A., & Theriault, G. (1988). Inheritance of the amount and distribution of human body fat. *International Journal of Obesity, 12,* 205–215.

Bouchard, C. L., Tremblay, A., Despres, J. P., Nadeau, A. L., Theriault, G., Dussault, J., Moorjani, S., Pinault, S., & Fournier, G. (1990). The response to long-term overfeeding in identical twins. *New England Journal of Medicine, 322,* 1477–1482.

Bowen, D. J., Tomoyasu, N., & Cauce, A. M. (1991). The triple threat: A discussion of gender, class, and race differences in weight. *Women and Health, 17,* 123–143.

Bradley, C. (1994). Contribution of psychology to diabetes management. *British Journal of Clinical Psychology, 33,* 11–21.

Bradley, C., & Lewis, K. S. (1990). Measures of psychological well-being and treatment satisfaction developed from the responses of people with tablet-treated diabetes. *Diabetes Medicine, 7,* 445–457.

Bray, G. A. (1976). *The obese patient.* Philadelphia: W. B. Saunders.

Bray, G. A. (1986). Effects of obesity on health and happiness. In K. D. Brownell & J. P. Foreyt (Eds.), *Handbook of eating disorders* (pp. 3–44). New York: Basic Books.

Brower, K. J. (1993). Anabolic steroids: Potential for physical and psychological dependence. In C. E. Yesalis (Ed.), *Anabolic steroids in sport and exercise* (pp. 193–213). Champaign, IL: Human Kinetics Publishers.

Brownell, K. D. (January 1988). Yo-yo dieting. *Psychology Today,* 20–23.

Brownell, K. D., (1993). Whether obesity should be treated. *Health Psychology, 12* (editorial), 339–341.

Brownell, K. D., & Kaye, F. S. (1982). A school-based behavior modification, nutrition education, and physical activity program for obese children. *American Journal of Clinical Nutrition, 35,* 277–283.

Brownell, K. D., Greenwood, M. R. C. Stellar, E., & Schrager, E. E. (1986). The effects of repeated cycles of weight loss and regain in rats. *Physiology and Behavior, 38,* 459–464.

Brownell, K. D., Marlatt, G. A., Lichtenstein, E., & Wilson, G. T. (1986). Understanding and preventing relapse. *American Psychologist, 41,* 765–782.

Brownell, K. D., & Rodin, J. (1992). Prevalence of eating disorders in athletes. In K. D. Brownell, J. Rodin, & J. H. Wilmore (Eds.), *Eating, body weight, and performance in athletes: Disorders of modern society*. Philadelphia: Lea & Fabiger.

Brownell, K. D., & Rodin, J. (1994). Medical, metabolic and psychological effects of weight cycling. *Archives of Internal Medicine, 154*, 1325–1330.

Brownell, K. D., Rodin, J., & Wilmore, J. H. (Eds.). (1992). *Eating, body weight, and performance in athletes: Disorders of modern society*. Philadelphia: Lea & Fabiger.

Brownell, K. D., & Wadden, T. A. (1992). Etiology and treatment of obesity: Understanding a serious, prevalent, and refractory disorder. *Journal of Consulting and Clinical Psychology, 60*, 505–517.

Bruch, H. (1973). *Eating disorders*. New York: Basic Books.

Buckley, W. E., Yesalis, C. E., & Bennell, D. L. (1993). A study of anabolic steroid use at the secondary school level: Recommendations for prevention. In C. E. Yesalis (Ed.), *Anabolic steroids in sport and exercise*. Champaign, IL: Human Kinetics Publishers.

Burke, G. L., Savage, P. J., Manolio, T. A., Sprafka, M., Wagenknecht, L. E., Sidney, S., Perkins, L. L., Liu, K., & Jacobs, D. R. (1992). Correlates of obesity in young black and white women: The CARDIA Study. *American Journal of Public Health, 82*, 1621–1625.

Buydens-Branchey, L., Branchey, M. H., & Noumair, D. (1989). Age of alcoholism onset: I. Relationship to psychopathology. *Archives of General Psychiatry, 46*, 225–230.

Cade, J., & Margetts, B. (1989). Cigarette smoking and serum lipid and lipoprotum concentration. *British Medical Journal, 298*, 1312.

Campbell, E. J. M., Scadding, J. G., & Roberts, R. S. (1979). The concept of disease. *British Medical Journal, 2*, 757–762.

Campfield, L. A., Smith, F. J., Guisez, Y., Devos, R., & Burn, P. (1995). Mouse OB protein: Evidence for a peripheral signal linking adiposity and central neural networks. *Science, 269*, 546–549.

Cannon, W. B. (1939). *The wisdom of the body*. Philadelphia: W. W. Norton.

Carey, K. B., & Maisto, S. A. (1985). A review of the use of self-control techniques in the treatment of alcohol abuse. *Cognitive Therapy and Research, 9*, 235–251.

Carmack, M. A., & Mertens, R. (1979). Measuring commitment to running: A survey of runners' attitudes and mental states. *Journal of Sport Psychology, 1*, 25–42.

Carmody, T. P., Senner, J. W., Malinow, M. R., & Matarazzo, J. D. (1980). Physical exercise rehabilitation: Long-term dropout rate in cardiac patients. *Journal of Behavioral Medicine, 3*, 163–168.

Carnegie, D. (1948). *How to stop worrying and start living*. New York: Simon & Schuster.

Carney, R. M., Rich, M. W., & Teveldea, A. (1987). Major depressive disorder in coronary artery disease. *American Journal of Cardiology, 60*, 1273–1275.

Carpenter, C. C. J., Mayer, K. H., Fisher, A., Desai, M. B., & Durand, L. (1989). Natural history of AIDS in women in Rhode Island. *American Journal of Medicine, 86*, 771–781.

Carter, W. R., Gonder-Frederick, L. A., Cox, D. J., Clarke, W. L., & Scott, D. (1985). Effects of stress on blood glucose in IDDM. *Diabetes Care, 8*, 411–412.

Casperson, C. J., Christenson, G. M., & Pollard, R. A. (1986). Status of the 1990 physical fitness and exercise objectives—Evidence from NHIS 1985. *Public Health Report, 101,* 587–592.

Cassileth, B. R., Lisk, E. J., Miller, D. S., Brown, L. L., & Miller, C. (1985). Psychosocial correlates of survival in advanced malignant disease? *New England Journal of Medicine, 312,* 1551–1555.

Cella, D. F., Orofiamma, B., Holland, J. C., Silberfarb, P. M., Tross, S., Feldstein, M., Perry, M., Maurer, L. H., Comis, R., & Oraz, E. J. (1987). The relationship of psychological distress, extent of disease, and performance status in patients with lung cancer. *Cancer, 60,* 1661–1667.

Center for the Advancement of Health. (1996). *Indexed bibliography on self-management for people with chronic disease.* Washington, DC: Author.

Centers for Disease Control. (1987, March 2). *AIDS weekly surveillance report.* Atlanta, GA: Author.

Centers for Disease Control. (1990). Risk behavior for HIV transmission among IV DUs not in drug treatment-limited states. *Morbidity and Mortality Weekly Report, 39,* 273–276.

Centers for Disease Control. (December 1991). *HIV/AIDS surveillance report (through November 30, 1991).* Atlanta, GA: Author.

Centers for Disease Control. (1992). *HIV/AIDS surveillance report, July, 1992.* Atlanta GA: Author.

Centers for Disease Control and Prevention. (1995). Diabetes Fact Sheet. Available on Internet: http://www.cdc.gov/nccdphp/ddt/facts.htm

Centers for Disease Control and Prevention. (1998). Trends in the HIV and AIDS epidemic, 1998. Available on Internet: http://www.cdcnpin.org/geneva 98/trends/start.htm#turn

Centers for Disease Control and Public Health Service. (April 1993). *HIV/AIDS surveillance.* Atlanta, GA: Author.

Chadwick, O., Yule, W., & Anderson, R. (1990). The examination attainments of secondary school pupils who use solvents. *British Journal of Educational Psychology, 60* (Part 2), 180–191.

Chandra, R. K., & Newberne, P. M. (1977). *Nutrition, immunity, and infection: Mechanisms of interactions.* New York: Plenum.

Chin, J. (1990). Current and future dimensions of the HIV/pandemic in women and children. *Lancet, 336,* 221–224.

Christoff, K. A., & Kelly, J. A. (1985). A behavioral approach to social skills training. In L. L. Abate & M. A. Milan (Eds.), *Handbook of social skills training and research* (pp. 361–387). New York: John Wiley.

Clarkson, T. B., Kaplan, J. R., Adams, M. R., & Manuck, S. B. (1987). Psychosocial influences on the pathogenesis of atherosclerosis among nonhuman primates. *Circulation, 76* (Suppl. 1), I-29–I-40.

Cloninger, C. R., Bohman, M., & Sigvardsson, S. (1981). Inheritance of alcohol abuse. *Archives of General Psychiatry, 38,* 861–868.

Cockburn, J., Gibberd, R. W., Reid, A. Z., & Sanson-Fisher, R. W. (1987). Determinants of non-compliance with short-term antibiotic regimens. *British Medical Journal, Clinical Research Edition, 295,* 814–818.

Cohen S., & McKay, G. (1984). Social support, stress, and the buffering hypothesis: A theoretical analysis. In A. Baum, S. E. Taylor, & J. E. Singer (Eds.), *Handbook of psychology and health*. Hillside, NJ: Erlbaum.

Cohen, S., & Wills, T. A. (1985). Stress, social support, and the buffering hypothesis. *Psychological Bulletin, 98*, 310–357.

Collins, R. L., Taylor, S. E., & Skokan, L. A. (1990). A better world or a shattered vision? Changes in perspectives following victimization. *Social Cognition, 8*, 263–285.

Cook, D. G., Shaper, A. G., Pocock, S. J., & Kussick, S. J. (1986). Giving up smoking and the risk of heart attacks: A report from the British Regional Study. *Lancet, 2*, 1376–1380.

Cooper, K. H. (1968). *Aerobics*. New York: Bantam Books.

Cooper, K. H., Pollock, M. L., Martin, R. P., White, S. R., Linnerud, A. C., & Jackson, A. (1976). Physical fitness levels vs. selected coronary risk factors. *Journal of the American Medical Association, 236*, 166–169.

Cousins, N. (1979). *Anatomy of an illness as perceived by the patient*. New York: W. W. Norton.

Cox, D. J., Gonder-Frederick, L. A., Julian D. M., Carter, W. R., & Clarke, W. L. (1989). Effects and correlation of blood glucose awareness training among patients with IDDM. *Diabetes Care, 12*, 313–318.

Cox, D. J., Gonder-Frederick, L. A., Julian, D. M., Cryer, P., Lee, J. H., Richards, F. E., & Clarke, W. (1991). Intensive versus standard blood glucose awareness training (BGAT) with insulin-dependent diabetes: Mechanisms and ancillary effects. *Psychosomatic Medicine, 53*, 453–462.

Cox, D. J., Irvine, A., Gonder-Frederick, L., Nowacek, G., & Butterfield, J. (1987). Fear of hypoglycemia: Quantification, validation, and utilization. *Diabetes Care, 10*, 617–621.

Crandall, R. C. (1986). *Running: The consequences*. Jefferson, NC: McFarland & Co.

Croog, S. H., & Levine, S. (1982). *Life after a heart attack: Social and psychological factors eight years later*. New York: Human Sciences Press.

Crossman, J., Jamieson, J., & Henderson, L. (1987). Response of competitive athletes to layoffs in training. Exercise addiction or psychological relief. *Journal of Sport Behavior, 10*, 28–37.

Cummings, C., Gordon, J. R., & Marlatt, G. A. Relapse: Prevention and prediction. (1980). In W. R. Miller (Ed.), *The addictive behaviors: Treatment of alcoholism, drug abuse, smoking, and obesity*. (pp. 291–321). Elmsford, NY: Pergamon Press.

Cummings, K. M., Emont, S. L., Jaen, C., & Sciandra, R. (1988). Format and quitting instructions as factors influencing the impact of a self-administered quit smoking program. *Health Education Quarterly, 15*, 199–216.

Cummings, P., & Psaty, B. M. (1994). The association between cholesterol and death from injury. *Annals of Internal Medicine, 120*, 848–855.

Curran, J. W., Jaffe, H. W., Hardy, A. M., Morgan, W. M., Selik, R. M., & Donders, T. J. (1988). The epidemiology of HIV infection and AIDS in the United States. *Science, 239*, 610–616.

Dark, K., Peeke, H. V., Ellman, G., & Salfi, M. (1987). Behaviorally conditioned histamine release. Prior stress and conditionability and extinction of the response. *Annals of the New York Academy of Sciences, 496*, 578–582.

Darwin, C. R. (1859). *On the origin of species by means of natural selection, or, the preservation of favored races in the struggle for life.* London: Murray.

Davis, C., Brewer, H., & Ratusny, D. (1993). Behavioral frequency and psychological commitment: Necessary concepts in the study of excessive exercise. *Journal of Behavioral Medicine, 16,* 611–628.

DCCT Research Group. (1990). Diabetes Control and Complications Trial (DCCT): Update. *Diabetic Care, 13,* 427–433.

DeClemente, C. C. (1981). Self-efficacy and smoking cessation maintenance: A preliminary report. *Cognitive Therapy and Research, 5,* 175–187.

Dembroski, T. M., MacDougall, J. M., Costa, P. T., & Grandits, G. A. (1989). Components of hostility as predictors of sudden death and myocardial infarction in the multiple risk factor intervention trial. *Psychosomatic Medicine, 51,* 514–522.

Despres, J. P., Moorjani, S., Lupien, P. J., Tremblay, A., & Modeau, A. (1990). Regional distribution of body fat plasma lipoprotein and cardiovascular disease. *Arteriosclerosis, 10,* 497–511.

Devlin, M. J., Walsh, B. T., Spitzer, R. L., & Hasin, D. (1992). Is there another binge eating disorder? A review of the literature on overeating in the absence of bulimia nervosa. *International Journal of Eating Disorders, 11,* 333–340.

Dews, P. B. (Ed.). (1984). *Caffeine.* New York: Springer-Verlag.

Dienstbier, R. A., LaGuardia, R. L., Barnes, M., Tharp, G., & Schmidt, R. (1987). Catecholamine training effects from exercise programs: A bridge to exercise-temperament relationships. *Motivation and Motivation, 11,* 297–318.

Dimatteo, M. R., Sherbourne, C. D., Hays, R. D., Ordway, L., Kravitz, R. L., McGlynn, E. A., Kaplan, S., & Rogers, W. H. (1993). Physicians' characteristics influence patients' adherence to medical treatment: Results from the Medical Outcomes Study. *Health Psychology, 12,* 93–102.

Dishman, R. K. (1986). Mental Health. In V. Seefeld (Ed.), *Physical activity and well being* (pp. 304–341). Reston, VA: American Association for Health, Physical Education, Recreation and Dance.

Dishman, R. K. (1990). Determinants of participation in physical activity. In M. C. Bouchard, R. J. Shephard, T. Sutton, & B. D. McPherson (Eds.), *Exercise, fitness and health* (pp. 75–101). Champaign, IL: Human Kinetics Publishers.

Doyne, E. J., Ossip-Klein, D. J., Bowman, E. D., Osbourn, K. M., McDougall-Wilson, I. B., & Neimeyer, R. A. (1987). Running versus weight lifting in the treatment of depression. *Journal of Consulting and Clinical Psychology, 55,* 748–754.

Duppert, P. M., Rappaport, N. B., & Martin, J. E. (1987). Exercise in cardiovascular disease. *Behavioral Modification, 11,* 329–347.

DuRant, R. W., Ashworth, C. S., Newman, C., & Rickert, V. I. (1994). Stability of the relationships between anabolic steroid use and multiple substance use among adolescents. *Journal of Adolescent Health, 15,* 111–116.

Ellis, A. (1962). *Reason and emotion in psychotherapy.* New York: Lyle Stewart.

Ellis, A., McInerney, J. F., DiGuiseppe, R., & Yeager R. J. (1988). *Rational-emotive therapy with alcoholics and substance abusers.* Elmsford, NY: Pergamon Press.

Emery, C. F., & Blumenthal, J. A. (1991). Effects of physical exercise on psychological and cognitive functioning of older adults. *Annals of Behavioral Medicine, 13,* 99–107.

Engel, G. L. (1977). The need for a new medical model: A challenge for biomedicine. *Science, 196,* 129–136.

Engel, G. L. (1980). The clinical application of the biopsychosocial model. *American Journal of Psychiatry, 137,* 535–544.

Epstein, L. H., Grunberg, N. E., Lichtenstein, E., & Evans, R. I. (1989). Smoking research: Basic research, interventions, prevention, and new trends. *Health Psychology, 8,* 705–721.

Epstein, L. H., Koeske, R., & Wing, R. R. (1984). Adherence to exercise in obese children. *Journal of Rehabilitation, 4,* 185–195.

Epstein, L. H., Wing, R. R., Penner, B. C., & Kress, M. J. (1985). Effect of diet and controlled exercise on weight loss in obese children. *Journal of Pediatrics, 107,* 358–361.

Estroff, T. W., & Gold, M. S. (1985–1986). Medical and psychiatric complications of cocaine abuse with possible points of pharmacological treatment. *Advances in Alcohol and Substance Abuse, 5,* 61–76.

The Expert Panel. (1988). Report of the National Cholesterol Education Program Expert Panel on detection, evaluation, and treatment of high blood cholesterol in adults. *Archives of Internal Medicine, 148,* 36–69.

Eysenck, M. H. (1973). Personality and the maintenance of the smoking habit. In W. L. Dunn (Ed.), *Smoking Behaviour: Motive and Incentives* (pp. 113–146). Washington, DC: Winston.

Fast facts. (June 1996). *Cancer Smart, 4,* 7.

Fawzy, F. I., Kemeny, M. E., Fawzy, N. W., Elashoff, R., Morton, D., Cousins, N., & Fahey, J. L. (1990). A structured psychiatric intervention for cancer patients: I. Changes over time in immunological measures. *Archives of General Psychiatry, 47,* 729–735.

Fehily, A., Phillips, K., & Yarnell, J. (1984). Diet, smoking, social class, and body mass index in the Caerphilly Heart Disease Study. *American Journal of Clinical Nutrition, 40,* 827–833.

Feinglos, M., & Surwit, R. (1988). *Behavior and Diabetes Mellitus.* Kalamazoo, MI: Upjohn Co.

Fetzer, J. N., Solt, P. F., & McKinney, S. (1985). Typology of food preferences identified by Nuti-Food sort. *Journal of the American Dietetic Association, 85,* 961–965.

Fiore, M. C., Novotny, T. E., Pierce, J. P., Hatziandreu, E. J., Patel, K. M., & Davis, R. M. (1989). Trends in cigarette smoking in the United States. *Journal of the American Medical Association, 261,* 49–55.

Fischl, M. A., Richman, D. D., Grieco, M. H., Gottleib, M. S., & Volberding, P. A. (1987). The efficacy of Azodothymidine (AZT) in the treatment of patients with AIDS and AIDS-related complex: A double-blind, placebo controlled trial. *New England Journal of Medicine, 317,* 185–191.

Folks, D. G., Blake, D. J., Freeman, A. M., Sokol, R. S., & Baker, D. M. (1988). Persistent depression in coronary bypass patients reporting sexual maladjustment. *Psychosomatics, 29,* 387–391.

Follick, M. J., Gorkin, L., Capone, R. J., Smith, T. W., Ahern, D. K., Stablein, D., Niaura, R., & Visco, J. (1988). Psychological distress as a predictor of ventricular arrhythmias in a post-myocardial infarction population. *American Heart Journal, 116,* 32–36.

Fortmann, S. P., Killen, J. D., Telch, M. J., & Newman, B. (1988). Minimal contact treatment for smoking cessation. A placebo controlled trial of nicotine polacrilex and self-directed relapse prevention: Initial results of the Stanford Stop Smoking Project. *Journal of the American Medical Association, 260,* 1575–1580.

Foster, G. D., Kendall, P. C., Wadden, T. A., Stunkard, A. J., & Vogt, R. A. (1996). Psychological effects of weight loss and regain: A prospective evaluation. *Journal of Consulting and Clinical Psychology, 64,* 752–757.

Frank, R. G., Umlauf, R. L., Wonderlich, S. A., & Ashkanazi, G. S. (1986). Hypnosis and behavioral treatment in a worksite smoking cessation program. *Addictive Behaviors, 11,* 59–62.

Frasure-Smith, N. (1994). Psychosocial factors and prognosis in established coronary heart disease: What do we know and what should we do? In R. B. Wilhams (Chair), *Psychological factors and prognosis in established coronary heart disease: What do we know and what should we do?* Symposium conducted at the Society of Behavioral Medicine's Fifteenth Anniversary Meeting, Boston, MA.

Frasure-Smith, N., Lesperance, F., & Talajic, M. (1993). Depression following myocardial infarction. *Journal of the American Medical Association, 270,* 1819–1825.

Freidman, M., & Rosenman, R. H. (1974). *Type A behavior and your heart.* New York: Alfred A. Knopf.

Freud, A. (1965). Normality and pathology in childhood: *Vol. 6 of the Writings of Anna Freud.* New York: International Universities Press.

Friedl, K. E. (1993). Effects of anabolic steroids on physical health. In C. E. Yesalis (Ed.), *Anabolic steroids in sport and exercise* (pp. 107–150). Champaign, IL: Human Kinetics Publishers.

Friedland, G. M., Saltzman, G., Vileno, J., Freeman, K., Schragees, L. K., & Klein, R. S. (1991). Survival differences in patients with AIDS. *Journal of Acquired Immune Deficiency Syndromes, 4,* 144–153.

Friedman, H. S., & Booth-Kewley, S. (1988). Validity of the type A construct: A reprise. *Psychological Bulletin, 104,* 381–384.

Friedman, M., Thoresen, C. E., Gill, J. J., Powell, L. H., Ulmer, D., Thompson, L., Price, V. A., Rabin, D. D., Breall, W. S., Dixon, T., Levy, R., & Bourg, E. (1984). Alteration of the Type A behavior and reduction in cardiac recurrences in postmyocardial infarction patients. *American Heart Journal, 108,* 237–248.

Friedman, M., Thoresen, C. E., Gill, J. J., Ulmer, D., Powell, L. H., Price, V. A., Brown, B., Thompson, L., Rabin, D., Breall, W. S., Bourg, E., Levy, R., & Dixon, T. (1986). Alteration of Type A behavior and its effect on cardiac recurrences in postmyocardial infarction patients. Summary results of the recurrent coronary prevention project. *American Heart Journal, 112,* 653–665.

Funk, S. C., & Houston, B. K. (1987). A critical analysis of the hardiness scale's validity and utility. *Journal of Personality and Social Psychology, 53,* 572–578.

Gardner, E. L., & Lowinson, J. H. (1991). Marijuana's interaction with brain reward systems: Update. *Pharmacology, Biochemistry & Behavior, 40,* 571–580.

Gawin, F. W. (1991). Cocaine addiction: Psychology and neurophysiology. *Science, 199,* 1580–1586.

Gawin, F. W., & Ellenwood, E. H. (1988). Cocaine and other stimulants: Actions, abuse, and treatment. *New England Journal of Medicine, 318,* 1173–1182.

Ghanadian, R., Puah, K. M., & O'Donoghue, E. P. M. (1979). Serum testosterone and dihydrotestosterone in carcinoma of the prostate. *British Journal of Cancer, 39,* 696–699.

Gillespie, C. (1991). Optimizing blood glucose monitoring. In C. Bradley, P. Home, & M. Christie (Eds.), *The technology of diabetes care: Converging medical and psychosocial perspectives* (pp. 49–56). New York: Harwood Academic Publishers.

Gillman, M. W., Cupples, L. A., Millen, B. E., Ellison, R. C., & Wolf, P. A. (1997). Inverse association of dietary fat with development of ischemic stroke in men. *Journal of the American Medical Association, 278,* 2145–2150.

Girdano, D. A., Everly, G. S., & Dusek, D. E. (1990). *Controlling stress and tension* (3rd ed.). Englewood Cliffs, NJ: Prentice-Hall.

Glass, D. C. (1989). Psychology and health: Obstacles and opportunities. *Journal of Applied Social Psychology, 19,* 1145–1163.

Glasser, W. (1976). *Positive addiction.* New York: Harper & Row.

Glassman, A. H., & Shapiro, P. A. Depression and the courses of coronary artery disease. *American Journal of Psychiatry, 155,* 4–11.

Goedert, J. J., Duliege, A. M., Amos, C. I., Felton, S., & Biggar, R. J. (1991). High risk of HIV-1 infection for first-born twins. The International Registry of HIV-exposed twins. *Lancet, 338,* 1471–1475.

Goetsch, V. L., VanDorsten, B., Pbert, L. A., Ulrich, I., et al. (1993). Acute effects of laboratory stress on blood glucose in noninsulin-dependent diabetes. *Psychosomatic Medicine, 55,* 492–496.

Gold, M. S. (1993). Opiate addiction and the locus coeruleus: The clinical utility of Clonidine, Naltrexone, Methadone, and Buprenorphine. *Psychiatric Clinics of North America, 16,* 65.

Goldman, F. M., & Kennedy, B. J. (1979). Group counseling in adult patients with advanced cancer. *Cancer, 43,* 760.

Gonder-Frederick, L. A., Carter, W. R., Cox, D. J., & Clarke, W. L. (1990). Environmental stress and blood glucose change in insulin-dependent diabetes mellitus. *Health Psychology, 9,* 503–515.

Gorczynski, R. M., Macrae, S., & Kennedy, M., (1982). Conditioned immune response associated with allogeneic skin graphs in mice. *Journal of Immunology, 129,* 704–709.

Gordon, T., Kannel, W. B., Dawber, T. R., & McGee, D. (1975). Changes associated with cigarette smoking: The Framingham study. *American Heart Journal, 90,* 322–328.

Gordon, W. A., Friedenbergs, I., Diller, L., Hibbard, M., Wolf, C., Levine, L., Lipkins, R., Ezrachi, O., & Lucido, O. (1980). Efficacy of psychosocial investigation with cancer patients. *Journal of Consulting and Clinical Psychology, 48,* 743–759.

Gorkin, L. (1994). Psychosocial factors and prognosis in established coronary heart disease: What do we know and what should we do? In R. B. William (Chair), *Psychosocial factors and prognosis in established coronary heart disease: What do we know and what should we do?* Symposium conducted at the Society of Behavioral Medicine's Fifteenth Anniversary Meeting, Boston, MA.

Greene, W. C. (September 1993). AIDS and the immune system. *Scientific American, 269*, 99–105.

Greenwald, H. P. (1992). *Who survives cancer?* Berkeley: University of California Press.

Grey, G. P., Bergfors, R., Levin, R., & Levine, S. (1978). Comparison of the effects of restricted morning or evening water intake on adrenocortical activity in female rats. *Neuroendocrinology, 25*, 236–246.

Griest, J. H., Klein, M. H., Eischens, R. R., Faris, J. T. Gurman, A. S., & Morgan, W. P. (1981). Running through your mind. In M. H. Sacks & M. L. Sachs (Eds.), *Psychology of running*. Champaign, IL: Human Kinetics Publishers.

Grilly, D. M. (1989). *Drugs and human behavior*. Needham Heights, MA: Allyn & Bacon.

Gruber, B. L., Hall, N. R., Hersh, S. P., & DuBois, P. (1988). Immune system and psychosocial changes in metastatic cancer patients using relaxation and guided imagery: A pilot study. *Scandinavian Journal of Behavior Therapy, 17*, 25–46.

Haan, N. (1969). A tripartite model of ego functioning: Values and clinical research applications. *Journal of Nervous and Mental Disease, 148*, 14–30.

Hackett, G., & Horan, J. J. (1979). Partial component analysis of a comprehensive smoking program. *Addictive Behaviors, 4*, 259–262.

Hall, S. M., Tunstall, C., Rugg, D., Jones, R. T., & Benowitz, N. (1985). Nicotine gum and behavioral treatment in smoking cessation. *Journal of Consulting and Clinical Psychology, 53*, 256–258.

Hamburg, M. A., & Fauci, A. S. (1990). HIV infection and AIDS: Challenges to biomedical research. In L. O. Gostin (Ed.), *AIDS and the health care system* (pp. 171–182). New Haven, CT: Yale University Press.

Hamm, P., Shekelle, R. B., & Stamler, J. (1989). Large fluctuations in body weight during young adulthood and 25 year risk of coronary heart disease in men. *American Journal of Epidemiology, 129*, 312–318.

Harlow, H. F., & Zimmerman, R. R. (1959). Affectional responses in the infant monkey. *Science, 130*, 421–432.

Hasin, D., Grant, B., & Endicott, J. (1990). The natural history of alcohol abuse: Implications for definitions of alcohol use disorders. *American Journal of Psychiatry, 147*, 1537–1541.

Haste, F. M., Brooke, O. G., Anderson, H. R., Bland, J. M., Shaw, A., Griffin, J., & Peacock, J. L. (1990). Nutrient intakes during pregnancy: Observations on the influence of smoking and social class. *American Journal of Clinical Nutrition, 51*, 29–36.

Havel, R. J., and Goldstein, A. (1959). The role of sympathetic nervous system in the metabolism of free fatty acids. *Journal of Lipid Research, 1*, 102–108.

Heather, N., & Robertson, I. (1983). *Controlled drinking* (Rev. ed.). London: Methuen.

Helgeson, V. S. (1993). Two important distinctions in social support: Kind of support and perceived versus received. *Journal of Applied Social Psychology, 23,* 825–845.

Hembree, W. C., Nahas, G. G., Zeidenberg, P., & Huang, H. F. S. (1979). Changes in human spermatozoa associated with high dose marijuana-smoking. In G. G. Nahas & W. D. Paton (Eds.), *Marijuana: Biological effects* (pp. 429–439). Elmsford, NY: Pergamon Press.

Henderson, B. E., Ross, R. K., & Bernstein, L. (1988). Estrogen as a cause of human cancer: The Richard and Hilda Rosenthal Foundation Award Lecture. *Cancer Research, 48,* 246–263.

Herbert, T. B., & Cohen, S. (1993). Stress and immunity in humans: A meta-analytic review. *Psychosomatic Medicine, 55,* 364–379.

Herd, D. (1989). The epidemiology of drinking patterns and alcohol-related problems among U.S. blacks. In *Alcohol use among U.S. ethnic minorities.* National Institute on Alcohol Abuse and Alcoholism Research Monograph No. 18 (DHHS Publication No. ADM 89–1435). Washington, DC: U.S. Government Printing Office.

Herman, C. P., & Mack, D. (1975). Restrained and unrestrained eating. *Journal of Personality, 43,* 647–660.

Herzog, D. B., Keller, M. B., Lavori, P. W., Kenny, G. M., & Sacks, N. R. (1992). The prevalance of personality disorders in 210 women with eating disorders. *Journal of Clinical Psychiatry, 53,* 147–152.

Hill, R. D., Storandt, M., & Malley, M. (1993). The impact of long-term exercise training on psychological function in older adults. *Journal of Gerontology, 48,* 12–17.

Hillbrand, M., Spitz, R. T., & Foster, H. G. (1995). Serum cholesterol and aggression in hospitalized male forensic patients. *Journal of Behavioral Medicine, 18,* 33–43.

Hinkle, L. E., & Wolfe, S. (1942). Importance of life stress in course and management of Diabetes Mellitus. *Journal of the American Medical Association, 148,* 513–520.

Hoebel, B. G., & Tietelbaum, P. (1966). Weight regulation in normal and hypothalamic hyperphagic rats. *Journal of Comparative and Physiological Psychology, 61,* 189–193.

Hole, J. W. (1993). *Human Anatomy and Physiology* (6th ed.). Madison, WI: Brown & Benchmark.

Hooker, W. D., & Jones, R. T. (1987). Increased susceptibility to memory intrusions and the Stroop interference effect during acute marijuana intoxication. *Psychopharmacology, 91,* 20–24.

House, J. S., Landis, K. R., & Umberson, D. (1988). Social relationships and health. *Science, 241,* 540–545.

Howe, A. (1996). "I know what to do, but it's not possible to do it"—general practitioners' perceptions of their ability to detect psychological distress. *Family Practice, 13:2,* 127–132.

Hsu, L. K. G. (1990). *Eating disorders.* New York: Guilford Press.

Human Capital Initiative Coordinating Committee. (1996). *Human Capital Initiative—Report 4. Doing the Right Thing: A Research Plan for Healthy Living.* Washington, DC: American Psychological Society.

Husain, M. M., Black, K. J., Doraiswamy, P. M., Shah, S. A., Rockwell, W. J. K., Ellinwood, E. H., & Krishnan, K. R. R. (1992). Subcortical brain anatomy in anorexia and bulimia. *Biological Psychology, 31,* 735–738.

Ickovics, J. R., & Rodin, J. (1992). Women and AIDS in the United States: Epidemiology, natural history, and mediating mechanisms. *Health Psychology, 11,* 1–16.

Imam, N., Carpenter, C. C. J., Mayer, K. H., Fisher, A., Stein, M., & Danforth, S. B. (1990). Hierarchical pattern of mucosal candida infections in HIV-seropositive women. *American Journal of Medicine, 89,* 142–146.

Istvan, J., & Matarazzo, J. D. (1984). Tobacco, alcohol and caffeine use: A review of their interrelationships. *Psychological Bulletin, 95,* 301–326.

Jacobs, D. (1987). Cost-effectiveness of specialized psychological programs for reducing hospital stays and outpatient visits. *Journal of Clinical Psychology, 13,* 397–403.

Jacobs, D. R. (1992). Correlates of obesity in young black and white women: The CARDIA Study. *American Journal of Public Health, 82,* 1621–1625.

Jacobson, E. (1929). *Progressive relaxation.* Chicago: University of Chicago Press.

Jacoby, R. (1993). The miserable hath no other medicine, but only hope: Some conceptual considerations on hope and stress. *Psychology of Stress, 9,* 61–69.

Jaffe, J. H. (1980). Drug addiction and drug abuse. In A. G. Gilman, L. S. Goodman, & A. G. Gilman (Eds.), *The pharmacological basis of therapeutics* (6th ed., pp. 150–175). New York: Macmillan.

Jaffe, L. R., Seehaus, M., Wagner, C., & Leadbeater, B. J., (1988). Anal intercourse and knowledge of acquired immunodeficiency syndrome among minority-group female adolescents. *Journal of Pediatrics, 112,* 1005–1087.

Jakubowski, P., & Lange, A. (1978). *The assertive option.* Champaign, IL: Research Press.

Jasnoski, M. L., & Kugler, J. (1987). Relaxation imagery and neuro-immunomodulation. *Annals of the New York Academy of Sciences, 496,* 722–738.

Jemmott, J. B., III, Jemmott, L. S., & Fong, G. T. (1992). Reductions in HIV risk-associated sexual behaviors among black adolescents: Effects of an AIDS prevention intervention. *American Journal of Public Health, 82,* 372–377.

Jemmott, L. S., & Jemmott, J. B., III (1990). Sexual knowledge attitudes and risky sexual behavior among inner-city black male adolescents. *Journal of Adolescent Research, 5,* 346–369.

Johnsgard, K. (1985). The motivation of the long-distance runner: I. *Journal of Sports Medicine, 25,* 135–139.

Julien, R. M. (1995). *A primer of drug action.* New York: W. H. Freeman & Co.

Kahn, H. S., Williamson, D. F., & Stevens, J. A. (1991). Race and weight change in US women: The roles of socioeconomic and marital status. *American Journal of Public Health, 81,* 319–323.

Kalichman, S. C., Kelly, J. A., Hunter, T. L., Murphy, D. A., & Tyler, R. (1993). Culturally tailored HIV-AIDS risk-reduction messages targeted to African-

American urban women: Impact on risk sensitization and risk reduction. *Journal of Consulting and Clinical Psychology, 61,* 291–295.

Kamin-Seigel, L., Rodin, J., Seligman, M. E. P., & Dwyer, J. (1991). Explanatory style and cell-mediated immunity in elderly men and women. *Health Psychology, 10,* 229–235.

Kannel, W. B. (1986). Epidemiologic insights into atherosclerotic cardiovascular disease from the Framingham Heart Study. In M. L. Pollock & D. H. Schmidt (Eds.), *Heart disease and rehabilitation* (2nd ed., pp. 3–27). New York: John Wiley.

Kaplan, H. I. (1975). Current psychodynamic concepts in psychosomatic medicine. In R. O. Pasnau (Ed.), *Consultation-liaison psychiatry.* New York: Grune & Stratton.

Kaplan, R. M., & Simon, H. J. (1990). Compliance in medical care: Reconsideration of self-predictions. *Annals of Behavioral Medicine, 12,* 66–71.

Karasek, R. A., Theorell, T. G., Schwartz, J. E., Pieper, C., & Alfredsson, L. (1982). Job, psychological factors and coronary heart disease: Swedish prospective findings and U.S. prevalence findings using a new occupational inference method. *Advances in Cardiology, 29,* 62–67.

Kaslow, R. A., Ostrow, D. G., Detels, R., Phair, J. P., Polk, B. F., & Rinaldo, C. R. (1987). The multicenter AIDS Cohort Study: Rationale, organization, and selected characteristics of the participants. *American Journal of Epidemiology, 126,* 310–318.

Kavanaugh, D. J., Gooley, S., & Wilson, P. H. (1993). Prediction of adherence and control in diabetes. *Journal of Behavioral Medicine, 16,* 509–522.

Keesey, R. E. (1980). A set-point analysis of the regulation of body weight. In A. J. Stunkard (Ed.), *Obesity* (pp. 144–163). Philadelphia: W. B. Saunders.

Kelly, J., St. Lawrence, J., Diaz, y., Stevenson, L., Hauth, A., Brasfield, T., Kalichman, S., Smith, J., & Andrew, M. (1991). HIV risk behavior reduction following intervention with key opinion leaders of a population: An experimental community level analysis. *American Journal of Public Health, 81,* 168–171.

Kelly, J. A., Murphy, D. A., Roffman, R. A., Solomon, L. J., Winett, R. A., Stevenson, L. Y., Koob, J. J., Ayotte, D. R., Flynn, B. S., Desiderats, L. L., Hauth, A. C., Lemke, A. L., Lombard, D., Morgan, M. G., Norman, A. D., Sikkema, K. J., Steiner, S., & Yaffe, D. M. (1992). Acquired immunodeficiency syndrome/human immunodeficiency virus risk behavior among gay men in small cities. *Archives of Internal Medicine, 152,* 2293–2297.

Kelly, J. A., Murphy, D. A., Sikkema, K. J., & Kalichman, S. C. (1993). Psychological interventions to prevent HIV infection are urgently needed. *American Psychologist, 48,* 1023–1034.

Kemmer, F., Bisping, R., Steingruber, H., Barr, H., Hardtmann, R., Schlaghecke, R., & Berger, M. (1984). Psychological stress and metabolic control in patients with type 1 Diabetes Mellitus. *New England Journal of Medicine, 314,* 1078–1084.

Kendall, P. C., & Hammen, C. (1995). *Abnormal psychology.* Boston: Houghton Mifflin.

Kennedy A., Gettys, T. W., Watson, P., Wallace, P., Ganaway, E., Pan, Q., & Garvey, W. T. (1997). The metabolic significance of leptin in humans:

Gender-based differences in relationship to adiposity, insulin sensitivity, and energy expenditure. *Journal of Clinical Endocrinology and Metabolism, 82 (4)*, 1293–1300.

Kennedy, S., Kiecolt-Glaser, J. K., & Glaser, R. (1988). Immunological consequences of acute and chronic stressors: mediating role of interpersonal relationships. *British Journal of Medical Psychology, 61* (Part 1), 77–85.

Kenyon, G. S. (1968). Conceptual models for characterizing physical activity. *Research Quarterly, 39*, 96–105.

Kerner, K. (1988). Current topics in inhalant abuse. In R. A. Crider & B. A. Rouse (Eds.), *Epidemiology of inhalant use. An update* (NIDA Research Monograph 85, pp. 8–29). Washington, DC: U.S. Department of Health and Human Services.

Keys, A. (Ed.). (1970). Coronary heart disease in seven countries. *Circulation, 4* (Suppl. 1), 1–112.

Keys, A., Anderson, J. T., & Grande, F. (1965). Serum cholesterol response to changes in the diet. II. The effect of cholesterol in the diet. *Metabolism, 14*, 759.

Keys, A. J., Brozek, J. A., Henschel, A., Michelson, O., & Taylor, H. L. (1950). *The biology of human starvation*. Minneapolis: University of Minnesota Press.

Kiecolt-Glaser, J., Dura, J., Speicher, C., Trask, J., & Glaser, R. (1991). Spousal caregivers of dementia victims: Longitudinal changes in immunity and health. *Psychosomatic Medicine, 53*, 345–362.

Kiecolt-Glaser, J. K., Fisher, L. D., Ogrocki, P., Stout, J. C., Speicher, C. E., & Glaser, R. (1987). Marital quality, marital disruption, and immune function. *Psychosomatic Medicine, 49*, 13–34.

Kiecolt-Glaser, J. K., Garner, W., Speicher, C., Penn, G. M., Holliday, J., & Glaser, R. (1984). Psychosocial modifiers of immunocompetence in medical students. *Psychosomatic Medicine, 46*, 7–14.

Kiecolt-Glaser, J. K., & Glaser, R. (1992). Psychoneuroimmunology: Can psychological interventions modulate immunity? *Journal of Consulting and Clinical Psychology, 60*, 569–575.

Kiecolt-Glaser, J. K., Glaser, R., Williger, D., Stout, J., Messick, G., Sheppard, S., Ricker, D., Romisher, S. C., Briner, W., Bonnell, G., & Donnerberg, R. (1985). Psychosocial enhancement of immunocompetence in a geriatric population. *Health Psychology, 4*, 25–41.

Kiecolt-Glaser, J. K., & Greenberg, B. (1984). Social support as a moderator of the after effects of stress in female psychiatric inpatients. *Journal of Abnormal Psychology, 33*, 192–199.

King, A. C., Haskell, W. L., Taylor, C. B., Kraemer, H. C., & DeBusk, R. F. (1991). Group-versus home-based exercise training in healthy older men and women: A community-based clinical trial. *Journal of the American Medical Association, 266*, 1535–1542.

King, A. C., Taylor, C. B., Haskell, W. L., & DeBusk, R. F. (1989). Influence of regular aerobic exercise on psychological health: A randomized, controlled trail of healthy middle-aged adults. *Health Psychology, 8*, 305–324.

Klesges, R. C., Eck, L. H., Clark, E. M., Meyers, A. W., & Hanson, C. L. (1990). The effects of smoking cessation and gender on dietary intake, physical activity, and weight gain. *International Journal of Eating Disorders, 9*, 435–445.

Klesges, R. C., & Klesges, L. M. (1988). Cigarette smoking as a weight loss strategy in a university population. *International Journal of Eating Disorders, 7*, 413–419.

Klesges, R. C., Meyers, A. W., Klesges, L. M., & Lavasque, M. E. (1989). Smoking, body weight and their effects on smoking behavior: A comprehensive review of the literature. *Psychological Bulletin, 106*, 204–230.

Kobasa, S. C. (1979). Stressful life events, personality and health: An inquiry into hardiness. *Journal of Personality and Social Psychology, 37*, 1–11.

Kobasa, S. C., & Maddi, S. R. (1977). Existential personality theory. In R. Corsini (Ed.), *Current Personality Theories* (pp. 242–276). Itasca, IL: Peacock.

Kobasa, S. C., Maddi, S. R., & Courington, S. (1981). Personality and constitution as mediators in the stress-illness relationship. *Journal of Health and Social Behavior, 22*, 368–378.

Kramsch, D. M., Aspen, A. J., Abramowitz, B. M., & Hood, W. B., Jr. (1981). Reduction of coronary atherosclerosis by moderate conditioning exercise in monkeys on an atherogenic diet. *New England Journal of Medicine, 305*, 1483–1489.

Krantz, D. S., Contrada, R. J., Hill, R. O., & Friedler, E. (1988). Environmental stress and biobehavioral antecedents of coronary heart disease. *Journal of Consulting and Clinical Psychology, 56*, 333–341.

Kristensen, P., Judge, M., Thim, L., Ribel, U., Christjansen, K., Wulff, B., Clausen, J., Jensen, P., Madsen, O., Vrang, N., Larsen, P., & Hastrup, S. (1998). Hypothalamic CART is a new anorectic peptide regulated by leptin. *Nature, 393*, 72–76.

Kruse, M. S., & Calden, M. E. (1986). Compliance to a clinically prescribed exercise program. *Fitness in Business, 1*, 57–61.

Kupecz, D., & Prochazka, A. (1996). A comparison of nicotine delivery systems in a multimodality smoking cessation program. *Nurse Practitioner, 21*, 73.

Lammers, C. A., Naliboff, B. D., & Straatmeyer, A. J. (1984). The effects of progressive relaxation on stress and diabetes control. *Behavioral Research and Therapy, 22*, 641–650.

Langer, E. J., & Roden, J. (1976). The effects of choice and enhanced personal responsibility for the aged: A field experiment in an institutional setting. *Journal of Personality and Social Psychology, 34*, 191–198.

LaRosa, J. (1997). Triglycerides and coronary risk in women and the elderly. *Archives of Internal Medicine, 157*, 961–968.

Larsen, J. (1998). Fad diets. Available on Internet: http://www.dietitian.com/faddiet.html

Larson, D. E. (Ed.) (1990). *Mayo Clinic family health book.* New York: William Morrow & Co.

Lazarus, R. S. (1971). The concepts of stress and disease. In L. Levi (Ed.), *Society, stress and disease: The psychosocial environment and psychosomatic disease: Vol 1* (pp. 53–58). London: Oxford University Press.

Lazarus, R. S. (1991). Progress on a cognitive-motivational-relational theory of emotion. *American Psychologist, 46*, 819–834.

Lazarus, R. S. (1993). Coping theory and research: Past, present, and future. *Psychosomatic Medicine, 55 (3)*, 234–247.

Lazurus, R. S., & Folkman, S. (1984). *Stress, appraisal and coping.* New York: Springer.

Lee, C. (1993). Factors related to the adoption of exercise among older women. *Journal of Behavioral Medicine, 16*, 328–334.

Leon, A. S. (1972). Comparative cardiovascular adaptation to exercise in animals and man and its relevance to coronary heart disease. In C. M. Bloor (Ed.), *Comparative pathophysiology of circulatory disorders* (pp. 143–174). New York: Plenum.

Leon, A. S. (1987). Age and other predictors of coronary heart disease. *Medicine and Science in Sports and Exercise, 19*, 159–167.

Leon, A. S., & Connett, J. (1991). Physical activity and 10.5 year mortality in the Multiple Risk Factor Intervention Trial (MRFIT). *International Journal of Epidemiology, 20*, 690–697.

Leon, A. S., Connett, J., Jacobs, D. R., Jr., & Rauramaa, R. (1987). Leisure-time physical activity and risk of coronary heart disease and death: The MRFIT. *Journal of the American Medical Association, 258*, 2388–2395.

LeShan, L. (1977). *You can fight for life: Emotional factors in the causation of cancer.* New York: M. Evans.

Levine, S., & Coe, C. L. (1989). Endocrine regeneration. In S. Cheron (Ed.), *Psychosomatic medicine: Theory physiology and practice: Vol. 1* (pp. 331–381). Madison, CT: International Universities Press.

Levy, S. M., Herberman, R. B., Lippman, M., D'Angelo, T., & Lee, J. (1991). Immunological and psychosocial predictors of disease recurrence in patients with early stage breast cancer. *Behavioral Medicine*, Summer, 67–75.

Lew, E. A., & Garfinkle, L. (1979). Variations in mortality by weight among 150,000 men and women. *Journal of Chronic Diseases, 32*, 563–576.

Lewis, B. S., & Lynch, W. D. (1993). The effect of physician advice on exercise behavior. *Preventive Medicine, 22*, 110–121.

Lewis, D. K., & Watters, J. K. (1991). Sexual risk behavior among heterosexual intravenous drug users ethnic and gender variations. *AIDS, 5*, 77–83.

Lichtenstein, E., & Brown, R. A. Smoking cessation methods: Review and recommendations. (1980). In W. R. Miller (Ed.), *The addictive behaviors: Treatment of alcoholism, drug abuse, smoking, and obesity* (pp. 169–206). New York: Pergamon Press.

Linden, W., Stossel, C., & Maurice, J. (1996). Psychological interventions for patients with coronary artery disease: A meta-analysis. *Archives of Internal Medicine, 156*, 745–752.

Lipkus, I. M., Barefoot, J. C., William, R. B., & Siegler, I. C. (1994). Personality measures as predictors of smoking initiation and cessation in the UNC Alumni Heart Study. *Health Psychology, 13*, 149–155.

Lissau-Lund-Sorensen, I., & Sorensen, T. L. I. (1992). Prospective study of the influence of social factors in childhood on risk of overweight in young adulthood. *International Journal of Obesity, 16*, 169–175.

Lissner, L., Odell, P. M., D'Agostino, R. B., Stokes, J., Kreger, B. E., Belanger, A. J., & Brownell, K. D. (1991). Variability of weight and health outcomes in the Framingham population. *New England Journal of Medicine, 324*, 1839–1844.

Lori, C. F., Lori, G. T., & Buchwald, K. W. (1990). The mechanism of epinephrine action vs. changes in blood sugar, lactic acid, and blood pressure during continuous intravenous injection of epinephrine. *American Journal of Physiology, 93,* 273–283.

MacDonald, P. C., Edman, C. D., Hemsell, D. C., Porter, J. C., & Siiteri, P. K. (1978). Androstenedione to estrone in premenopausal women with and without endometrial cancer. *American Journal of Obstetrics and Gynecology, 130,* 563–576.

MacQueen, G., Marshall, J., Perdue, M., Siegel, S., & Bienenstock, J. (1989). Pavlovian conditioning of rat mucosal mast cells to secrete rat mast cell protease II. *Science, 243,* 83–85.

Mahoney, M. J. (1977). Cognitive therapy and research: A question of questions. *Cognitive Therapy and Research, 1,* 1–3.

Mann, J. (1992, June). *AIDS in the world 1992: A global epidemic out of control?* (Report of the Global AIDS Policy Coalition). Cambridge, MA: Harvard University School of Public Health.

Manuck, S. B., Kaplan, J. R., & Clarkson, T. B. (1983). Social stability and coronary artery atherosclerosis in cynomolgus monkeys. *Neuroscience and Biobehavioral Review, 7,* 485–491.

Manuck, S. B., Muldoon, M. F., Kaplan, J. R., Adams, M. R., & Polefron, J. M. (1989). Coronary artery atherosclerosis and cardiac response to stress in cynomulgus monkeys. In A. W. Siegman & T. M. Dembroski (Eds.), *In search of coronary prone behavior* (pp. 207–227). Hillsdale, NJ: Lawrence Erlbaum Associates.

Margolis, S., & Achuff, S. C. (1998). *Coronary heart disease.* The Johns Hopkins White Papers. Baltimore, MD: The Johns Hopkins Medical Institutions.

Margolis, S., & Goldschmidt-Clermont, P. J. (1994). *Coronary heart disease.* The Johns Hopkins White Papers. Baltimore, MD: The Johns Hopkins Medical Institutions.

Marlatt, G. A. (1985). Relapse prevention: Theoretical rationale and overview of the model. In G. A. Marlatt & J. R. Gordon (Eds.), *Relapse prevention* (pp. 3–70). New York: Guilford.

Mason, J. W. (1971). A re-evaluation of the concept of non-specificity in stress theory. *Journal of Psychiatric Research, 8,* 323–333.

Matarazzo, J. D. (1980). Behavioral health and behavioral medicine: Frontiers for a new health psychology. *American Psychologist, 35,* 807–817.

May, G. S., Eberlein, K. A., & Furberg, C. D. (1982). Secondary prevention after myocardial infarction: A review of long-term trials. *Progress in Cardiovascular Disease, 24,* 331–351.

Mayne, S. T., Janerich, D. T., Greenwald, P., Chorost, S., Tucci, C., Zaman, M. B., Melmed, M. R., Kiely, M., & McKneally, M. F. (1994). Dietary betacarotene and lung cancer risk in U.S. nonsmokers. *Journal of the National Cancer Institute, 86,* 33–38.

Mayou, R. (1981). Effectiveness of cardiac rehabilitation. *Journal of Psychosomatic Research, 25,* 423–427.

McCann, I. L., & Holmes, D. S. (1984). Influence of aerobic exercise on depression. *Journal of Personality and Social Psychology, 46,* 1142–1147.

McCaul, K. D., Glasgow, R. E., & Schefer, L. C. (1987). Diabetes regimen behaviors: Predicting adherence. *Medical Care, 25,* 868–881.

McCray, E., & Onorato, I. M. (1992). Sentinel surveillance of human immunodeficiency virus infection in sexually-transmitted disease clinics in the United States. *Sexually Transmitted Diseases, 19,* 235–241.

McCullagh, P., North, T. C., & Mood, D. (1988). *Exercise as a treatment for depression: A meta-analysis.* Paper presented at the meeting of the North American Society for the Psychology of Sport and Physical Activity, Knoxville, TN.

McGrady, A., Graham, G., & Bailey, B. (1996). Biofeedback-assisted relaxation in insulin-dependent diabetes: A replication and extension study. *Annals of Behavioral Medicine, 18,* 185–189.

McGue, M., Pickens, R. W., & Svikis, D. S. (1992). Sex and age effects on the inheritance of alcohol problems: A twin study. *Journal of Abnormal Psychology, 101,* 3–17.

Meyerowitz, W., & Jaramillo, J. D. C. (1992). Antidepressant treatment and weight loss. *Current Therapeutic Research, 52,* 169–174.

Miley, W. (1989). Reduction of blood glucose levels in chronically ill Type 2 diabetics by brief biofeedback-assisted relaxation training. *Rehabilitation Psychology, 34,* 17–24.

Miller, N. (1969). Learning of visceral and glandular responses. *Science, 163,* 434–445.

Miller, W. R., & Hester, R. K. (1980). Treating the problem drinker. Modern approaches. In W. R. Miller (Ed.), *The addictive behaviors: Treatment of alcoholism, drug abuse, smoking, and obesity* (pp. 11–141). Oxford, England: Pergamon Press.

Miller, W. R., & Sanchez, V. C. (1994). Motivating young adults for treatment and lifestyle change. In G. S. Howard & P. E. Nathan (Eds.), *Alcohol use and misuse by young adults* (pp. 55–81). Notre Dame, IN: University of Notre Dame Press.

Miller, W. R., Taylor, C. A., & West, J. C. (1980). Focused versus broad-spectrum behavior therapy for problem drinkers. *Journal of Consulting and Clinical Psychology, 48,* 590–601.

Morabia, A., & Wynder, E. L. (1990). Dietary habits of smokers, people who never smoked, and exsmokers. *American Journal of Clinical Nutrition, 52,* 933–937.

Morgan, C. L. (1894). *An introduction to comparative psychology.* London: E. Arnold.

Morgan, R. E., Palinkas, L. A., Barrett-Conner, E. L., & Wingard, D. L. Plasma cholesterol in older men. *Lancet, 341,* 75–79.

Morgan, W. P. (1979). Negative addiction in runners. *The Physician and Sports Medicine, 7(2),* 57–68.

Morgan, W. P. (1985). Affective beneficence of vigorous physical activity. *Medicine and Science in Sports and Exercise, 17,* 94–101.

Morris, J. N., Pollard, R., Everitt, M. G., Chave, S. P. W., & Semmence, A. M. (1980). Vigorous exercise in leisure-time: Protection against coronary heart disease. *Lancet, 2,* 1207–1210.

Muldoon, M. F., & Manuck, S. B. (1992). Health through cholesterol reduction: Are there unforeseen risks? *Annals of Behavioral Medicine, 14,* 101–108.

Murphy, J. M., Gatto, G. J., Waller, M. B., McBride, W. J., Lumeng, L., & Li, T. K.

(1986). Effects of scheduled access on ethanol intake by the alcohol pre-ferring P line of rats. *Alcohol, 3,* 331–336.

Nahas, G. G. (1984). Toxicology and pharmacology. In G. G. Nahas (Ed.), *Mari-juana in science and medicine* (pp. 109–246). New York: Raven Press.

Nakano, K. (1990). Effects of two self-control procedures modifying Type A be-havior. *Journal of Clinical Psychology, 16,* 652–657.

National Center on Addiction and Substance Abuse at Columbia University. (June 1996). Substance abuse and the American woman. Available on In-ternet: http://www.casacolumbia.org/pubs/jun96/womfor.htm

The National Diabetic Data Group. (1985). *Diabetes in America* (Publication No. 85–1468). Bethesda, MD: U.S. Department of Health and Human Services.

National Institute on Alcohol Abuse and Alcoholism. (1996). *Drinking and driving* (NIAAA Publication No. 31 PH362). Washington, DC: U.S. Department of Health and Human Services.

National Institute on Drug Abuse. (1991). *Anabolic steroids—A threat to body and mind* (DHHS Publication No. ADM 91–1810). Washington, DC: U.S. De-partment of Health and Human Services.

National Institute on Drug Abuse. (1994). *Inhalant abuse—its dangers are nothing to sniff at* (NIDA Research Report No. 94–3818). Washington, DC: U.S. Department of Health and Human Services.

National Institutes of Health Technology Assessment Conference Statement. (1992). *Methods for voluntary weight loss and control, March 30–April 1 1992.* National Institutes of Health, Office of Medical Applications of Research. Bethesda, MD: Author.

Neuman, P. A., & Halvorson, P. A. (1983). *Anorexia Nervosa and bulimia.* New York: Van Nostrand Reinhold.

Nisbett, R. E. (1970). Hunger, obesity, and the ventromedial hypothalamus. *Psy-chological Review, 79,* 433–453.

Noakes, T. D., Lionel, M. B., Opie, H., Rose, A. G., & Kleynhans, P. H. T. (1979). Autopsy-proved coronary atherosclerosis in marathon runners. *New En-gland Journal of Medicine, 301,* 86–89.

Noakes, T. D., & Opie, L. H. (1979). Marathon running and the heart: The South African experience. *American Heart Journal, 98,* 669–671.

North, T. C., & McCullagh, P. (1988). Aerobic and anaerobic exercise as a treat-ment for depression: A meta-analysis. Paper presented at the meeting of the Association of Applied Sport Psychology, Nashua, NH.

Novello, A. C. (1990). Surgeon General's Report on the health benefits of smoking cessation. *Public Health Reports, 105,* 545.

O'Connor, G. T., Buring, J. E, Yusuf, S., Goldhaven, S. Z., Olmstead, E. M., Paf-fenbarger, R. S., & Henneken, C. H. (1989). An overview of randomized trials of rehabilitation with exercise after myocardial infarction. *Circulation, 80,* 234–244.

Oldridge, N. B. (1982). Compliance and exercise in primary and secondary pre-vention of coronary heart disease: A review. *Preventive Medicine, 11,* 56–70.

Oldridge, N. B. (1986). Compliance with exercise programs. In M. L. Pollock & D. H. Schmidt (Eds.), *Heart disease and rehabilitation* (pp. 629–646). New York: John Wiley.

Oldridge, N. B., Wicks, J. R., Hanley, C. Sutton, J. R., & Jones, N. L. (1978). Non-compliance in an exercise rehabilitation program for men who have suffered a myocardial infarction. *Canadian Medical Association Journal, 118,* 361–364.

O'Leary, A. (1985). Self-efficacy and health. *Behavior Research and Therapy, 23,* 437–451.

Oliveros, S. C., Iruela, L. M., Caballero, L., & Baca, E. (1992). Fluoxitine-induced anorexia in a bulimic patient [letter to the editor]. *American Journal of Psychiatry, 149,* 1113–1114.

Olsen, E. (1982). Fitness report from the morgue. *Runner, 4,* 57–63.

Opie, L. H. (1975). Sudden death and sport. *Lancet, 1,* 263–266.

Ornish, D. (March 1996). *Master Lecture: Reversing Coronary Heart Disease.* The Fourth International Congress of Behavioral Medicine, Washington, DC.

Ornish, D., Brown, S. E., Scherwitz, L. W., Billings, J. H., Armstrong, W. T., Ports, T. A., McLanahan, S. M., Kirkeeide, R. L., Brand, R. J., & Gould, K. L. (1990). Can lifestyle changes reverse coronary heart disease? *Lancet, 336,* 129–133.

Ornish, D., Scherwitz, L. W., Doody, R. S., Kerten, D., McLanahan, S. M., Brown, S. E., DePurcy, G., Sonnemaker, R., Haynes, C., Lester, J., McAlister, G. K., Hall, R. J., Burdine, J. A., & Gotto, A. M. (1983). Effects of stress on management training and dietary changes in treating ischemic heart disease. *Journal of the American Medical Association, 249,* 54–60.

Overmeier, J. B., & Seligman, M. E. P. (1967). Effects of inescapable shock upon subsequent escape and avoidance learning. *Journal of Comparative and Physiological Psychology, 63,* 23–33.

Paffenbarger, R. S., Hyde, R. T., Wing, A. L., & Steinmetz, C. H. (1984). A natural history of athleticism and cardiovascular health. *Journal of the American Medical Association, 252,* 491–495.

Paffenbarger, R. S., Laughlin, M. E., Gima, A. S., & Black, R. A. (1970). Work activity of longshoremen as related to death from coronary heart disease and stroke. *New England Journal of Medicine, 282,* 1109–1113.

Paffenbarger, R. S., Wing, A. L., & Hyde, R. T. (1978). Physical activity as an index of heart attack risk in college alumni. *Amrican Journal of Epidemiology, 108,* 161–175.

Paffenbarger, R. S., Jr. (1986). Exercise in the primary prevention of coronary heart disease. In M. L. Pollock & D. Schmidt (Eds.), *Heart disease and rehabilitation* (pp. 349–367). New York: John Wiley.

Paffenbarger, R. S., Jr., & Hyde, R. F. (1984). Exercise in the prevention of coronary heart disease. *Preventive Medicine, 13,* 3–22.

Paffenbarger, R. S., Jr., Hyde, R. T., Wing, A. L., & Hsieh, C-C. (1986). Physical activity, all-cause mortality, and longevity of college alumni. *New England Journal of Medicine, 314,* 605–613.

Paganini-Hill, A., Chao, A., Ross, R. K., & Henderson, B. E. (1987). Vitamin A, beta-carotene, and risk of cancer: A prospective study. *Journal of the National Cancer Institute, 79,* 443–448.

Palmer, J. L., & McCulloch, D. K. (1991). Prediction and prevention of IDDM. *Diabetes, 40,* 943–947.

Pascual-Leone, A., Dhuna, A., & Allafullah, J. (1990). Cocaine-induced seizures. *Neurology, 40,* 404.

Pate, R. R., Pratt, M., Blair, S. N., Haskell, W. L., Macera, C. A., Bouchard, C., Buchner, D., Ettinger, W., Heath, G. W., King, A. C., et al. (1995). Physical activity and public health. *Journal of the American Medical Association, 273,* 402–407.

Patel, C., Marmot, M. G., & Terry, D. J. (1985). Trial of relaxation in reducing coronary risk: Four year follow-up. *British Medical Journal, 290,* 1103–1106.

Peavey, B. S., Lawlis, G. F., & Goven, A. (1985). Biofeedback-assisted relaxation: Effects on phagocytic capacity. *Biofeedback and Self-Regulation, 10,* 33–47.

Peel, S. (1992). Alcoholism, politics, and bureaucracy. The consensus against controlled drinking therapy in America. *Addictive Behavior, 17,* 83–93.

Pendry, M. L., Multsman, I. M., & West, L. J. (1982). Controlled drinking by alcoholics? New findings and a revaluation of a major affirmative study. *Science, 217,* 169–175.

Perkins, K. A. (1985). The synergistic effect of smoking and serum cholesterol on coronary heart disease. *Health Psychology, 4,* 337–360.

Perkins, K. A. (1992). Effects of tobacco smoking on caloric intake. *British Journal of Addiction, 87,* 193–205.

Peters, R. K., Cady, L. D., Bischoff, D. P., Bernstein, L., & Pike, M. C. (1983). Physical fitness and subsequent myocardial infarction in healthy workers. *Journal of the American Medical Association, 249,* 3052–3056.

Peterson, C., & Seligman, M. E. P. (1987). Explanatory style and illness. *Journal of Personality, 55,* 237–265.

Peterson, C., Seligman, M. E. P., & Vaillant, G. E. (1988). Pessimistic explanation style is a risk factor for physical illness: A thirty-five year longitudinal study. *Journal of Personality and Social Psychology, 55,* 23–27.

Pierce, J. P., Fiore, M. C., Novotny, T. E., Hatziandreu, E. J., & Davis, R. M. (1989). Trends in cigarette smoking in the United States: Educational differences are increasing. *Journal of the American Medical Association, 261,* 56–60.

Pinel, J. P. J. (1993). *Biopsychology.* Boston: Allyn & Bacon.

Pi-Sunyer, F. X. (1991). Health Implications of obesity. *American Journal of Clinical Nutrition, 53,* 404–413.

Polivy, J., Heatherton, T. F., & Herman, C. P. (1988). Self-esteem, restraint, and eating behavior. *Journal of Abnormal Psychology, 97,* 354–356.

Polivy, J., & Herman, C. P. (1983). *Breaking the diet habit: The natural weight alternative.* New York: Basic Books.

Polivy, J., & Herman, C. P. (1987). Diagnosis and treatment of normal eating. *Journal of Consulting and Clinical Psychology, 55,* 635–644.

Pollock, V. E., Volavka, J., Goodwin, D. W., Mednick, S. A., Gabrielli, W. F., Knop, J., & Schulsinger, F. (1983). The EEG after alcohol administration in men at risk for alcoholism. *Archives of General Psychiatry, 40,* 857–861.

Pomerleau, O. F., & Pomerleau, C. S. (1984). Neuroregulators and the reinforcement of smoking: Toward a biobehavioral explanation. *Neuroscience and Biobehavioral Reviews, 8,* 503–513.

Pope, H. G., & Katz, D. L. (1988). Affective and psychotic symptoms associated with anabolic steroid use. *American Journal of Psychiatry, 145,* 487–490.

Porgesz, B., Begleiter, H., Bihari, B., & Kissin, B. (1987). The N_2 component of the event-related brain potential in abstinent alcoholics. *Electroencephalography & Clinical Neurophysiology, 66,* 121–131.

Powell, K. E., Spain, K. G., Christenson, G. M., & Mollencamp, M. P. (1986). The status of the 1990 objectives for physical fitness and exercise. *Public Health Reports, 101,* 15–21.

Powley, T. L. Opsahl, C. A., Cox, J. E., & Weingarten, H. P. (1980). The role of the hypothalamus in energy homeostasis. In P. J. Morgane & J. A. Panksepp (Eds.), *Handbook of the Hypothalamus-3A: Behavioral studies of the hypothalamus* (pp. 211–298) New York: Marcel Dekker.

Preble, E. (1990). Impact of HIV/AIDS on African children. *Social Science and Medicine, 31,* 671–680.

Presley, C. A., & Meilman, P. W. (1992). *Alcohol and drugs on American college campuses: A report to college presidents.* Carbondale: Southern Illinois University.

Prosser, G., Carson, P., Philips, R., Gelson, A., Buch, N., Tucker, H., Neophytou, M., Lloyd, M., & Simpson, T. (1981). Morale in coronary patients following an exercise programme. *Journal of Psychosomatic Research, 25,* 587–593.

Quinn, T. C., Glasser, D., Cannon, R., Matuszak, D., Dunning, R., Kline, R., Campbell, C., Israel, E., Fanci, A., & Hook, E. (1988). Human immunodeficiency virus infection among patients attending clinics for sexually transmitted diseases. *New England Journal of Medicine, 318,* 197.

Quinn, T. C., Groseclose, S. L., Spense, M., Provost, V., & Hook, E. W. (1992). Evolution of the human immunodeficiency virus epidemic among patients attending sexually-transmitted disease clinics: A decade of experience. *Journal of Infectious Diseases, 165,* 541–544.

Rand, C. S. W., & Stunkard, A. J. (1983). Obesity and psychoanalysis: Treatment and four-year follow-up. *American Journal of Psychiatry, 140,* 1140–1144.

Ratliffe-Crain, J., & Baum, A. (1990). Individual differences and health: Gender, coping, and stress. In H. S. Friedman (Ed.), *Personality and disease* (pp. 226–253). New York: John Wiley.

Ray, O., & Ksir, C. (1993). *Drugs, society, and human behavior.* St. Louis: Mosby.

Rhoads, J. L., Wright, D. C., Redfield, R. R., & Burke, D. S., (1987). Chronic vaginal candidiasis in women with human immunodeficiency virus infection. *Journal of the American Medical Association, 257,* 3105–3107.

Rimm, E. B., & Masters, J. C. (1979). *Behavior therapy: Techniques and empirical findings* (2nd ed). New York: Academic Press.

Robbins, J. M., & Joseph, P. (1980). Commitment to running: Implications for the family and work. *Sociological Symposium, 80,* 87–108.

Robbins, J. M., & Joseph, P. (1985). Experiencing exercise withdrawal: Possible consequences of therapeutic and mastery running. *Journal of Sport Psychology, 7,* 23–39.

Rodin, J. (1980). The externality theory today. In A. J. Stunkard (Ed.), *Obesity* (pp. 226–239). Philadelphia: W. B. Saunders.

Rodin, J. (1985). Insulin levels, hunger, and food intake: An example of feedback loops in body weight regulation. *Health Psychology, 4,* 1–24.

Rogers, M. P., Reich, P., Strom, T. B., & Carpenter, C. B. (1976). Behaviorally conditioned immunosuppression: Replication of a recent study. *Psychosomatic Medicine, 38,* 447–452.

Rohner-Jeanrenaud, E., & Jeanrenaud, B. (1997). Central nervous system and body weight regulation. *Annals of Endocrinology (Paris), 58 (2),* 137–142.

Root-Bernstein, R. S. (1993). *Rethinking AIDS: The tragic cost of premature consensus.* New York: Free Press.

Rosenbaum, L. (1983). Biofeedback assisted stress management for insulin-treated diabetes mellitus. *Biofeedback and Self-Regulation, 8,* 519–532.

Rosenman, R. H., Brand, R. J., Jenkins, C. D., Freidman, M., Straus, R., & Wurm M. (1975). Coronary heart disease on the Western collaborative group study: Final follow-up experience of 8½ years. *Journal of the American Medical Association, 233,* 872–877.

Ross, C. E., & Mirowski, J. (1983). Social epidemiology of overweight: A substantive and methodological investigation. *Journal of Health and Social Behavior, 21,* 288–298.

Roth, D. L., & Holmes, D. S. (1987). Influence of aerobic exercise training and relaxation training on physical and psychological health following stressful life events. *Psychosomatic Medicine, 49,* 355–365.

Russell, M., Dark, K. A., Cummins, R. W., Ellman, G., Calloway, E., & Peeke, H. V. S. (1984). Learned histamine release. *Science, 225,* 733–734.

Sachs, M. L. (1984). The runner's high. In M. Sacks & M. Sachs (Eds.), *Running as therapy* (pp. 273–287). Lincoln: University of Nebraska Press.

Sapolsky, R. M. (1992). *Stress, the aging brain and the mechanisms of neuron death.* Cambridge, MA: MIT Press.

Sarason, B. R., Sarason, J. G., & Pierce, G. R. (1990). Traditional views of social support on their impact on assessment. In B. R. Sarason, J. G. Sarason, & G. R. Pierce (Eds.), *Social support: An interactional view* (pp. 9–25). New York: John Wiley.

Sato, T., Flood, G., & Makinodan, X. (1984). Influence of psychological stress on immunological recovery in mice exposed to low dose x-irradiation. *Radiation Research, 98,* 381–388.

Sato, T., Igarashi, N., Miyagawa, K., Nakajima, T., & Katayoma, T. (1988). Catecholomine and thyroid metabolism in a case of anorexia nervosa endocrinology, *Japonica, 35,* 295–301.

Schachter, S., Goldman, R., & Gordon, A. (1968). Effects of fear, food deprivation, and obesity on eating. *Journal of Personality and Social Psychology, 10,* 107–116.

Schafer, W. (1992). *Stress management for wellness* (2nd ed.). New York: Holt, Rinehart & Winston.

Schallert, T., Whishaw, I. Q., & Flannigan, K. P. (1977). Gastric pathology and feeding deficits induced by hypothalamic damage in rats. Effects of lesion type, size, and placement. *Journal of Comparative and Physiological Psychology, 91 (3),* 598–610.

Schelling, T. C. (1992). Addictive drugs: The cigarette experience. *Science, 256,* 427.

Schneider, A. M., & Tarshis, B. (1995). *Elements of physiological psychology.* New York: McGraw-Hill.

Schuckit, M., & Gold, E. O. (1988). A simultaneous evaluation of multiple markers of ethanol/placebo challenges in sons of alcoholics and controls. *Archives of General Psychiatry, 45,* 211–216.

Seligman, M. E. P. (1975). *Learned helplessness: On depression, development, and death*. San Francisco: W. H. Freeman.

Seligman, M. E. P., & Maier, S. F. (1967). Failure to escape traumatic shock. *Journal of Experimental Psychology, 74*, 1–9.

Selye, H. (1936). A syndrome produced by diverse nocuous agents in nature. *Nature (London), 148*, 84–85.

Selye, H. (1946). The general adaptation syndrome and the diseases of adoption. *Journal of Clinical Endocrinology, 6*, 117–196.

Selye, H. (1973). The evolution of the stress concept. *American Scientist, 61*, 692–699.

Siegel, J. M. (1993). Companion animals: In sickness and in health. *Journal of Social Issues, 49 (1)*, 157–167.

Sime, W. E. (1984). Psychological benefits of exercise training in the healthy individual. In J. D. Matarazzo, S. M. Weiss, J. A. Herd, W. E. Miller, & S. M. Weiss (Eds.), *Behavioral health: A handbook of health enhancement and disease prevention* (pp. 488–507). New York: John Wiley.

Simons, A. D., Epstein, L. H., McGowan, C. R., Kupfer, D. J., & Robertson, R. J. (1985). Exercise as a treatment for depression: An update. *Clinical Psychology Review, 5*, 553–568.

Simonton, O. C., Matthews-Simonton, S., & Creighton, J. L. (1978). *Getting well again*. New York: Bantam.

Sims, E. A. H., & Horton, E. S. (1968). Endocrine and metabolic adaptation to obesity and starvation. *American Journal of Clinical Nutrition, 21*, 1455–1470.

Singer, J. E., & Lord, D. (1984). The role of social support in coping. In A. Baum, S. E. Taylor, and J. E. Singer (Eds.), *Handbook of psychology and health: Vol. IV* (pp. 383–398). Hillsdale, NJ: Lawrence Erlbaum Associates.

Sjorstrom, L. (1992). Morbidity and mortality of severely obese subjects. *American Journal of Clinical Nutrition 551 (Supplement)*, 5085–5155.

Smith, J. C. (1993). *Understanding stress and coping*. New York: Macmillan.

Smith, T. W., & Christensen, A. J. (1992). Cardiovascular reactivity and interpersonal relations: Psychosomatic processes in social context. *Journal of Social and Clinical Psychology, 11*, 279–301.

Smith, T. W., & Leon, A. S. (1992). *Coronary heart disease: A behavioral perspective*. Champaign, IL: Research Press.

Snyder, C. R., Harris, C., Anderson, J. R., Holleran, S. A., Irving, L. M., Sigmon, S. T., Yoshinobi, L., Gibl, I., Langelle, C., & Harvey, P. (1991). The will and the ways: Development and validation of an individual-differences measure of hope. *Journal of Personality and Social Psychology, 60*, 570–585.

Sobell, M. B., & Sobell, L. C. (1973). Alcoholics treated by individualized behavior therapy: One year treatment outcome. *Behavior Research and Therapy, 11*, 519–618.

Sobell, M. B., & Sobell, L. C. (1993). *Problem drinkers: Guided self-charge treatment*. New York: Guilford Press.

Sobell, M. B., & Sobell, L. C. (1976). Second year treatment outcome of alcoholics treated by individualized behavior therapy: Results. *Behavior Research and Therapy, 14*, 195–215.

Solomon, R. L., & Corbit, J. D. (1973). An opponent-process theory of motivation: II. Cigarette addiction. *Journal of Abnormal Psychology, 81*, 158–171.

Sorensen, T. I. A., Holst, C., Stunkard, A. J., & Skovgaard, L. T. (1992). Correlations of body mass index of adult adoptees, and their biological and adoptive relatives. *International Journal of Obesity, 16*, 227–236.

Sorlie, P. Gordon, T., Kannel, W. B. (1980). Body build and mortality—the Framingham study. *Journal of the American Medical Association, 243*, 1828–1831.

Spanos, N. P., Mondoux, T. J., & Burgess, C. A. (1995). Comparison of multicomponent hypnotic and non-hypnotic treatments for smoking. Special issue: To the memory of Nicholas Spanos. *Contemporary Hypnosis, 12*, 12–19.

Spiegel, D., & Bloom, J. R. (1983). Group therapy and hypnosis reduce metastatic breast cancer pain. *Psychosomatic medicine, 45*, 333–339.

Spiegel, D., Bloom, J., Kraemer, H., & Gottheil, E. (1989). Effect of psychosocial treatment on survival of patients with metastatic breast cancer. *Lancet, 2*, 888–891.

Spitzer, R. L., Devlin, M., Walsh, B. T., Hasin, D., Wing, R., Marcus, M., Stunkard, A. J., Wadden, T., Yanovski, S., Agras, W. S., Mitchell, J., & Nonas, C. (1992. Binge eating disorder: To be or not to be in DSM-IV. *International Journal of Eating Disorders, 10*, 627–630.

Stabler, B., Lane, J. D., Morris, M. A., Litton, J., & Surwit. R. S. (1988). Type A behavior pattern and chronic glycemic control in individuals with IDDM. *Diabetes Care, 11*, 361–362.

Stall, R., Coates, T., & Hoff, C. (1988). Behavioral risk reduction for HIV infection among gay and bisexual men. *American Psychologist, 43*, 878–885.

Stamler, J., Wentworth, D., & Neaton, J. D. (1986). Is relationship between serum cholesterol and risk of premature death from coronary heart disease continuous and graded? *Journal of the American Medical Association, 256*, 2823–2828.

Steig, R., & Williams, R. (1983). Cost effectiveness study of multidisciplinary pain treatment of industrial-injured workers. *Seminars in Neurology, 3*, 370–376.

Stellar, E. (1954). The physiology of motivation. *Psychological Review, 61*, 5–22.

Stephens, T. (1987). Secular trends in adult physical activity: Exercise boom or bust? *Research Quarterly for Exercise and Sport, 58*, 94–105.

Stephens, T., Jacobs, D. R., and White, C. C. (1985). A descriptive epidemiology of leisure-time activity. *Public Health Reports, 100*, 147–158.

Stunkard, A. J., Harris, J. R., Pederson, N. L., & McClearn, G. E. (1990). A separated twin study of the body mass index. *New England Journal of Medicine, 322*, 1483–1487.

Stunkard, A. J., & Koch, C. (1964). The interpretation of gastric motility: I. Apparent bias in the reports of hunger by obese persons. *Archives of General Psychiatry, 11*, 74–82.

Stunkard, A. J., Sorensen, T. J. A., Hanis, C., Teasdale, T. W., Chakraborty, R., Schull, W. J., & Schulsinger, F. (1986). An adoption study of human obesity. *New England Journal of Medicine, 314*, 193–198.

Stunkard, A. J., & Wadden, T. A. (1992). Psychological aspects of severe obesity. *American Journal of Clinical Nutrition 55* (supplement), 5245–5325.

Suarez, E. C., & Williams, R. B. (1992). Interactive models of reactivity: The relationship between hostility and potentially pathogenic physiological responses to social stressors. In N. Schneiderman, P. McCabe, & A. Baum

(Eds.), *Perspectives in behavioral medicine: Stress and disease processes in medicine* (pp. 175–195). Hillsdale, NJ: Lawrence Erlbaum Associates.

Subar, A. F., Harlan, L. C., & Mattson, M. E. (1990). Food and nutrient intake differences between smokers and non-smokers in the U.S. *American Journal of Clinical Nutrition, 53*, 1104–1111.

Suinn, R. (1990). *Anxiety management training.* New York: Plenum.

Suinn, R. (1996). Psychological services in primary health care. Briefing presented on Capitol Hill, Washington, DC.

Suls, J., & Fletcher, B. (1985). The relative efficacy of avoidant and nonavoidant coping strategies: A meta-analysis. *Health Psychology, 4*, 249–288.

Surgeon General's Report on Physical Activity and Health. (1996). From the Centers for Disease Control and Prevention. *Journal of the American Medical Association, 276*, 522.

Surwit, R. S., & Feinglos, M. N. (1988). Stress and autonomic nervous system in type II diabetes. *Diabetes Care, 11*, 83–85.

Surwit, R. S., McCaskill, C. C., Ross, S. L., & Feinglos, M. N. (1991). Behavioral and pharmacologic manipulation of glucose tolerance. *Proceedings of the 14th International Diabetes Federation Congress*, Washington, DC.

Surwit, R. S., & Schneider, M. S. (1993). Role of stress in the etiology and treatment of Diabetes Mellitus. *Psychosomatic Medicine, 55*, 380–393.

Sutocky, J. W., Shultz, J. M., & Kizer, K. W. (1993). Alcohol-related mortality in California, 1980 to 1989. *American Journal of Public Health, 83*, 817–823.

Syme, S. L. (1987). Coronary artery disease: A sociocultural perspective. *Circulation, 76* (Suppl. 1), 112–116.

Szmukler, G. L. (1987). Some comments on the link between anorexia nervosa and affective disorder. *International Journal of Eating Disorders, 6*, 181–189.

Taylor, C. B., Sallis, J. F., & Needle, R. (1985). The relationship of physical activity and exercise to mental health. *Public Health Reports, 100*, 195–202.

Taylor, S. E. (1990). Health Psychology: The science and the field. *American Psychologist, 45*, 40–50.

Taylor, W. N. (1982). *Anabolic steroids and the athlete.* Jefferson, NC: McFarland & Co.

Teasdale, T. W., Sorensen, T. I. A., & Stunkard, A. J. (1992). Intelligence and educational level in relation to body mass index of adult males. *Human Biology, 64*, 99–106.

Telch, C. F., Agras, W. S., & Rossiter, E. M. (1988). Binge eating increases with increasing adiposity. *International Journal of Eating Disorders, 7*, 115–119.

Temoshok, L. (1985). Biopsychosocial studies of cutaneous malignant melanoma: Psychosocial factors associated with prognostic indicators, progression, psychophysiology, and tumor-host response. *Social Science and Medicine, 20*, 833–840.

Temoshok, L., & Dreher, H. (1992). *Type C and cancer.* New York: Random House.

Thaxton, L. (1982). Physiological and psychological effects of short term exercise addiction on habitual runners. *Journal of Sport Psychology, 4*, 73–80.

Thompson, J. K., & Blanton, P. (1987). Energy conservation and exercise dependence: A sympathetic arousal hypothesis. *Medicine and Science in Sport and Exercise, 19*, 91–99.

Thompson, P. D., & Mitchell, J. H. (1984). Exercise and sudden cardiac death. *New England Journal of Medicine, 311,* 914–915.

Tillman, P. S., & Pequegnat, W. (1996). Interventions to Prevent HIV Risk Behaviors. *Current Bibliographies in Medicine 96–7* (U.S. Department of Health and Human Services & National Library of Medicine Reference Section). Washington, DC: U.S. Government Printing Office.

Todd, T. (1987). Anabolic steroids: The gremlins of sport. *Journal of Sport History, 14,* 87–107.

Todd, T. (1994). Growing young. *Texas Monthly, 22,* 46–50.

Tomporowski, R. D., & Ellis, M. (1986). The impact of long-term exercise training on psychological function in older adults. *Journal of Gerontology, 48,* 12–17.

Trayburn, P., & James, W. P. T. (1981). Thermogenesis: Dietary and non-shivering aspects. In L. A. Cioffi, W. P. T. James, & T. P. VanItalie (Eds.), *The body weight regulatory system: Normal and disturbed mechanisms* (pp. 97–105). New York: Raven Press.

Trowell, H., Southgate, D. A., Wolever, T. M., Leeds, A. R., Gossull, M. A., & Jenkins, D. J. (1976). Letter: Dietary fiber redefined. *Lancet, 1,* 967.

Turk, D. C., & Nash, J. N. (1996). Psychological issues in chronic pain. In R. K. Portenoy (Series Ed.), *Contemporary Series in Neurology: Vol. 48. Pain management: Theory and practice* (pp. 323–335). Philadelphia: F. A. Davis.

Turk, D. C., & Rudy, D. E. (1990). Neglected factors in chronic pain treatment outcome studies—Referral patterns, failure to enter treatment, and attrition. *Pain, 43,* 7–26.

Ulin, P. R., (1992). African women and AIDS: Negotiating behavior change. *Social Science and Medicine, 34,* 63–73.

U.S. Bureau of the Census. (1984). *Statistical abstracts.* Washington, DC: U.S. Government Printing Office.

U.S. Congressional Budget Office. (1992). *Projections of national health expenditures.* Washington, DC: U.S. Congressional Budget Office.

U.S. Department of Health and Human Services. (1984). *Executive summary: Aging and health promotion: Market research for public education.* Washington, DC: U.S. Government Printing Office.

U.S. Department of Health and Human Services. (1988). *The health consequences of smoking: Nicotine addiction.* Washington DC: U.S. Government Printing Office.

U.S. Department of Health and Human Services. (1990). *Seventh annual report to the U.S. Congress on alcohol and health from the Secretary of Health and Human Services.* Rockville, MD: National Institute on Alcohol Abuse and Alcoholism.

U.S. Department of Health and Human Services. (1993). *Respiratory health effects of passive smoking: Lung cancer and other disorders. Smoking and tobacco control* (NIH Publication No. 93–3605, Monograph 4). Washington, DC: Environmental Protection Agency.

U.S. Senate Special Committee on Aging. (1988). *Developments in aging: Vol 1.* Washington, DC: U.S. Government Printing Office.

Vaillant, G. E. (1983). *The natural history of alcoholism.* Cambridge, MA: Harvard University Press.

Valenstein, E. S. (1973). *Brain control.* New York: John Wiley.

Wadden, T. A., & Stunkard, A. J. (1985). Social and psychological consequences of obesity. *Annals of Internal Medicine, 103*, 1062–1067.

Walker, W. B., & Franzini, L. B. (1985). Low risk aversive group treatments, physiological feedback, and booster sessions for smoking cessation. *Behavior Therapy, 6*, 263–274.

Walsh, B., & Devlin, M. J. (1992). The pharmacologic treatment of eating disorders. *Psychiatric Clinics of North America, 15*, 149–160.

Ward, I. (1972). Prenatal stress feminizes and demasculinizes the behavior of males. *Science, 175*, 82–84.

Ward, J. L., & Weisz, J. (1980). Maternal stress alters plasma testosterone in fetal males. *Science, 207*, 328–329.

Waterhouse, J., Muir, C., Correa, P., & Powell, J. (Eds.). (1976). *Cancer incidence in five continents* (Vol. 3). Lyon: International Agency for Research on Cancer.

Weekley, C. K., Klesges, P. C., & Reylea, G. (1992). Smoking as a weight-control strategy and its relationship to smoking status. *Addictive Behaviors, 17*, 259–271.

Weiner, H. (1992). *Perturbing the organism.* Chicago: University of Chicago Press.

Weinstein, W. S., & Meyers, A. W. (1983). Running as a treatment for depression: Is it worth it? *Journal of Sport Psychology, 5*, 288–301.

Weissman, C. S., Nathanson, C. A., Ensminger, M. E., Teitelbaum, M. A., Robinson, J. C., & Plichta, S., (1989). AIDS knowledge, perceived risk and prevention among adolescent clients of a family planning clinic. *Family Planning Perspectives, 21*, 213–217.

Wells, J., Howard, G., Nowlin, W., & Vargas, M. (1986). Presurgical anxiety and postsurgical pain and adjustment: Effects of a stress inoculation procedure. *Journal of Consulting and Clinical Psychology, 54*, 831–835.

West, K. M. (1978). *Epidemiology of diabetes and its vascular lesions.* New York: Elsevier.

West, V., Fellows, B., & Easton, S. (1995). The British Society of Experimental and Clinical Hypnosis: A national survey. *Contemporary Hypnosis, 12*, 143–147.

Whichelow, M. J., Golding, J. F., & Treasure, F. P. (1988). Comparison of some dietary habits of smokers and nonsmokers. *British Journal of Addiction, 83*, 295–304.

Willett, W. C., Polk, F., Underwood, B. S., Stampfer, M. J., Pressel, S., Rosner, B., Taylor, J. O., Schneider, K., & Hames, C. G. (1984). Relation of serum vitamins A and E and carotenoids to the risk of cancer. *New England Journal of Medicine, 310*, 430–434.

William, R., & Miller, W. R. (1993). Alcoholism: Toward a better disease model. *Psychology of Addictive Behaviors, 7*, 129–136.

Williams, R. B., Jr., Barefoot, J. C., & Shekelle, R. B. (1985). The health consequences of hostility. In M. A. Chesney & R. H. Rosenman (Eds.), *Anger and hostility in cardiovascular and behavioral disorders* (pp. 173–185). Washington, DC: Hemisphere.

Williams, R. H., & Porte, D. (1974). The pancreas. In R. H. William (Ed.) *Textbook of Endocrinology* (5th ed., pp. 502–626). Philadelphia: W. B. Saunders.

Willis, J. D., & Campbell, L. F. (1992). *Exercise psychology*. Champaign, IL: Human Kinetics Publishers.

Wilson, G. T. (1992). Diagnostic criteria for bulimia nervosa. *International Journal of Eating Disorders, 11*, 315–319.

Wing, R., Epstein, L., Nowalk, M., & Lambarski, D. (1996). Behavior self-regulation in the treatment of patients with Diabetes Mellitus. *Psychological Bulletin, 99*, 78–89.

Wing, R. R., Epstein, L. H., Nowalk, M. P., Koeske, R., & Hagg, S. (1985). Behavior change, weight loss, and physiological components in type II diabetic patients. *Journal of Consulting and Clinical Psychology, 53*, 111–122.

Witaker, A., Davis, M., Schaffer, D., Johnson, J., Abrams, S., Walsh, B. T., & Kalikow, K. (1989). The struggle to be thin: A survey of anorexic and bulemic symptoms in a non-referred adolescent population. *Psychological Medicine, 19*, 143–162.

Woods, S. C., Smith, P. H., & Porte, D. (1981). The role of the nervous system in metabolic regulation and its effects on diabetes and obesity. In M. Brownless (Ed.), *Handbook of Diabetes Mellitus: Vol. 3* (pp. 208–271). New York: Garland.

World Health Organization. (1987, March 26–27). *Prevention of cardiovascular disease among the elderly*. Report of a World Health Organization meeting. Geneva, Switzerland: Author.

World Health Organization. (December 1997). Report on the global HIV/AIDS epidemic. In point of fact no. 86. Available on Internet: http://www.unaids.org/highband/document/epidemia/report 97. html

Yehuda, R., Giller, E., & Mason, J. W. (1993). Psychoneuroendocrine assessment of posttraumatic stress disorder: Current progress and new directions. *Progress in Neuro-Pharmacology & Biological Psychiatry, 17 (4)*, 541–550.

Yesalis, C. E., Courson, S. P. & Wright, J. (1993). History of anabolic steroid use in sport and exercise. In C. E. Yesalis (Ed.), *Anabolic steroids in sport and exercise* (pp. 35–47). Champaign, IL: Human Kinetics Publishers.

Young, R. J. (1979). The effect of regular exercise on cognitive functioning and personality. *British Journal of Sports Medicine, 13*, 110–117.

Zhu, T., Korber, B. T., Nahamias, A. J., Hooper, E., Sharp, P. M., & Ho, D. D. (1998). An African HIV-1 sequence from 1959 and implications for the origin of the epidemic (letter). *Nature, 391*, 594–596.

Zucker, R. A., & Gomberg, E. S. L. (1986). Etiology of alcoholism reconsidered: The case for a biopsychosocial process. *American Journal of Psychiatry, 41*, 783–793.

Index

Addiction: drug, 90–91; nicotine, 82; positive, 89; running, 22–23. *See also* Alcohol abuse and dependence

Aging: disease and, 145, 198, 204; exercise and, 31–32

Agoraphobia, 141

AIDS/HIV infection: emergence of, 179–80; HIV virus and, 185–86; immune function and, 181–85; incidence and prevalence, 180–81; minorities and, 191–92; predisposing factors in, 185–86; risk-reducing behaviors and, 9; transmission and exposure, 185–86, 190–91; women's treatment for, 192

Alcohol abuse and dependence: abstinence versus controlled drinking, 75, 78–79; biomedical approaches to, 75–76; brief motivational counseling and, 79; as compulsive disease, 75–76; defining criteria, 73; drug treatments for, 76; gender, ethnic, and age factors in, 71–73; genetics and, 73–75, 76–77; lack of research on, 69; medical model versus social learning/behavioral model of, 77–78; in minority populations, 76–77; pharmacological intervention for, 75; pregnancy and, 73; problem drinkers and, 80; psychosocial and cultural factors in, 76–77; stress and, 20

Alcoholics Anonymous, 78

Alcoholism. *See* Alcohol abuse and dependence

American Psychological Association's Division of Health Psychology, 8

Amotivational syndrome, marijuana and, 91

Anorexia: bulimia and, 59; defined, 58; physiology and treatment of, 61; symptoms and predictive factors in, 60

Antibodies, immunity and, 182, 183–84

Antigens, immune responses and, 182–83

Antisocial personality disorder, 74

Anxiety, in psychoanalytic theory, 124–25

Aristotle, 4

Assertiveness training, 134–35

Atherosclerosis: cholesterol and, 164; diabetes and, 147

Athletes: anabolic steroid use by, 70–71, 92–95; eating disorders of, 58, 63–65

Attribution theory, 128–29

Autoimmune diseases, 187–88

Aversion therapy, 86–87

Basal cell carcinoma, 195–96

Beck, Aaron, 124, 134

Behavior modification: drastic versus gradual, 218; psychologists' role in, 9; psychosocial interventions, 188–90; techniques, 50–53, 197

Behavioral disorders, cholesterol levels and, 169

Behavioral medicine, development of, 7–8

Behavioral patterns: Type A, 114–17, 173, 176, 216–17; Type C, 206

Benson, Herbert, 220

Benson relaxation response, 133

Bernard, Claude, 102

Beta carotene, antioxidant effects of, 203

Biofeedback, 8, 9, 131–32, 189; diabetes management and, 152

Biomedical model: alcoholism and, 75–76; shortcomings of, 6–7

Biopsychosocial model, 6–7

Blood pressure, 163–64, 165

Body Mass Index, 37, 45–47

Breathing techniques, 132

Bulimia: anorexia and, 59; defined, 57–58; dieting and, 62; purging and, 58; treatment of, 62–63

Califano, Joseph A., Jr., 69, 219

Cancer, 195–211; death rates, U.S., 200 (figure), 201 (figure); description of, 196–98; detection and prevention, 197; diet and, 198–99, 203, 204; emotional state and, 205–10; exercise and, 204; incidence and prevalence, 197–98; psychological interventions, 208–10; risk factors in, 198–202; stage schemes for, 196–97; stress–immunity––cancer link, 207–10; types of, 198

Cannon, Walter B., 102

Cardiovascular disease: causes of, 164; personality–disease relationships and, 216–17; smoking and, 202. *See also* Coronary heart disease

Cardiovascular reactivity, 173

Caregiver stress, 219–20

Carnegie, Dale, 123–24

Carpenter, Karen, 57

Cholesterol: cigarette smoking and, 170–71; coronary heart disease and, 164, 168–69

Chronic illness, patient's responsibility in, 220

Chronic pain: biopsychosocial model of, 7; stress management techniques and, 133

Cigarette smoking, 81–89; behavioral interventions, 86–89; cognitive behavioral relapse prevention program, 89; coronary heart disease and, 25, 26, 165, 170–71, 175; exercise adherence and, 29; health effects of, 199–202; lifestyle behaviors and, 81–82; multimodal cessation plan, 88–89; personality factors in, 86; reasons for, 82–86; second-hand smoke exposure, 202; smoke-free environments and, 85–86; statistics, 81; teenage, rise in, 202; weight and, 49, 52

Cocaine, 70, 75, 89–90

Cognitive Behavioral Therapy (Beck), 124

Cognitive restructuring, 123–24, 133–34

Colon cancer, 204

Cooper, Kenneth, 15

Coronary heart disease, 159–78; anatomy and physiology, 160–64; artery bypass surgery, 167; biological treatments for, 166–68; cholesterol and, 164, 168–69; cigarette smoking and, 170–71, 175; development of, 164–66; diabetes and, 165, 171–72; diet and, 168–69, 175; exercise and, 23–26, 165–66, 174–75; hypertension and, 169–70; physical activity and,

171; psychosocial stressors and, 114–17, 172–73; rehabilitation, 173–76; risk factors, 164–66, 168–73; running and, 26–28; social interactions and, 172–73; Type A behavioral pattern (TABP) and, 114–17, 173, 176

Darwin, Charles, 102
Depression: diabetics and, 153–54; exercise and, 20–21; reactive, 128
Descartes, René, 4
Diabetes, 141–56; adult onset (Type 2), 142, 146–47, 151–53; anatomy and physiology, 142–47; cardiovascular disease and, 165, 171–72; development of, 142–43; diseases and long-term effects of, 147–48, 153; genetics of, 145–46; gestational, 141–42; glucose metabolism and, 148–50; hyperglycemia and, 142, 148–50; incidence and prevalence of, 145; insulin and, 142–45; juvenile-onset (Type 1), 145, 150; stress and, 148–53; warning signs of, 149; weight control and, 146–47, 154–55
Diabetes management and treatment, 147, 148, 155; psychological factors in, 153–54; treatment adherence in, 155; weight control in, 154–55
Diabetes risk test, 143–44
Diabetic ketoacidosis, 145, 153
Diabetic neuropathy, 147
Diet: cancer and, 198–99, 203; cholesterol and, 168–69; coronary heart disease and, 168–69, 175; fiber in, 204
Drug abuse, 89–90; AIDS and, 190–91; detrimental effects of, 70; lack of research on, 69; stress and, 20; weight control and, 52–53

Eating disorders: of athletes, 58, 63–64; personality disorders and, 59. See also Anorexia; Bulimia
Ellis, Albert, 124, 134
Emotional well-being: cancer and, 205–10; of diabetic patients, 153–54; exercise and, 20–21, 32

Exercise, 15–33; addiction, 22–23; adherence, 28–31; aerobic revolution in, 15, 17; aging and gender issues in, 31–32; benefits, 17–18; cancer and, 204; coronary heart disease and, 23–26, 165–66, 171, 174–75; cross-training, 15, 21; daily requirement, 16; emotional fitness and, 20–21, 32; motivation for, 17, 20; physicians' influence on, 30; reasons for lack of, 18–19, 28–29; recommendations, 19; running boom and, 15–16; self-test, 24–25; stress reduction and, 19–20; toughness response and, 21; weight control and, 49–50

Fasting, 53–54
Fen-Phen, 85
Finnish Alpha-Tocopherol studies, 203
Fixx, Jim, 28
Freud, Anna, 124
Freud, Sigmund, 124

Gall, Franz Joseph, 5
Gender: eating disorders and, 64–65; social support systems and, 130; weight control and, 35, 48–49. See also Women
General systems theory, 6
Guided imagery, 133, 188

Hardiness, concept of, 127–28
Health care system: access in, 219; costs (U.S.), 8; psychological services and programs in, 8–9; self-help in, 220
Health psychology, defined, 215
Heart: anatomy of, 160 (figure); arrhythmias of, 162–63; electrical activity in, 162 (figure)
Heart attack, 162; depression and, 176–77; treatment for, 166–68. See also Coronary heart disease
Heart transplants, 167–68
Henrich, Christy, 58
Heroin, 90

HIV infection. *See* AIDS/HIV infection

Homeostatis, 102

Hope, stress reduction and, 129

Hostility, coronary heart disease and, 173

Human Capital Initiative Coordinating Committee (HCICC), 217, 218, 219

Human growth hormone, 93, 94

Hypertension, 147, 164, 169–70

Hypervigilance, stress and, 126

Hypoglycemic coma, 145

Hypothalamic-pituitary-adrenal axis (HPA), stress and, 117–18

Immune system, 181–85; AIDS and, 181–85; diabetes and, 145; negative stressors and, 207–8; nervous system interactions with, 186–88; psychosocial interventions and, 188–90, 208–10

Immunity: cell-mediated, 182, 184–85; general and specific, 183–84; stress–immunity–cancer link, 207–10; substance abuse and, 208

Inhalant abuse, 91–92

Insulin, weight gain and, 37, 43

Jacobson, E., 132–33

Johnson, Magic, 186

Lifestyle balancing, 89

Lifestyle behaviors: cigarette smoking and, 81–82; health care costs and, 217–19; modification of, 9, 50–53, 197, 218; weight control and, 48, 52, 65. *See also* Exercise

Localization of function, 5

Lung cancer, 197, 199

Lupus, 187–88

Macrophages, immune responses and, 182, 183, 189–90

Marijuana, 70, 90–91

Melanoma, 196

Mental illness, early views on, 4–5

Mental imagery techniques, 205

Metastasis, 196

Miller, Neal, 8, 131

Mind-body interaction: behavioral medicine and, 8; Cartesian impasse and, 4; controversy of, 205–6; historical views on, 4–5

Minorities, AIDS and, 191–92

Monocytes, immunity and, 183

Morgan's Canon, 5–6

Multiple Risk Factor Intervention Trial (MRFIT), 115

Muscle relaxation therapy, 132–33, 152, 188–89, 216

Myocardial infarction, 162, 164

National Institutes of Health (NIH), 69; weight control and, 48, 50

Natural killer (NK) cell activity: disease outcome and, 207–8; immunity and, 183, 184–85

Nervous system: sympathetic, stress and, 102, 103 (figure), 114; Type 2 diabetes and, 148–50, 152

Neurogenic theory of compulsive disease, 76

Nicotine addiction, 70. *See also* Cigarette smoking

Obesity, 36–47; cancer and, 199; contributing factors in, 36–37, 38; coronary heart disease and, 171; diabetes and, 146–47; evolution and, 38; genetics and, 42, 45, 47; health risks of, 44–47; intelligence and, 47; leptin's role in, 43–44; physiological model of, 42–44; psychoanalytic model of, 38–39; psychosocial risks of, 53–54; set-point weight and, 38, 42–43; social learning and, 38–42. *See also* Weight control and dieting

Occam's Razor, 5

Opponent process, 84

Pancreatic cancer, 197

Percutaneous Transluminal Coronary Angioplasty, 166–67

Personality: disease and, 216–17; exercise and, 29; smoking and, 86
Personality disorders: alcoholism and, 73–74; anabolic steroid use and, 93–94; eating disorders and, 59
Phagocytosis, immunity and, 182, 183, 189–90
Phenylpropanolamine, weight loss and, 52
Phrenology, 5
Pinel, Phillipe, 4–5
Plato, 4
Pneuma theory, 4
Post-traumatic stress disorder, 102, 117–18
Prozac, 52, 85
Psychology of well being, 215; origins of, 4–5; roles for, 8–9
Psychoneuroimmunology, 186–88
Psychosocial Adjustment to Illness Scale (PAIS), 177
Psychosocial stressors, cardiovascular disease and, 172–73
Pythagoras, 4

Rational Emotive Therapy (Ellis), 124, 134
Reductionism, principle of, 5–6
Relaxation techniques, 132–33, 152, 188–89, 216
Renal disease, diabetes and, 148
Retrovirus, 182
ReVia (drug), 76
Running: addiction, 22–23; coronary heart disease and, 26–28; versus cross-training, 21; motives for, 17; physical and mental impacts of, 15–16; runner's high, 23; as therapy, 20

Schultz, H. H., 133
Seattle Longitudinal Assessment of Cancer Survival (SLACS), 205
Self-change programs, 80
Self-efficacy: as predictor of treatment adherence, 155; stress coping and, 129
Self-esteem, dieting and, 41–42
Selye, Hans, 102–4, 105, 111

Sexual dysfunction, heart attack and, 177
Sexually transmitted diseases, AIDS and, 181
Social support, disease and, 172–73
Steroids, abuse of, 70–71, 92–95
Stress: caregiver, 219–20; coronary heart disease and, 114–17; corticoid secretions and, 111–12; diabetes and, 148–53; fight-or-flight response and, 102, 106; hormones and, 112–13; hypothalamic-pituitary-adrenal axis (HPA) and, 117–18; immune function and, 187, 188–89, 208–10; individual responses to, 108; measurement, 113–14; mood-altering chemicals and, 20; pathological change and, 112; peptides and, 113; physiological responses to, 102–6, 114–17; self-assessment, 107; stages of, 105–6; stress–immunity–cancer link, 207–10
Stress coping strategy(ies), 123–36, 215–16; aerobic exercise, 19–20; assertive behavior, 134–45; biofeedback, 131–32; breathing techniques, 132; cognitive restructuring, 133–34; defense mechanisms in, 124–25; explanatory style in, 128–29; guided imagery, 133; hardiness trait in, 127–28; human–pet companionship and, 130–31; internal characteristics and, 127–29; learned helplessness and, 128, 129; measurement of, 126; of diabetics, 150–53; problem-focused versus emotion-focused, 126–27; psychological services, 8–9; Rational-Emotive-Behavioral Therapy, 134; relaxation therapy, 132–33; self-efficacy and hope in, 129; sense of control in, 108, 109; social support, 130; substance abuse as, 208; Type C behavior pattern and, 206
Stress research and theory, 101–20: animal studies in, 110–11; general adaptation syndrome in, 105–10, 117; historical overview, 102–4; in-

terpersonal relationships in, 107–8; nonlinear cause–effect relationship in, 104–5, 106; process approach in, 125–27; psychoanalytic, 124–25

Substance abuse. *See* Alcohol abuse and dependence; Drug abuse

Sympathetic arousal hypothesis, 22–23

Todd, Terry, 92

Treatment adherence: models of, 217; self-efficacy and, 155

Type A behavioral pattern (TABP): cardiovascular disorders, 114–17, 173, 176, 216–17; self-assessment of, 116

Type C behavioral pattern, cancer and, 206

Vision problems, diabetes and, 147–48

Weight: ideal, 44–45, 55; reasonable, 55; set-point, 38, 42–43, 83, 85

Weight control and dieting: athletes' concerns with, 58, 63–65; behavioral modification techniques in, 50–53; costs and benefits, 53–55; diabetics and, 154–55; failure in, 52; fasting controversy in, 53–54; gender factor in, 35, 48–49, 64–65; lifestyle and, 48, 52, 65; methods and strategies, 48–49, 51 (table), 55–56, 65; multidimensional approach to, 53; self-esteem and, 41–42; smoking and, 82–85; spot reducing controversy in, 56; "yo-yo" dieting, 37–38, 54. *See also* Anorexia; Bulimia; Eating disorders; Obesity

Weiner, Mason, 104–5

Women: AIDS and, 190–93; disease and, 219; exercise and, 31–32; weight concerns of, 36, 48–49

About the Author

WILLIAM M. MILEY is Professor of Psychology at The Richard Stockton College of New Jersey.

ISBN 0-275-96275-X

9 780275 962753

90000>

EAN

HARDCOVER BAR CODE